INTEGRITY

INTEGRITY

VOLUME 2
The Second Year
January–June 1947

CAROL ROBINSON & ED WILLOCK, *EDITORS*

First Published by
Integrity Publishing Co., New York, 1947
Edited by Edward F. Willock and Carol Jackson Robinson
Illustrations by Ed Willock
2020 © by Arouca Press

All rights reserved:
No part of this book may be reproduced or transmitted,
in any form or by any means, without permission

ISBN: 978-1-7770523-1-7 (pbk)
ISBN: 978-1-7770523-8-6 (hc)

Arouca Press
PO Box 55003
Bridgeport PO
Waterloo, ON N2J3G0
Canada
www.aroucapress.com
Send inquiries to info@aroucapress.com

Book and cover design
by Michael Schrauzer

CONTENTS

EDITOR'S NOTE VII

JANUARY 1947 1
Editorial 3
A Christian Abnormal Psychology, *Carol Robinson* 5
Book Reviews 63

FEBRUARY 1947 71
Editorial 73
The Rise of Cataldo, *A Story, Ed Willock* 77
Protestantism and Economic Life,
  Jerem O'Sullivan-Barra. 86
Contemporary American Protestantism,
  Carol Robinson 106
Why I am Not a Catholic,
  Various Anonymous Contributors. 125
Book Reviews 133

MARCH 1947 141
Editorial. 143
Making Concupiscence Pay, *Irene Mary Naughton* 149
To Be Specific, *Ed Willock*. 162
Song For Those In Search of Riches, *Thomas J. Beary* . . . 176
I'd Rather Be a Menial, *Carol Robinson* 177
Ours Not To See The Triumph of the Truth,
  Elizabeth Odell. 192
Calvary Canticle, *Elizabeth Odell* 193
Correspondence 194
Book Reviews 205

APRIL 1947 211
Editorial. 213
Resurrection: 1947, *Rev. Benedict Ehmann* 215

The Size of It, *Mr. Little (Pseudonym)* 226
Road to Reality, *James P. Egan* 231
The Psychology of Anti-Semitism, *Arthur Sheehan* 238
The Deceived, *Gerard Sedley* 245
A Retreat to Principle, *Bruce Vawter* 248
Man's Providence, *Carol Robinson* 261
Book Reviews 271

MAY 1947 283

Editorial 285
A Holy Thing, *John M. Oesterreicher* 290
Among So Many, *Neil MacCarthy* 293
Towards a New Generation, *Mary Mannix* 301
Life with Mother, *Dorothy Willock* 308
Sins of Flesh and Commerce, *Carol Robinson* 313
Our Child is Mentally Defective, *Anonymous* 329
The Family Has Lost Its Head, *Ed Willock* 335
Book Reviews 347

JUNE 1947 355

Editorial 357
Our Lady of Wisdom, *Herbert Thomas Schwartz* 359
Commencement Address for a Catholic College,
   Elizabeth Odell 374
Life in an Education Factory, *Sandra Kelley* 376
The Thirst for Theology, *Carol Robinson* 392
The Real McCoy, *Catherine Christopher* 408
Advice to Her Daughter On Starting to School,
   Catherine Walsh 408
Secular Education – Some Years After, *M.B.W* 409
Book Reviews 423

Editor's Note

THIS IS THE SECOND VOLUME OF A multi-volume project to republish all of the *Integrity* issues published from 1946 to 1956. The original editors were Carol Jackson Robinson (1911–2002) and Edward Willock (1916–1960). Dorothy Dohen (1924–1984) succeeded them as editor in 1952.

This volume features the first six issues for 1947. We have included a number of footnotes in order to provide more context into what was written at that time — events or people which may not be as readily known in 2020.

We wish to acknowledge the work of The Angelus Press for first re-introducing *Integrity* to the general public. Our work differs insofar as we wish to re-introduce the *entire* corpus to the general public since these issues are relatively difficult to find and could be of lasting importance to future generations who wish to read about the intellectual climate of the Catholic Church in the United States after World War II.

The *Integrity* writers become more focused in their analysis of issues such as: the family, education, the socio-economic order, fatherhood, Protestantism, and the relationship between the Faith's practice and its involvement in the governance of society. Such issues were perhaps overlooked at that time by the more mainstream Catholic periodicals, but if the feedback we have received from the first volume is any indication, *Integrity* has not lost any of its relevance.

Our goal is to initiate a discussion among informed Catholics about the issue of the integration of daily life and Faith in the modern world.

We are certainly aware that some of the conclusions made by these authors will be hotly debated, but for us the important point is that a serious effort was made to look at these issues from a Catholic view. Can we fault them for wishing to critique modern society as Catholics? How precisely are we to view contemporary problems affecting the life of the believer? Is the Faith merely a set of devotional principles with no bearing on society at large? Let the reader decide if their attempt at tackling such a wide-range of problems was successful or not.

We would be remiss not to acknowledge the contributions of those who helped with the transcription of these issues. Their generosity and time given to help with this volume will not be forgotten.

Lesson from the Book of Wisdom

Blessed is the man that is found without blemish, and that hath not gone after gold, nor put his trust in money nor in treasures. Who is he, and we will praise him? For he hath done wonderful things in his life. Who hath been tried thereby, and made perfect, he shall have glory everlasting: he that could have transgressed and hath not transgressed and could do evil things, and hath not done them, therefore are his goods established in the Lord, and all the Church of the saints shall declare his alms.

Ecclesiasticus 31: 8–11

EDITORIAL

IF ANYONE WERE TO ASK WHAT IS the prevailing intellectual or spiritual influence in this country today it would be hard to answer. We are a Protestant country but Protestantism is no longer the dominant mentality. Catholics are numerous but the Catholic view of life obtains hardly anywhere. Secularism is very much with us but it is a this-world philosophy without specific content. Materialism is rife but is more a way of life than a way of thinking.

We of *Integrity* incline to think that the most pervasive contemporary influence is Freudianism or pseudo-Freudianism. It has infiltrated into the schools. It is gaining ascendency over the medical profession (at a time when the medical profession is tempted to coalesce into a united socialized group). It was held in high honor in the armed forces where psychiatric verdicts, though often very foolish, were never questioned. It is the rock foundation of all social work, sociology, and advanced personnel techniques. It forms the structural basis of novels and detective fiction, and has its affiliations with modern music. It has perverted the ballet and preoccupied the theatre. The movies have been lately intent on it. Even the Protestant clergy are toying with it as a vehicle for giving spiritual help.

People have been pecking at Freudianism for a long time, applauding this, deploring that. The pecking has done no good and, because it was merely pecking, much harm. It is amazing how many people, and how many Catholics, have been taken in by a psychology, and philosophy, so wildly at odds with human experience and Christian principles. But so it is.

Someone has to do more than peck, so we have undertaken a large Christian view of the field which Freudianism purports to explain. Our view is long on principles, devoid of juicy case histories. It is shamefully condensed. It is psychology which tends more toward the philosophical than the clinical.

This study pre-supposes the classical psychology as set forth by St. Thomas, but has purposely avoided technical explanations, for fear of obscuring the main issues. It deals only with functional mental disorders; not with those which have an organic base. We hope in the future to clarify and amplify some specific aspects of this complex problem.

THE EDITORS

A Christian Abnormal Psychology
The Bankruptcy of Modern Psychiatry

OF ALL MODERN PROBLEMS NONE IS more serious than the alarming growth of mental disorders, slight and not so slight. Asylums are packed, psychoanalysts are doing a lucrative business, psychiatrists have taken on a new dignity, and psychology is a popular field of graduate and undergraduate study. A demented relative used to be a closet skeleton. No longer. Uncle Alexander, but yesterday carted off (by the combined force of ten strong men) to a "psychoneurotic institution" is only "sick." It's just like a cold, but a little more inconvenient. Especially for Uncle Alexander.

How we kid ourselves! It's like pretending that there is no atom bomb, or that we can get along amicably with atheistic Russia, or that there always was as much cancer as now only we didn't recognize it. And so we manage to pretend that the loss of reason, that the terrible, unbearable, mental and spiritual torture of thousands doesn't really hurt. What's worse, we try to pretend that it "just happened," and that it has nothing to do with our decline of morals, our cult of luxury, our liberal education, our disdain of discipline, and our all-pervading, wanton disregard of God.

An army of experts has arisen to deal with the situation. They are working in the dark. It is curious that we have so long tolerated their groping; that we are impressed by the curious vocabulary they have made up for themselves; that we pay such enormous sums to them and are content with so little in return. A psychiatrist enjoys the prerogatives of the undertaker: we are grateful to each for taking over an unsavory job; and we are more than willing that the details of the operation remain a mystery.

Would it be impertinent to inquire the ideal toward which psychiatry is presumably working; would it be presumptuous to demand that abnormal psychologists specify their norm? Here is the opening sentence in a current college text of abnormal psychology:

> In all of the treatises on abnormal psychology there arises the problem of determining what activities are normal and what activities are abnormal... The fact that no solution has been reached (on this) is due in a large measure to our lack of knowledge of the normal individual.[1]

It is as though a medical doctor had no idea what health was and might be misled into thinking that a dead person had recovered, merely because his convulsions had ceased.

The root of the difficulty is this matter of the norm, and the reason is that the science of psychiatry arose in the post-Christian era, after the truth about the nature and purpose of man had been lost, lost at least to the fathers of that science.

Most references to "medieval" treatment of the insane in textbooks are wildly inaccurate. Snake pits were a device of the ancients; the chained inmates of Bedlam were a post-Reformation scandal; and diabolism as an all-pervasive explanation was 17th century. True history does honor to the Church. The admirable Gheel system of allowing freedom of the village to harmless lunatics was started by a cult to St. Dymphna, and still persists. Medieval references to the care of the insane were simple and salutary, including such advice as playing music to cheer the melancholy. Above all what honors the Church is that mental disease never became a major problem while the world still lived within the framework which She made.

[1] Dorcas & Shaffer, *Textbook of Abnormal Psychology*. Used at Fordham.

A Christian Abnormal Psychology

Freud is the father of modern psychiatry. His philosophy has a pervasive influence even where his technique is rejected. Freud did not know what a man is, much less what a normal man is; or what the purpose of life is; or that God exists. His standard of a "cure" is that a neurotic patient should achieve a satisfactory sex life.

Not everyone agrees with Freud, but all take him as a standard of reference, good or bad. The reason for his influence is that he did offer some sort of comprehensive explanation of mental disease, even though the explanation is materialistic, atheistic, and sensual. The real alternative to Freud is another comprehensive explanation, not just a modification or criticism of his system. Freud is not accidentally wrong; he is essentially wrong. Accidentally and occasionally he is right. He had his insights, but his explanations were off-center.

You can't build a rival system to Freud's starting experimentally. Freud didn't build his system experimentally either. He already had a philosophy in the light of which he made up his principles.

The first work on a Christian abnormal psychology must be to build a comprehensive general explanation rooted in truths that we do certainly know. Then in the light of this, let us explain the abnormalities and work out the cures. This paper proposes a rough framework.

A world in a spiritual void,
   grew madder by the day;
Along came Sigmund Freud,
   And sped it on its way.

PART I. THE NORM

Ought a man to adjust himself to his environment, or conspire to make over or escape from his environment? A neurotic is usually conspicuously out of step or is he, perhaps, the only one in step? How can you know unless you have objective standards as to what constitutes a good environment. The normal man cannot be studied in isolation from his normal habitat because his mental balance is affected by his environment.

Because we live in cities which are ugly and disordered, and made by men, we lose sight of the harmony of the universe as made by God. God designed everything harmoniously. There is a rhythm in the movement of the planets, an order within atoms; there is a procession in the season, an ebb and flow in tides, a balance of elements in the soil and a reciprocal relationship among members of a family. There are little things and big things, and all sizes in between. There are organic things and inorganic things. There are material things and spiritual things.

Is man little or big? Neither. He is the measure of the little and the big. He is the standard of reference of maximal and minimal. Within the macrocosm which is the universe, he is a microcosm, a little universe, containing within himself all gradations of material being while he is himself the most complex organic structure in the universe.

All other material things are made for man. He is kingpin of the visible universe, even if not its absolute master. Only when men's thinking is warped do they fancy themselves inferior and subordinate to the material universe.

There is a whole invisible universe above man, in which he also shares. In relation to it he is on the bottom rung. The unique position of man in the universe is that it is he alone who bridges the material and spiritual orders, with one foot in each. He is highest in the material order by virtue of the complexity of his organism; lowest in the spiritual order because of the cumbersome way he attains knowledge, through his senses and through reason.

The world isn't just a jumble of things; it's an ordered and very intricate arrangement of things. God makes a synthesis of things. He doesn't just put them together; He also supplies a principle of operation. Not just planets but also a law of gravity, an internal tendency according to a certain mode of physical attraction of forces. Not just animals, but animals with instincts which lead them to do what they are made to do. The whole universe is like that; filled with principles by which they operate. Everything operates according to reason — only it is God's reason, reflected in the thing by instinct or law.

The catch is man. He too is a synthesis, more intricate than all the others. He, too, has a vital principle, his soul. But he has the power to understand what he ought to do and he has the free will to do it, or not to do it. This is how it comes about that man is in the moral order, and that a new law, the moral law, is operative in regard to him. Man's freedom makes it possible for him to upset, possibly destroy, the harmony of the universe.

Man may soon succeed in destroying the harmony of the physical universe, which will be an end of him and it. He has already considerably upset the balance of nature. He has created chaos in his relationships with his own kind, chaos which we know as world war. He can destroy himself and he sometimes does. When he kills his body, it is suicide. When he turns away from God, it is mortal sin. When he destroys the harmony of his own nature, it is insanity.

All things are made for man, but man is made for God. Man preserves the harmony of the universe and operates within it only so long as he himself is ordered to God and respects God's laws on the various levels. The great sin of our time is presumptuous disregard of God's natural, moral and physical laws. We set ourselves up as gods and try to create a harmony of our own, ordered to our own pleasure. That is why, in every field, there is profound disorder.

Insofar as the harmony of the sub-human world is disturbed, it redounds on man and creates a tension in his nature too. For instance, enormous cities are a strain on most men, if only because they surround men with cement and steel, from which men are remote in the scale of being, and separate them from the organic world with which they have a closer natural relationship. It is not strange that gardening, that farm animals and pets, and that all the manifold changes of the seasons, should have a soothing effect on men. These things (and not subways and skyscrapers) form their natural habitat.

However, most of the strains on human nature come from disordered human relationships. Here too, there are organic laws which must be observed. The arrangement of society is not arbitrary in its fundamentals, but only in its accidentals. One thing that *is* arbitrary is the form of government. It is silly to attach an exaggerated importance to democracy, while permitting divorce. The family is a matter of necessity; democracy is a matter of preference.

There are four elements essential to an ordered society: the family, the community, authority, a functional nature. We shall treat of each briefly, only insofar as it relates to mental disorders.

The family. The basic unit of society is the family, and not the individual, as liberal economics would have it. The practical necessity for the family is the bearing and rearing of children; but the practical necessities of nature are all reflected in the psychological make-up of human beings. Men and women are not really whole individuals in a psychological sense, but meant to complement each other in a permanent stable, family unit. Children need the security of parental love as much as they need the physical care of adults. These things are all pretty obvious and the greatest effort in history to dispense with the family, the Russian experiment, failed dismally. We still have the family, but I wonder if we appreciate how much we owe to it for whatever stability we do have in society.

However, our families are not healthy, and this is reflected almost immediately in mental disorders. Marriage is not stable, thanks to the possibility of divorce, which affects all marriages and carries a threat to all women. Further, even where there is no immediate threat of divorce, domestic unhappiness is rife, and this can be traced to all sorts of factors, chief among which is the unholiness of family life. The practice of birth control is another serious disorder, for what marriage can survive on the basis of adolescent romanticism?

The Community. There needs to be a community life beyond the family. Men especially need a little world where they are known by their first names, where they are accepted for what they are, where people care whether they live or die, are happy or unhappy. It should be an organic community, like a village or a really active parish, or a self-contained small town. But organic communities have nearly disappeared with over-centralization. Five hundred people rushed together in the same subway train, packed into the same Broadway nightclub, decorously arranged in the same suburb, or lined up in rows in the same insurance office, are not a community. Ten mothers of infant babies in the same park, an alumni association, an air-raid warden crew, or the local chapter of the Knights of Columbus, are only faintly so.

In place of community we are offered "one world." It is too big. Even half a world is too big. It does not matter psychologically how the large nations are apportioned, so long only as a man can carry on his ordinary affairs in a pint-sized puddle to which he has some relevance. Let there be a million such puddles compromising one state, if only each man has his own puddle and doesn't have to crack his brain to comprehend Japanese affairs of state, or Indonesian economics. The man who prefers the kitchen gossip of the tabloids to a full account of the proceedings of the United Nations Assembly is at least biting off something he can chew. Perhaps he would lift his intellectual level to politics and economics if these were small-scale enough.

Loneliness reflects the absence of community life, and also the absence of a healthy family life of the sort which can embrace aging grandparents and indigent great uncles. It is all too common in large cities, especially among unmarried women and old people. If you really face the truth of the problem you have to admit that most loneliness should never have been in the first place. Unless a woman brings social ostracism upon herself by some terrible deed or deficiency, she should be accepted and at home someplace with all her eccentricities (of which she would have much fewer) and faults. Both the usual diagnosis (that lonely Miss X has a personality defect that can probably be remedied by a charm school or psychoanalysis) and the usually recommended cure (attendance at artificial gatherings full of other forlorn souls), is calloused, uncomprehending, and unlikely to succeed.

Authority and function. Christianity teaches that every man has a particular job to do in the world and that he will be judged according to how well he does it. The corollary proposition is that it takes all kinds to make a world and that there is indeed a natural diversity among men. Not all men are fit to rule; not all men are fit to contemplate.

Here contemporary American society is at its greatest odds with the Church. Anyone can be president of the United States; anyone can make a million dollars; and all people ought to desire both. In consequence we have a society in which very intelligent men are doing stupid work (because only a handful of people run everything), which is a strain on them; in which many stupid men (through graft or inheritance) are doing work far beyond their intelligent capacity, which is a strain on *them*; in which a very few intelligent men have vast responsibilities, and die early of coronary thrombosis. We have a society in which the president is hopelessly overburdened and where every last clerk and truck driver feels duty bound to decide all matters of state along with him. Nobody has security. Everybody suffers from envy. No one is contented with his state of life (and, indeed, few people can boast a state in life). Avarice is universal. This is background for thousands upon thousands of neuroses and psychoses which would never have occurred in a simpler and more reasonable society.

The Normal Man

Man is composed of body and soul, in a substantial unity. Psycho-somatic medicine (which is the last but one fad in psychological circles) is an elegant way of saying the same thing. The psyche is the soul (divested usually of its true spiritual nature) and the somatic part refers to the body. One influences the other, as doctors are rediscovering. However, the relationship between body and soul is one of true unity, not just of mutual influence. The philosophical way of putting it is that the soul is the *substantial form* of the body. Without a soul the body cannot operate, and soon corrupts, as is evident in death which is the separation of soul and body. The soul is the vital principle of operation in the whole man. The body is the soul's avenue of knowledge and the vehicle of much of its operation.

In most cases the body and soul operate as a unit. It is not surprising then that a man down with the flu is depressed in spirits, or that a man habitually lost in lust will lose his mind.

THE NORMAL MAN IS THE HIERACHICAL MAN, OF WHOM THE EXEMPLAR IS THE SAINT.

The pictures below give a rough illustration of the hierarchical man and his disordered opposite. In this crude presentation the hierarchical man is grossly oversimplified, while his opposite is unnecessarily chaotic. In reality certain localized defects, if severe, would suffice for a mental breakdown.

The important thing to note in the pictures is that a man's balance depends on the right ordering of all his parts; the lower subordinate to and governed by the higher. Thus the passions (emotions) should be subject to reason. The reason, in turn, should be subject itself to God.

This is a man compared to a household in which, 1) the entire activity is ordered to GOD. The spiritual faculties: 2) the INTELLECT meditates so that it may make true judgments, 3) the Will grows strong so as to make decisions, and controle the PASSIONS, 4) of which some are dormant, while some are operating in an orderly way. 5) & 6).

There are two sorts of spiritual disorders in man: mental disease and sin. Mortal sin is a matter specifically of the will's direction. Mental disease may mean a disorder in the functioning of the mind or of the will, or it may mean failure of the reason to govern the passions.

Sin and insanity are related disorders but not parallel disorders. The saint is the most sane of men, because the concept of sanctity includes perfect sanity. That is why peace is the fruit of holiness, because peace is defined as the tranquility of order, which tranquility consists in all the appetitive movements in one

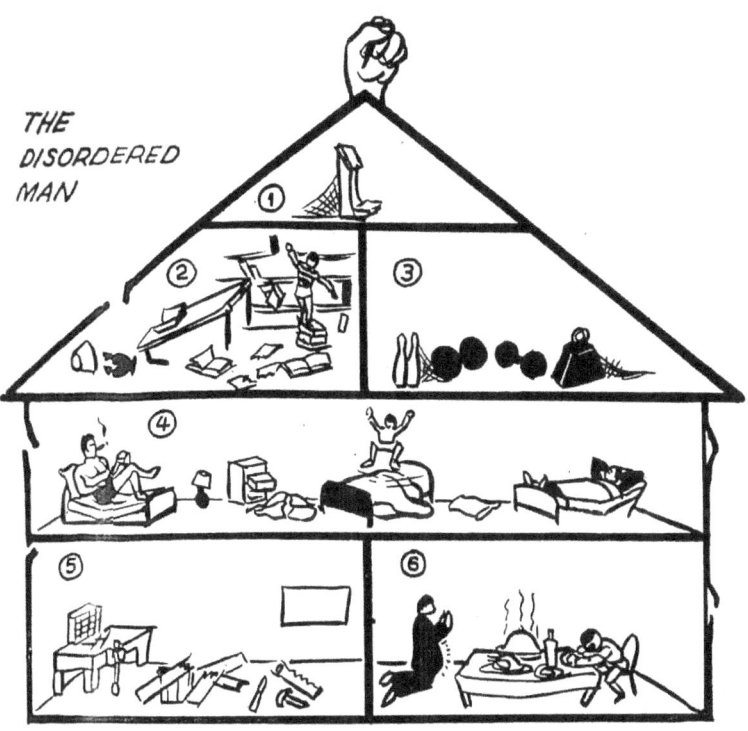

This is a man compared to a disordered household, which 1) ignores God. The PASSIONS run wild 2) making true judgments impossible. 3) & 4) The WILL grows flabby and the INTELLECT does not operate. 5) There is no work, but destruction. 6) Worship is toward SENSE PLEASURES.

man being set at rest together. Otherwise the two disorders are not necessarily coincidental. A man can be grievously proud, yet sane. A demented man can be in the state of grace.

DIFFERENCES IN PEOPLE
1. Differences in Intellectual Capacity

Other things being equal, the simple-minded and the very intelligent men are the most easily unbalanced. A simple intellect cannot handle complex and subtle ideas because it is unable to resolve seeming contraries and make subtle distinctions. There are quite a few simple people in the world. For their own happiness, sanity and sanctity, they should lead simple, peaceful, ordered lives according to truths authoritatively given them by others. The Catholic Church has always guarded the simple, and the near-simple. She has protected them when she could from religious controversy (while the wise could debate about such matters publicly), from reading harmful books, and even from the mental and moral tangles of Hollywood. When She made a society the simple were mostly on the land, close to animals and fields, folk-music and dancing, and their guardian the Church. Even today the mildly demented among them can occasionally find sanctuary working in peace, silence, and simplicity for a monastery or convent.

Heaven help the simple today! The schools want them to make up their own minds about the gravest problems of life and eternity. The newspapers and radio invite them to consider matters too difficult for international statesmen to settle. Everyone has to have an opinion about everything, whether or not it is within his province or competence.

The very intelligent have a different problem, peculiar to societies like ours. Intelligence drives the mind to the discovery of basic principles, to correlating, comparing, weighing, testing. A philosophical genius could easily go mad in Harvard or Yale, where every professor consciously or unconsciously contradicts his colleagues, to say nothing of the internal inconsistencies in his own theories. In a world devoid of fundamental certainties, and even implicitly denying the possibility of discovering truth, its best brains are tempted to blow themselves out. When high intellectual quality is combined, as it often soon is, with escape via the sense pleasures, the hazards are even greater. Again it is the Church which could have saved them, and would have in another age. The mind driven to distraction by Nietzsche and Hegel would have found rest, joy and adventure in the certainty of the Faith and the lucidity of the *Summa Theologica*.

2. Sex Differences

Men and women, being made to complement each other, have sort of half-natures. What one lacks the other is meant to supply. It works out neatly when they pair off to start families, as was intended. The man stands on his own two feet and goes about taking care of the welfare of his family and society. He is given to manliness, courage and enterprise. He is objective in his reasoning, usually accurate in his judgments, and not much interested in personalities. His wife's intelligence is more diffuse. Her judgments are made with the spontaneous assistance of her heart and her senses. They are often more penetrating than her husband's, but sometimes not so accurate. She is subject to moods and depressions traceable to physiological sources and considerably modified by the presence of a loving husband. She cheerfully will give herself entirely for her husband and children.

The very possibility of divorce unsettles all marriages. It is the woman who suffers chiefly from the prospect of impermanence in marriage, since hers is the dependent nature. Her normal womanliness, domesticity and tenderness can be twisted into instability, emotionalism and vacillation, fertile grounds for neuroses. Current ideals of married love as reflected in movies, magazine stories and divorce courts, are completely cock-eyed morally and psychologically. The ideal woman as portrayed therein just doesn't exist. She is radiantly and persistently beautiful. She never becomes old. She never becomes pregnant. She falls in love only with worthy and devastatingly handsome men, who reciprocate an hundredfold. It is all very adolescent and imaginary. In real life not all girls are beautiful, but all of them are aching for a totality of devotion to someone. They ought to expend their generosity in a secure domestic situation. If a woman's marriage is not secure or if she is not married her need for devotion will find another outlet, which ought to be in piety. There is sound psychological basis for calling women "the devout female sex." Psychologically, if one may say so, they need God more than men do, because their nature demands that they give themselves. Here it is interesting parenthetically to note that God does really supply much of what is wanting in the natural order, such as fulfillment to a woman's nature and solace to the afflicted.

A woman's mental balance is related to her necessity of self-giving. Even the selfish, gold-digger type of woman cannot escape her own nature, and usually ends up hopelessly devoted to some quite worthless member of the opposite sex. As for most women, their happiness, and often their mental balance, depends on what they choose to worship. A husband, securely held by bonds other than adolescent physical charms, plus a house-full of children in constant need of attention, is the safest environment for the majority of women. The alternative is the convent, which supplies a framework for selfless devotion to a high ideal, and does in fact provide most of its nuns with a full, joyful life of serenity. One of the greatest lacks among most non-Catholics is a framework, like a community of nuns within which to lead a selfless life. Even the works of mercy have become professionalized, so that a girl who wants to spend herself as a nurse or social worker usually finds herself instead making rather a good thing of a career to which the sick and the poor are incidental. This is the fundamental reason for the discontent among nurses and social workers. They are unhappy not so much because they are underpaid, but because they are paid.

Unmarried girls who go in for business careers are in a much worse state. There is nothing satisfactory about giving yourself wholly to International Business Machines or R. H. Macy. It is usually only possible to bring yourself to spend yourself for their causes via a personal devotion, whether from afar or all too dangerously near, to the first vice president, or the section manager or the supervisor of the filing department. This fact is well recognized in shrewd personnel practice, and accounts for the unusual charm found among the company's representatives whose special duty it is to persuade office girls to work overtime.

Never mind the disorder it may cause in the affections of plain little Miss Brown, whose life seems so drab on the exterior, but whose day dreams are wildly exciting and not a little adulterous.

There is another grave tension on the modern woman, and that is the strain of trying to be like a man. Its most pronounced manifestations are found among successful business women. They are either calloused and hard (much more unattractively so than men who are calloused and hard), or they are strained to the point of, or beyond, a nervous breakdown. Self-sufficiency and objectivity, which are necessary in high positions in our competitive society, are not natural feminine characteristics.

Women trying to imitate men is at its worst in matters of sex. Traditional morals, double standard and all, are consistent with the psychology of the sexes. A man's passions are distinct from his intellectual judgment and he can be promiscuous without involving his whole nature. He does not fall in love with every girl he makes love to. It is not so with women. Their hearts go right along with their feelings, and drag the intellect after, causing no end of trouble, and possibly unbalancing them. Nor do women who try to be calloused about these things (possibly at the behest of a psychoanalyst whom Heaven forgive!) succeed in becoming like men. Rather are they degraded to something below the human species.

Men's mental balance stands more strain in personal and domestic affairs than does women's, because men are more objective and self-sufficient, in general less sensitive. For unbalance in men one should look to other factors. The war is the most important factor now. In it men were brutalized and demoralized, shocked and paralyzed with fear. Another common and general cause is industrialism, which frustrates the initiative, responsibility and creativity of men, and carries the constant threat of insecurity. Not having a functional, secure place in the world of affairs puts a man in roughly the same position as a woman who is insecure in her home.

3. Temperamental Differences

Four basic temperaments have been recognized since ancient times. Most modern efforts to classify people according to bodily structure or the bumps on their heads or some other physical factors are efforts to discover a measurable basis for temperamental differences and have so far been unsuccessful. Evidently the differences of temperament though of the body rather than of the soul (and therefore inheritable) are diffuse.

Knowledge of temperament provides a guide as to how to treat different people; whether to console a person or be harsh with him; whether to spank a child or gently reprimand him. Temperamental differences are very important in relation to sanity. Why is only one child out of six neurotic as a result of identical home conditions? Why does one girl on the assembly line have hysterics after two days and the next girl remains placid after five years? Usually temperament is the deciding factor.

Certain factors modify or cloud one's native temperament. You cannot easily discern the temperament of a holy person, because he will have overcome the defects of it. Gross sinners are so much alike that temperament is not evident. Mental disease also can blur temperamental distinctions.

The four basic temperaments[2] are the choleric, melancholic, sanguine and phlegmatic. Most people are a mixture of two temperaments one modifying the other.

The Choleric is the executive type, with great drive, ambition and capability; with powers of organization and a love of commanding. He has two minds and no heart, very little human sympathy. He has great pride and is given to anger. Choleric people direct the great enterprises of the world. In our day that means big business. The handful of men who direct our gigantic commercial enterprises are mostly choleric. This type rarely

---

[2] For an admirable and more detailed description of the temperaments, see *The Four Temperaments*, by the Rev. Conrad Hock. Bruce Publishing Company, Milwaukee, Wisconsin.

goes insane because, despite strong passions, the choleric operate chiefly by intellect and will. These men do a superhuman amount of work. They break down physically rather than mentally, usually from heart trouble.

The Melancholic is more the thoughtful type. His temperament is the most unfortunate from the point of view of mental balance. Melancholic people react slowly, feel deeply, and tend excessively to the passion of sorrow. They naturally see the dark side of things, often to the point of warping their judgments. When they go overboard in their sorrow they are candidates for involutional melancholia, a madness of despair with suicidal tendencies.

Melancholic people are naturally reflective, serious, passive, reserved, irresolute, diffident, pusillanimous, given to solitude and easily falling into day dreaming. For all that many saints and great creative thinkers have been melancholic.

People of this temperament need God more than others. When they are "emotionally unbalanced" their need for religion is acute, and indeed it is doubtful if anything else can help them. Excessive talking about their troubles, as in psychoanalysis, can only aggravate the difficulty. Naturally speaking it is almost impossible to restore a melancholic to mental balance once he has reached the psychotic stage.

The Sanguine is charming and superficial. These people have weak passions but are quick. They have great optimism, usually unfounded; love fine clothes and good manners, are cheerful and vain. Except in that they are unstable they are proof against mental disorders. However their instability, if increased by careless upbringing or by unstable economic and domestic conditions, can eventually cause a breakdown.

The Phlegmatic is slow but not deep. People of this temperament have weak passions. They are the office workers who seem to have an infinite capacity for being bored, who can do the same monotonous work for years on end with solicitude only for a full lunch hour. These are the children it is quite safe to spank and even then you won't make much as an impression.

It takes a lot to unbalance a phlegmatic person. However should he lose his mental balance, it will be almost impossible for him to recover, because of the difficulty of arousing him to make an effort.

A man with an upsurging "id",
   Sought relief from the life he had hid.
"Oh go right ahead",
   The psychiatrist said,
"You've just done what your libido bid!"

But he answered them short
   With a violent retort,
"If I have then no guilt,
   What a monster you've built.
Did I sin? Well, I certainly did!"

PART II. DISORDERS SEATED IN THE INTELLECT

Functional mental disorders involve the spiritual nature of man. They are disorders either within the mind itself (defective operation of the intellectual faculty or the will) or of the mind's jurisdiction over the passions (emotions).

The three elements chiefly involved are the intellect, the will and the passions. The inter-relationship of these three elements is very close. Nevertheless we shall make logical distinctions between them for purposes of orderly discussion. This division will be useful in explaining the origin of mental disorders although it may have no clinical value.

The Nature of the Intellectual Faculty

The intellect is not simply a faculty for knowing but a faculty for knowing *truth*. It is determined as to universal truth, but not as to particular truths. That means that in the presence of the Beatific Vision the mind can no longer be deceived. Here on earth the mind can accept error for the grain of truth that is usually in it. Nothing, as erroneous, can be accepted by the mind. So, for instance, self-contradictory statements are instantly rejected. The fact that the mind is made to know truth is the reason why what really is true always seems to put the mind at rest, seems to correspond with something already in the mind.

The way the mind works is just the opposite from the way of the senses. The senses are concerned with particulars; *this* rose, and *that* bottle of scotch. The mind's first concern is with universals. The mind has to have some universal goal or objective before it can even begin to operate. You have to know you are going to Chicago before you can decide which route to take. It is as simple as that. The way it is put philosophically is that the end is the last in the order of execution, first in order of intention, and that you have to have the first general intention before you can make lesser particular intentions.

This means that nobody can live without a purpose in life, and that there can be only one last end, although a man can have a lot of proximate ends so long only as they are ordered somehow to the final goal.

Now the mental disorders which we are going to consider as chiefly in the intellectual faculty are all related to this matter of the last end. If a man cannot find a last end he is incapable of mature operation; if his last end is false he will suffer more or less; if his last end is vague and indistinct he will not be able to derive secondary principles of operation from it.

God and False Gods

Our last end and perfect happiness is God. As St. Augustine has said: "Thou hast made us for Thyself, O Lord, and our hearts are restless till they rest in Thee."

If we set up something else as our final goal that something else becomes a god to us. This fact is quite often striking, so that we say, for instance, that a man *worships* his belly when his life is devoted to fine eating. All final ends have a sort of infinity about them. Thus, not the ambition to have enough clothes to cover our nakedness, which could easily be arranged; but to be well dressed, which tends toward infinity. So also not to make a hundred dollars a week, unless this goal be very remote; but to make a million dollars or just to make money in general. You have to take your last end seriously, worship it, even to the extent of sacrificing for it, and let it give order to your life.

Here we come upon the question of sanctity and sanity again. Mortal sin is the deliberate turning away from God as one's last end, and the consequent turning to another last end. Because of the deliberate element, however, the sin is in the will rather than in the intellect. It is possible through ignorance to have a badly distorted view of God as your last end, and yet not be in mortal sin. This is especially the case in inculpable paganism and material heresy. However, most false gods do indicate a distorted will, even if not an incipient mental disorder. The road to Hell is not necessarily via the insane asylum.

On the other hand, you are in a bad way if you have no final goal at all, a state which is not uncommon today. You can vacillate only so long before you slow down to a full stop. A person who hesitates to accept the goals currently offered by a materialistic world, yet lacks opportunity or drive to discover better, may well be in a better state spiritually than his eager-beaver confreres. It sometimes seems almost as though God allowed some to lose their sanity as a merciful escape from an intolerable situation in which they declined to compromise. These are the people who would have found God if we had made God known in the market-place as we ought. Perhaps they will recover their sanity again, and sanctity too, if we go out and minister to them in charity.

From a purely psychological point of view (which is not the final criterion) it is better to have a false end than no end at all. Almost any end will preserve an hierarchy within one's nature even if it is distorted a bit. This doesn't mean you can choose a

A Christian Abnormal Psychology

final end at random. You have to have some conviction about it or it's as good as no end at all.

From the final goal derives the first intention, and from that all the secondary goals and secondary intentions. Let us say that a man has decided his goal is making money. How neat it is. Everything falls into place. He moves to the suburbs, buys his wife a fur coat, chooses a dark-blue tie, joins the Masons, and sends his son to Yale, all as remotely or directly auxiliary to the accumulation of wealth. Such a man will keep his sanity up unto the very gates of Hell unless he loses confidence in his goal, or despairs of reaching it. Since the making of money has no natural limit but can continue to infinity, it is a good goal for keeping up one's interest. There is little danger that it will be realized and the emptiness of it seen. On the other hand, in these times of economic uncertainty, there is the prospect of despair. A bad stock market crash might send our man insane. But we shall come to despair presently. One more word about our example. Notice that he will practice austerity in the pursuit of his ideal. If he really believes, he will not be a jolly drunkard or waste money on wild women. The austerity will increase his chances of sanity on the whole, as it will keep his emotions in order. Hitler and Stalin have not been conspicuously sullied by lust and carousing in their steadfast pursuit of power. Maybe this explains why they have not gone mad in their madness. Sense indulgence can be very debilitating.

Psychologically, esoteric religions like theosophy are useful, if you can bring yourself to believe them. They preserve the sense of mystery which really does shroud God. It is more restful to the mind to consider too many things mysterious and above it,

Harvard man with world on his shoulders.

than to try to analyze and dissect the sort of god liberal education usually offers: a god at once responsible for the entire universe and yet capable of our complete comprehension, some sort of a mathematical formula perhaps. Clearly such a god is no god at all, since blind forces and mathematical formulae are considerably inferior to the men who are, in the concepts of the same liberal school, the finest emergent evolution types yet: the contemporary gods. What such thinking resolves itself into is that we are god, and therefore we are our own last end. It's a sort of egomania, a madness per se. Self-worship is by all odds the worst form of worship, save only Devil worship. Even unaccompanied by malice it is a menace to sanity, especially to those who think or feel deeply. Many a college graduate is wandering around with mental indigestion from trying to figure out, comprehend, coordinate and encompass the world of which he appears to himself to be the focal point. It leads to headaches and swelling of the brain; then to mental torment, and possibly to madness. If our student has a strong moral sense he is also carrying the world around on his shoulders: a very heavy, sometimes crushing load. His to wipe out venereal disease, his to put an end to war, and all the time he may be a person of no influence or position whatever even for initiating such crusades. It's not so much a matter of pride as of having been maneuvered into the control position of the universe through having unfortunately attended the best colleges. What a relief it would be to learn that God's Providence presides over all things. It would even be a relief to believe that the goddess of the Atlantic Ocean will wipe out all suffering if only men go about their daily business with confidence and blow kisses oceanward each day at high noon.

Of the many possibilities for false worship there is one more which ought to be mentioned and that is worship of another person. This most tempting form of false worship can be recognized by the fact that one orders one's life to the person in question; just as Hitler's youth directed their whole lives to the Feuhrer. We have the same unhealthy element in our love affairs. Our popular songs tend more to "I worship and I adore you," than to "You are so beautiful."

We have said before that melancholic people especially need a strong religion to balance their despondent nature. Lacking it they are the ones most likely to go overboard in false worship of another person. Especially is this true of melancholic women when they fall in love. Since men find it wearing to play the dual role of love and god, the women's hearts are often broken. They then easily fall into despair and sometimes want to kill themselves.

Freud had a misdirected insight into this problem. He saw the tendency of some women to expect mere men to be more than husbands and lovers and guessed the women were looking for fathers, which sounds plausible because of the fatherliness of God. To explain it Freud cooked up a theory about how every young girl has to go through a period of falling in love with her father before she can fall in love properly with young men. It is like Freud to have made fathers (who are handy, to be sure) suddenly dispensable to the psychical development of their daughters, while waving away a traditional prejudice in favor of God's indispensability.

What's Wrong With True Worship?

Since Catholics know the only true God and have their last end all set and certain, they should be marvelously well balanced, at least spiritually. One can understand how bad Catholics might run into trouble but when pious Catholics have nervous breakdowns, when even nuns and priests go insane, does it not call for some explanation? We think it does, despite the fact that deeply religious people have the lowest insanity rate.

You need not only to have a final end, but to have one from which distinct secondary principles can be derived. The true final end, and the most universal one is God but it is also the farthest away in a sense, because it really is the final end, and many are the paths which lead to God, according to the nature and work and temperament and circumstances of every man. In between a man and his final end of God there is a complicated maze which he must tread according to certain derivative principles. Otherwise God is meaningless as a final end. All right, where are the principles? There are the ten commandments, largely prohibitory, except for the injunction to love God with our whole hearts (which in turn needs a multitude of derivative applications as regards daily life). There are the precepts of the Church, which have limited application. But where are the guiding principles for choosing a job? For a social life? For much of professional life, and for many other spheres of activity? For the most part they have not been worked out in regard to our society, for we live in a society which the Church did not make, which is not built on Catholic foundations, or even on the foundations of the natural law. There is that wide gap between religion and daily life which *Integrity* is always talking about, and which is creating a terrific tension in all our lives. This is probably the root reason why lay Catholics have mental breakdowns. The more penetrating and sensitive they are the more sharply they feel the contrast between the nobility of their religion and the sordidness of their economic aspirations; between the intensity of their spiritual life and the dullness of mechanical work and play. But if they do not recognize it as a tension, they lead double lives and feel it dimly. Most of them are trying to serve both God and Mammon. It is impossible, psychologically and on the authority of revelation. To do so would be to have two final ends contradicting each other. They are in this spot. They have a distant goal, which is God, but no precise rules, other than prohibitory and devotional, for getting there. Meanwhile they have a temporal life to live. So they accept the working principles of Mammon, and shift to a godly economy for devotional purposes. Or they try to make a synthesis between spiritual progress and worldly success. Now the Protestants can do this because in a sense they are responsible for the underlying principles of our economic order. *Catholics cannot, because their religion continually confronts them with the antithesis which exists between the spirit of the world and the spirit of God.* When Catholics attempt a synthesis they merely try to lead Catholic lives within a secular framework by the vigorous practice of minor virtues; try to fit God into a Mammon scheme of things. They are like a man who, having taken a bride, sees her only clandestinely, while daily appearing in public with another woman. Besides the scandal, it is a strain, and one which could easily provoke a nervous breakdown.

With religious the situation is a little different, but comparable. They don't need temporal principles so much as lay people do. What they need, and what they frequently do not get, is theology. They need not only to aim at God, but to know how to progress toward Him in prayer and sanctification, and they need to

INTEGRITY, January 1947

Young man lacking a final end.

know this pretty specifically. The same thing holds for pious souls in the world who are engaged in works of mercy or are otherwise removed from the usual temporal activities. They are starved from lack of religious instruction commensurate with their fervor and desire. They need dogma, spiritual direction, instruction in advancing in prayer, and liturgy. Instead they usually get, or fall into, either mediocrity or sentimentality or both. Mediocrity means a lessening of fervor, a deadening of the ideal. Sentimentality means reducing religious practice to the sense level of feeling. Devotionalism is an exploitation of the emotions, which is dangerous for one's spiritual health, and sometimes leads to a crazed state. The more intelligent a person is, the more dangerous it is to feed him pious fluff in religion because humility keeps a pious person from discarding what his intelligence tells him is nonsense. Instead he tries to erect a system without substance, to mull over and reflect on and live by, ideas which are too puny for him. Such a person often falls into scrupulosity.

No Life Without Purpose

It isn't always easy to find a last end, and sometimes it is impossible. In that case the person is bogged down completely and literally cannot operate. You cannot do the first things unless you have a last end. You cannot, for instance, keep your room clean, or yourself neat, or get to appointments on time, or read the latest book, or look for a job, if you are unable to decide what is the purpose of life. It is quite irrational of parents to say to their neurotic children, "Take your mind out of the clouds and at least clean your room. That's easy enough." It isn't easy. It's impossible if you don't see any reason for living anyhow. It may be hard to save a person who is headed for what will presently be diagnosed as schizophrenia, but the only real cure is to provide an ultimate reason for living. The victim is often enough an idealistic adolescent who declines to accept the drab commercial future envisioned by his parents, and yet has not had sufficient contact with vital religion to give credence to his noble feelings. His idealism ought to be caught up and encouraged (and could easily be by religion, or by the pseudo-religion which is Communism). But the conservative world wants to make him settle down to being worldly; to bow to commercialism and defer to the omnipotence of respectability. When they fail, he makes his exit from the rational world; when they succeed he takes his place in a humdrum office, and may never again become "unbalanced." It is not for us to measure the spiritual cost of his compromise, but sometimes when reading case histories of psychiatric "cures," you have an oppressive sense that the doctor has been the devil's advocate.

Marking Time

For the person who is not able to find a final end, because of those offered tempt to belief or desirability, there are two ways to stave off slowing down to a full stop, or losing control of a confused mind. Both are temporary measures, but given time, what cannot a man discover?

The one way out is to postpone the necessity of choosing a final end, which always involves postponing one's full maturity. The army offers a convenient respite, for instance. It has its own mysterious ends, which one can generally presume to be good. All you have to do is obey. The purpose of life can wait. Who knows if one will come back alive? How many young men were at loose ends in regard to their lives' purpose and work is evidenced by the general lethargy among returned veterans, for the army is not a likely place to discover the purpose of life if you don't know it already. Many of them are falling into another temporary groove:

education. Education for what? Education to prepare for a life that you don't know the purpose of, in many cases. You vaguely hope that college will tell you the purpose of life. But that is the last thing a modern college will tell you. So get a B.A. you go on to your M.A., still hoping. Then you get your Ph.D. and have a nervous breakdown, which can gracefully be attributed to overwork.

Or you can escape via the senses. We shall discuss this outlet under the passions, because there are several different ways of being precipitated into it. One thing only we would like to point out here. Sense pleasures really can be set up as final ends, by drastic foreshortening of life. "I decline to look beyond midnight tonight, and my one ambition until then is to get drunk."

Girl foreshortening her final end.

PART III. DISORDERS SEATED IN THE WILL

Psychiatry can never be an exact science because of the freedom of the will. The will is the only really capricious element in the universe. Men may justifiably hope to be able exactly to predict the weather, but not human conduct. There are two factors involved which are essentially beyond their powers of prognostication: free will and the grace of God. Many psychiatrists deny the existence of both. The wonder is that they have any success at all.

Realize that the will is a blind faculty. It desires, but it cannot desire what it does not know. Therefore it is tied absolutely to the intellect. This does not mean that it is governed by the intellect, but rather the reverse, although the influence is mutual. Nevertheless it is dependent for its knowledge, and were the knowledge to be entirely cut off, the will would be impotent and the person mad.

A Christian Abnormal Psychology

The intellect moves the will as presenting its object to it. The will desires good and it is determined to the universal good. But short of God, who is the universal good, the will can choose any particular thing as good, so long only as the intellect can be brought to present the good side so the will can choose it. Short of God everything has its good and bad aspects (just as all errors have a grain of truth); the only thing is that the will has to choose something *as good*. This is verified over and over again in common experience.

The good thing about castor oil is that it may make you well. The bad thing is the awful taste. As long as you think about the bad taste you can't take the medicine. But if you want to get well badly enough you may be able to bring yourself to act. Exterior influences on the will always have to modify the intellectual stalemate which prevents action. They bring pressure to bear. They rush up reserve arguments, to twist the intellectual judgment and move the will. That's why fear is so useful. A mother's threat of a spanking may make the prospect of taking castor oil attractive by contrast with the alternative.

Things done through fear are truly voluntary, though under some pressure. It is otherwise with coercion. If you force medicine down the throat of the screaming and protesting child, the act of taking castor oil is completely involuntary, however effective medicinally.

The will and intellect cooperate only in practical judgments and not in speculative matters. The act is simultaneous, neither will nor intellect having chronological primacy. But there is a primacy of knowledge on the part of the intellect; a primacy of election on the part of the will. Once the judgment has been formed the will has to follow along, but it is the will which moves the intellect to make the judgment.

The Matter of the Guilty Conscience

When the practical judgment of the intellect is a moral one, the conscience is involved. The conscience isn't a special faculty, it's simply the name for the practical moral judgment of the intellect. But it has a particular insistence about it which gives it almost a personality.

It will be useful to recall here that man belongs to the moral order, since he has a free will. It is a matter of indifference which subway you take home (because that is not a moral question) but it is not a matter of indifference whether or not you steal money. Animals have instincts to lead them to do what they ought to do. We have a conscience which merely informs us. Nor do we have to obey, because we have free wills. But just disobey and see what trouble you get into. First of all, it's a sin ever to go against your conscience. Often enough it's also neurotic trouble. Here's how the conscience operates:

A Christian Abnormal Psychology

By the time conscience has become remorse of conscience the disorder which is sin has set in and the disorder which is lack of peace is swinging into operation.

The cure for remorse of conscience is absolution which literally does wipe the slate clean, restore peace and grace. Absolution (it comes from God of course, who else could do these things?) is normally and most easily obtained in the confessional, but obtainable extraordinarily with perfect contrition, by direct recourse to God.

The alternatives to absolution are hardness (which is a building up of resistance to, a dulling of, the conscience), or some sort of nervous disorder, minor or major.

It is not strange that today, when the moral order is so largely ignored or denied, that there should be many disorders and derangements stemming from tortured and twisted consciences. Anyone who has had any contact with the insane can testify to the overt manifestation of this. Men's instincts are better in this regard than much formal education. The drive to confess and be forgiven seeks curious outlets, but it has a healthy origin. It accounts for the appeal of revivalist Protestantism, with its mass meetings at which "sinners" are urged publicly to manifest their sorrow and change of heart. Whoever has seen the sordid, undignified, and over-emotional exhibition put on by evangelists cannot, even so, help but feel that the humiliation endured by the repentant sinners abundantly suffices for perfect contrition and perhaps often does indeed win them the absolution which comes so easily to Catholics. Amid more luxurious surroundings, the Oxford Group provides a confessional for the better heeled. Alcoholics Anonymous has a similar provision, treated somewhat gingerly by members, who seem to prefer to relate their colorful misdeeds on public lecture platforms. Even blurting out one's tale at random helps, insofar as it relieves the tension. Most such accounts do contain contrition of a sort anyhow, what with the frequent expression of "I ought not to have," "What a fool I was," "My weakness was so great," etc. Any such recital is beneficial to a person's mental health, at least the first time. The danger is that what verges on indecent spiritual exposure to begin with will become a habit and the person may easily come to brag about what he formerly recited with shame. Then he is in the same spot as those who never had any contrition but were loose-tongued about their immorality only to show what virile fellows they were: a state morally grave and mentally dangerous.

Is it odd that pent-up remorse of conscience should seek a physical outlet? There is a real unity between our bodies and souls. An intensity which is frustrated spiritually will seek relief physically, and usually an appropriate one. When a moral cleansing is in order it may find expression in physical cleansing; in washing hands all the time, or bathing with undo frequency. A neurotic's new year's resolutions are often about bathing, or laundering or neatness. They are the physical parallel of the Catholic penitent's post-confession resolutions to be careful about morning and evening prayers and to receive the sacraments more frequently. Look at our society. There never was such a mania for cleanliness, such a preoccupation with plumbing, such an interest in bathrooms. Can this be unrelated to our unrelieved guilty consciences?

Some consciences are naturally stronger than others. All men have a moral sense, but some men show little evidence of it, while others seem driven by theirs.

Those of lax conscience are known to confessors as recidivists. They are the people who confess the same sins over and over again without much contrition and with no real effort at amendment. Pathological personalities are their psychological counterpart. They are the people who persistently steal or forge checks or commit other crimes without noticeable remorse. They usually have a background of lax upbringing which serves to aggravate their native defects. These are really moral problems. They fall into psychiatric hands partly through the sentimentality which says that all bad people are really only sick.

The ultra-sensitive consciences provide fertile material for sanctity under proper spiritual guidance. Otherwise they fall into scrupulosity. A person with a "New England conscience" who hasn't very specific objective moral standards is excellent potential neurotic material.

The Matter of an Erroneous Conscience

A conscience may be wrong, either in a vacillating, uncertain way, or triumphantly.

The first case is pretty general in this day of moral chaos. A person has to make his moral judgements catch as catch can, because the conscience keeps on working even in a semi-vacuum, just as the speculative intellect, starved for substantial food, will keep trying to understand and philosophize about the monotonous work the person is doing, or the petty affairs of his associates. One basis of conscience formation is whispered gutter confidences, usually about sex, and almost always fantastically wrong. Another is what other people think and do — a very fluctuating standard. The movies set the standard now, with advertisements a close second. "Inner feelings" are another poor criterion. What are "inner feelings"? Something you ate, or idle phantasms passing through the imagination. A vague conscience looking into itself for moral standards will get awfully confused. The person will not be able to distinguish between temptation and sin (the consent of the will). Just because a person idly thinks that his brother may be killed in the war does not mean that he wishes his brother were dead. It does not follow from a passing physical attraction that you have consented to the idea of fornication. Here is the trouble with scrupulous people. They cannot distinguish between temptation and sin.

It is interesting to note here that the Freudians hasten to accuse where the Church insistently absolves and hastens to console. The former doesn't hesitate to say: "You really wish he were dead." "You really hate your mother, don't you?" "You are secretly in love with your brother's wife and that is why you put salt in your brother's coffee. You wanted to poison him."

But a priest would remind you that what pops up in your imagination doesn't constitute sin unless consented to, and he would forbid you to worry about inadvertently putting salt in your brother's coffee just because you were lost in admiration of his wife's fresh beauty in her new blue dress.

Or, again, you form your conscience by your sense of shame. A sense of shame is a good thing, but it can be wrong too. Sex as such often seems shameful to people because they have come by their sex information surreptitiously, or not at all. The Catholics of the last generation have been almost as remiss as non-Catholics, thanks to Puritan influence in both cases, in the matter of sex instruction. Sins of omission in this regard do really account for much mental torture. Now the pendulum has swung and the mental torture is from excesses in the other direction. For a brief moment we had a generation immodest, promiscuous, appallingly outspoken, carefree and gay. The immodesty and promiscuity linger on; tongues continue unrestrained, but the whole business has lost its air of innocence. What happened to the sense of shame? It is still missing, but it will return automatically in its proper role, with a return of a balanced view of sex and the cultivation of the virtue of modesty.

What about consciences which are conscientiously wrong? What about people who are sure they are right, only they are not? What about those who practice birth control as their civic duty, divorce their wives in the spirit of self-sacrifice, put their cancerous aunts painlessly to death, and practice cannibalism with religious fervor? Well, they won't have guilty consciences. Most non-Catholics who practice birth control, for instance, really feel quite virtuous about it. And, as a matter of fact, they really are not sinning as long as they are sincere in their ignorance. They can, however, be guiltless in the sight of God without getting the slightest sympathy from nature, which always takes its toll. So if their practices are against nature, unnatural, they can expect to suffer natural consequences, the grief or the loneliness or the nervous disorders which they bring upon themselves. Birth control, for instance, is a much greater threat to mental health than a nursery full of children is to physical health. It also indirectly undermines the stability of marriage and the security of a woman's position. The possibilities of unhappiness and neurosis as the result of practicing homosexuality are far greater, because it is a graver perversion of nature. Other practices, like cannibalism and euthanasia, cause social disorders perhaps along with psychological ones.

What's in the Unconscious?

It is interesting to consider the unconscious in connection with the conscience. There seems no doubt but that the deeps of our nature are not readily accessible to our scrutiny and that they might contain matter in conflict with our conscious life.

The moral judgment which we call the conscious is not under our control but operates according to certain moral considerations of its own. One thing the conscience is very strong and insistent about: that good must be done and evil avoided. We would like here to make the hypothesis that the conscience also has, but dimly, all the natural moral laws as regards the human person, as part of its initial equipment. So, for instance, if you could isolate a person from any sort of moral instruction, he would instinctively react against lying (which is an unnatural abuse of the power of speech), against homosexuality, against birth control, etc. No doubt he would soon become corrupted, or his progeny would (owing to original sin and the insistence of the passions). But the right rules would continue to lie deep within him. If this hypothesis is true then there is deep-set conflict within people who are following the dictates of an erroneous conscience in good faith. The corollary is that peace, that blessed interior peace that comes from being completely at one with yourself, is the prerogative of the just. It would mean, for instance, that people who practice birth control are dimly disturbed in their unconscious. It would mean that all Communist party members are potential neurotics, if only because of their deliberate denial of the objective criterion of truth.

Here seems a good place to discuss psychoanalysis, which dabbles in the unconscious.

Psychoanalysis

Psychoanalysis is a method without a very coherent, or generally agreed upon philosophy. It supposes that causes of mental disease lie deep in the personality, in the unconscious, and that they can be brought into the conscious mind by prolonged, uninhibited talking. Freud is the father and hero of psychoanalysis.

How can psychoanalysis cure conflicts? Conflicts involve conscience and morality. But psychoanalysis is an amoral process at best, at frequent worst it has sort of an inverse morality. Where there is an express conflict of conscience the psychoanalyst will grant absolution, of his sort. It is done by denying the conscience, not the guilt. Nothing is evil to the Freudians; it's only your *attitude* that matters.

In the case of the conflicts mentioned above, where the conscience is making feeble protest from below against its own conscious operation on false information, one has the feeling that the very heart of the conscience is being run down and destroyed by psychoanalysis for it even goes so far in extreme cases as to try to destroy the basic principle that good must be done and evil avoided. At this point psychoanalysis, and any other form of psychiatry that goes along with it, is no longer fit subject for joking, but very close to, and possibly involved in, diabolical activity.

One of Gertrud von le Fort's novels, *The Veil of Veronica*[3], treats of this matter. Veronica's Aunt Edelgart hesitates to join the Church for twenty years. Finally she takes instructions and then

3   Sheed and Ward, 1934. This quotation is taken from pages 297 and 298.

refused to make her confession. Follows a period of intense spiritual suffering, to cure which she goes to a psychiatrist. From him she obtains a sort of peace, followed by diabolical disturbances. She is finally freed, not without violence, and enters the Church, making a public confession on her death bed, of which this is an excerpt:

> With my sense of guilt I still believed in God. But a sense of guilt is not the last form of Faith; the last form of Faith begins when one can no longer bear the sense of guilt, when its torments becomes so excruciating that one is driven to hate it. At this time, I thrust away from me everything that could remind me of God: Crucifix and Rosary and Missal, for the sight of them was like a devouring fire. And this is the last form of Faith. Only when his hatred of God is extinguished, does man become a complete unbeliever. And here the truly awful derision in which he, who had me in his power, held me, begins to show itself; I, now in my fear unlocked myself to mortal man — not however to man in his compassion, but to man in his presumption. To this presumption I exposed those deeps of my soul which God alone has reserved to Himself the power to adjust. Instead of flying to the Sacrament, I fled to science: I confessed to the doctor, and I received from him the only absolution which the world has power to give, namely the absolution of the psychiatrist, in the eyes of which there is no sin that cannot be forgiven, because, there being no such thing as the soul, it cannot refuse itself to God. And this absolution conferred on me that terrible peace in which thousands live today whose disease is simply this, that they have despised the peace of God! For even those who are furthest away

from Him have an Either-Or in relation to God, otherwise they would not be living.

From that day forward, I no longer believed in anything, not even in him in whose hands I was — the doctor had soon talked me out of my belief in him. Nor was I any longer animated by feelings of hatred towards God, but on the contrary I started going to church again — the doctor had likewise advised this, albeit in moderation. I suffered no more from an inner conflict and sadness, but I ate and drank and slept. I ceased to have struggles or temptations, for the simple reason that he in whom I no longer believed, from now on paid no further attention to me, but cast me aside like a worm or a lump of earth. And I myself did not regard myself as other than such. For as what else could I regard myself — there was nothing anywhere but that in the whole universe there was nothing left but matter alone grey, blind matter!

To return to the psychoanalytic technique as such. It presupposes that you cannot cure a spiritual trouble of which you do not know all the sordid details. That is not true. For one thing, it should not be hard to guess the trouble, for people are much alike and there are only a certain number of things that bother them. A good confessor can guess pretty accurately what is tying the tongue of his unseen penitent, because he knows men. If the psychiatrist is long in doubt it is because he does not know men, and he has an erroneous theory he has to fit the facts into. If a psychiatrist does know the truth about life and men, and can guess what the trouble is with his patient, what is wrong with handing out some information that might be helpful? Let the doctor, or a priest, supply data to a patient tormented by metaphysical problems. Likewise on the matter of sex. Or, if the doctor suspects the person to be tormented with good reason, let him tell about the mercy of God and how to make acts of contrition. These things are, of course, common sense, and likely often done. But they are contrary to the psychoanalytic theory which would persist in airing a person's dirty laundry, and probably much soiled linen as well that wasn't there to begin with, because concentration on sex matters sends the imagination into tail spins.

Let's leave the unconscious alone. Aren't we trying to invent a science of darkness where we ought to be availing ourselves of mystical theology instead? Our earthy and less than earthy parallel to what happens in high spiritual states is suspicious, for the devil imitates. How differently God deals with our unconscious (or if you want to call it that). In the first place He accepts our relationship on the conscious level and only holds us accountable for what we knowingly do. If the enormity of our pride is so near to us that we cannot see it, God waits, and he keeps pouring grace through the sacraments into that same depth of our being in which Freud discovers so much that is vile. Only after a long time (until we can bear it?) does God set out to purify our innermost nature. He does not trust us to direct the process, but he does it to us, we only suffering it to be done. This is the dark night that mystical theology talks about. The end result is high sanctity. What have the psychoanalysts to show for their efforts? Is it sometimes the death of the soul? They say one of the fruits of psychoanalysis is self-knowledge. But is it? Truly to know yourself is to know what the saints know, which is that you are nothing. You learn it through knowing God, that He is everything.

Diabolism

There is a regular chant in psychiatric textbooks to the effect that the Catholic Church for many ages obscured problems of mental disease because of the superstitious belief in the devil. They are wrong twice. The Church never did attribute all insanity to diabolism. And there is really a devil. He does obsess and possess people. Even today.

Quite often one hears of experiences in insane asylums which can only be explained preternaturally. For instance, patients have been known to become very violent when the Blessed Sacrament was brought into their section of the hospital, even though they did not see the priest and had no way of knowing he had entered.

Evidently some of the insanity today is not insanity at all, but diabolical possession. How much? Probably not very much. This is the last explanation which must be given when all others fail (and if the conditions indicate it). Purely natural factors are quite sufficient to account for the undue amount of insanity today, quite apart from this explanation. On the other hand, there are two factors which would lead one to look for diabolical activity. First is the fact that around seventy percent of Americans are now unbaptized, which means the devil has a certain jurisdiction over them. The other is that Freudian psychiatrists are providing grist for the mill.

Diabolical possession means that the devil (or a number of devils) takes possession and control of a person's body; during which time the person himself is usually unconscious, although he may be dimly aware of what is going on. There are intervals, usually violent, when the devil thus takes over. There are other intervals of calm and lucidity when the devil, still evidently remaining, does not interfere with a person's normal functioning.

If you wanted to find diabolical possession in America, the obvious place to look is among the mentally diseased, since that is what possession would look like to our secular minds. The next stop would be to find a classification of patients corresponding to the known characteristics. As it happens, there is such a classification. It is known as multiple personality and its chief mark is the alternating possession of the same body by distinctly different persons. It is a rare and spectacular "disease," about which physicians have sundry conflicting theories. The public is acquainted with it chiefly in Dr. Jekyll and Mr. Hyde. Treatment is attempted with analysis, hypnosis and other methods. If it really is diabolical possession, how futile and yet how dangerous to the doctors, are their efforts.

We had Jane psychoanalyzed
For she was acting queer.
We found that Jane is crazy,
In a different way than we are.

PART IV. DISORDERS ARISING THROUGH THE PASSIONS

Here is where emotional difficulties come in. A passion has no necessary connection with torrid love stories, but is roughly equivalent to an emotion (if strong) or a feeling (if weak). It is an act of the sensitive appetite, a desire on the sense or animal level, of men.

The passions represent joint action of our psychical and physiological natures (as when blood rushes to the head in anger). A lot of contemporary effort is being wasted trying to account for emotional difficulties solely on the physiological level, which is like trying to account for murder by metabolism.

Our passions, though not the highest sphere of our lives, are in a sense the predominant sphere. The idea is to regulate them by reason. To the degree that we do subject our passions to reason we are truly human, we preserve our hierarchical nature, our balance, our sanity. On the other hand, when our passions get out of control we are for that very reason in a bad way. Disordered passions can cause trouble all the way up to and including insanity depending on to what extent they cloud or distort the intellect and so pervert the will. When the passions take over and obliterate the reason, there is madness simply.

Disorders of sin and insanity run a close parallel in the matter of the passions. All the sins of weakness belong to the order of uncontrolled passions and the correspondence between the degree of material sin and the degree of nervous disorder is often startling. So here again we are reminded that religion is the guardian of sanity. As a matter of fact the Church retains a full understanding of man's nature in regard to the passions. It is intended in man that the passions should be governed by reason, but there is a certain conflict of ends between the two. ("The spirit is willing, but the flesh is weak.") It was to correct this internal warfare that God gave us the gift of integrity, which we lost by original sin. It is to regain some semblance of integrity that discipline and mortification are necessary in our lives.

The world is completely at odds with the Church in this matter of mortification. Whereas we gain control of ourselves only with difficulty in any case, the world with its false compassion is raising havoc with our natures. A philosophy of self-indulgence runs all through education. Advertising exploits our passions on a gigantic and scientific scale. Advertising and mortification work on exactly the same principles toward different ends. "Feast! Save yourself labor! Buy our cigarettes which show you pictures of such luscious girls!" cry the advertisements. "Fast! Be diligent! Keep your mind pure!" says the Church. No wonder religion is unpopular in these days of ascendant commercialism. Advertising wants to perfect everything except man. Incidentally, a very good case can be made on these grounds for the essential immorality of modern advertising.

The ultimate effect of all this stimulation of sense desires (Heaven help us it is even called "The American Way of Life.") is the multiplication of sorrows. Material things, attractive at first, eventually pall and provoke despair. Spiritual things at first repel then attract and satisfy.

Inhibitions

You might argue that advertising corrupts people only as incidental to its own profit and not from deliberate denial of man's nature. The same cannot be said about some psychiatry which is intent on glorifying the passions at the expense of the reason. According to this notion, it is unhealthy to restrain the passions; and if restrained there will be neurotic manifestations. Hence the popular idea that it is unhygienic to be without sex life.

The truth of the matter of inhibitions is this: every passion involves some bodily change, as counterpart to the spiritual effect. An inhibition is an attempted suppression of the physical part of the passion rather than of the passion itself. It is the suppression not of anger, but of the appearance of anger. It is the presence of aplomb to hide the reality of embarrassment. But you cannot suppress the physical element in passion and you only succeed in diverting it elsewhere, into ulcers or tics. Inhibitions are usually charged in regard to sex passions, but this is true only insofar as people entertain sex desires which circumstances prevent their satisfying. It is not true in the case of people who for reasons of a higher good, decline to entertain this passion at all. Here again the Church's moral teaching is consonant with our nature: purity of thought is essential to chastity.

Looking at the matter in a large perspective however, it is true that the intensity of human nature is suppressed in the modern world. Human nature is intense. Vitality is its mark. Yet all the way down the line the intensity is frustrated. Our souls are denied a noble cause. Our love is denied worthy objects. Our intellects are deadened, especially in our work. Our creativity is stultified. Our marriages are barren. Our bodies grow flabby from over-stuffed furniture and super-comfortable automobiles. We can't even play games and invent amusements. We are passive. We are spectators. We are robots.

But vitality will out. Some people stand up and scream. Some get drunk. Some go in for sex. Some read the tabloids, getting their daily dose of violent death, execution, rape, murder, and all the rest. How near is mass violence to the surface of American life?

INTEGRITY, January 1947

Sentimentality, Sex and Lust

Love is basic to all the other passions. Ultimately all human action springs from love. This accounts for the plausibility of the Freudian theory. Freud could not have explained so much by, for instance, hope, as he did by sex, because sex is the most vehement form of this basic passion of love.

Besides the love which is a passion, there is also a rational love seated in our will. It is with this rational love that we love God, and other men for God's sake. We also with this love cherish people in that love of friendship which seeks to give itself and not to possess. When love to which belong on this rational level because of its object, drops to the sense level, you have a disorder known as sentimentality. We Americans are maudlin in our sentimentality.

This dropping of love from the rational to the sense level has happened often in religion. It comes from an overemphasis on devotional matters. It is characteristic of the "love is my only dogma" type of liberal Protestantism, which tries to solve all its problems by "love" in the absence of principles. What else can this love be but feeling, and chiefly, as it has turned out, the feeling of pity. Pity is a good enough feeling, but needs the guidance of reason. Sentimental pity (more often than malice) is back of the enthusiasm for birth control and euthanasia. Sentimentalists lose full control of their reason. They are fuzzy thinkers of the "how heartless you are to let this poor woman suffer so from cancer," school. They shudder at the mention of Hell. Naturally it does not fit in with their doctrine of love, because it doesn't appeal to their feelings.

All of us are infected with fuzzy thinking and sentimentality to some degree. It is at least a remote cause of mental disorder, and it makes the cure of neurotics enormously more difficult than it would be otherwise. There is nothing left for it but patiently to instruct and discipline the sloppy modern mind.

Sex is the most vehement form of passionate love since it has to insure, from the natural point of view, that we carry on

A Christian Abnormal Psychology

Passions under control....

the race. Although sex is on the sense level it is capable of being caught up with the love of friendship on the rational level, and even divinized through the *sacrament* of matrimony. It is in this way that Christianity has exalted sex. It is wonderful to meditate on the fact that God has not despised our animal nature but has transformed it. He has done the same thing with eating, which is a rather ludicrous procedure considered in itself. On the human level, however, it is a social as well as a biological function. And since the Eucharistic banquet was initiated, eating itself has been elevated to something of a ceremony.

During the decline of the Roman Empire, the primary passions were grossly disordered, with lust and gluttony especially prevalent. Pagan rites included revolting obscenities and sex symbols were everywhere. It took centuries of Christian austerity to restore simple goodness to simple natural phenomena and to purify the minds of men.

It seems as though the Freudians are bent on making everything obscene again. Freud even has a whole set of sex symbols for the interpretation of dreams. Many people's minds are already so diseased that they cannot see a tall building or a vegetable stand without sex associations.

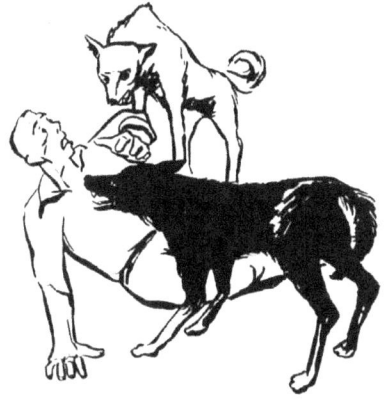

Passions in control.

Instead of lifting sex up to a holy familial love, our age is ruthlessly pulling it down to sheer lust, which is sex from which as much reason as possible has been eliminated.

Nothing so distorts the intellect as lust. The imagination keeps feeding the intellect images calculated to distort the judgment. And it is no easy matter to purify a mind of lust once it has been saturated; in fact, it is very difficult to get such a person to want to rise out of his mire. Where there is any will to recover, the Church's method is the emergency treatment: constant and continuous attendance at the sacraments, penance as often as one falls, and daily Communion. When a man is beyond self-help God will lift him up so long as he merely consents. The world's methods are quite other. The world invites the mind to the consideration of lust, now everywhere in books, magazines, advertisements, and even radio jokes. Some psychiatrists do the worst possible thing. They urge as a remedy for preoccupation with sex, still more preoccupation with it.

Another reason for sex disorders lies in the fact that people confined by their philosophies to the physical level, the materialists, sometimes have messianic expectations in regard to sex. It's like having a deep yearning which is really for a college education and a house in the country, but which you hope to satisfy with chocolate pecan sundaes (because everyone assures you that houses in the country and college educations don't really exist and that chocolate pecan sundaes are the highest good). Under these circumstances your appetite for chocolate pecan sundaes is insatiable. Maybe nymphomaniacs can be accounted for here.

Fear and Insecurity

Fear chills and paralyzes. This is its physiological aspect. In extreme cases it can turn the hair white, cause more or less permanent shock or amnesia. There were a lot of cases of this during the war. The diagnosis is simple enough. And because the effects are chiefly bodily, physical measures are effective in the cure.

A Christian Abnormal Psychology

Fear is a special problem today in its aspect of widespread insecurity. It is popular to talk about insecurity as though it were a problem inherent in economics instead of a fear inherent in men, and to try to cure it by guaranteed annual wages and such. This is an exact parallel to our trying to cure unhappiness among nurses by raising their wages, without bothering to account for the fact that they were much happier when they were paid less. There is hardly a contemporary problem which is not now basically and blatantly spiritual. Insecurity is one of them.

Mr. Roosevelt's "We have nothing to fear but fear itself," is a very inaccurate statement. There are a lot of things to be afraid of: atomic bombs, death, economic ruin, starvation, cancer, and the rest. They all fulfill the conditions for exciting the passion of fear: they are evil; they threaten; they are not yet upon us. We are falling all over ourselves to eliminate these causes of fear, but without self-reform. The only way to eliminate many of them (all of them can't be eliminated) is for our society to turn again to God and right itself. This doesn't have much popular appeal. Instead we plan to guarantee security where there is no security. We try long and patiently to get Russia to sign a treaty, although we have no reason to suppose that she will honor it. We try to guarantee wages without regard to the economic balance of the industry. We pile up insurance in the face of currency inflation. We huddle together in large cities where we make excellent targets. We tend toward socialist government by way of assembling all our bad eggs in one basket.

Meanwhile our lives are utterly in God's hands, as always, whether we face the fact or not. As long as we do God's Will, things will work out well. Since we pretend He isn't there, we continue to suffer the consequences of our own muddling.

Where insecurity is an individual psychological problem there is no cure short of trust in God. People who are worried at 18 about job security at 60 should not be taken seriously on an economic plane. They are in the same boat with people who are afraid to cross streets or walk over bridges. There is only one condition under which they can be freed, not from fear itself (which is often a good thing and is taken care of by the virtue of courage), but from morbid fear. Trust in God. "No harm can come to a good man." "In the sight of the unwise they seemed to die, but they are at peace. Alleluia."[4] All sorts of things may happen to us. But that ultimately it will all turn out all right, and that God will give us grace to sustain us in trials, are certainties of faith. Without these certainties who can cure fear? Men will kill themselves for fear of death (for such is the paradoxical character of the human animal).

Despair

Despair is a little further along the road that fear travels. Evil is already upon you in despair, and the sorrow it causes by its presence threatens to overwhelm. The sudden tension and semi-paralysis caused by fear is replaced by deep bodily as well as spiritual depression. People who despair are always tired, weighted down quite literally by their own depression. They want to sleep all the time. Neurasthenia is the name usually given them. Doctors who fail to take into account spiritual realities try all sorts of cures. One doctor's remedy for this was simply prolonged rest, during which his patients were not even allowed to feed themselves. Since despair usually carries a wave of self-pity along with it, it is hard to suppose he helped them.

Despair is the prevailing mood of western civilization. It is not the sin against hope kind of despair, which directly doubts God's power to save. In America, it is usually natural despair; the despair of making a million dollars, of settling in Westchester, of obtaining international peace, of finding a husband, or of advancing in the social scale, or of buying love and happiness. We brought it on ourselves by placing our hope in materialistic

---

4 In reference to Wisdom 3: 1 which is also used for the text of the Common of Martyrs in the Roman Missal. — Ed.

things. Of itself our despair has nothing to do with God, but it might lead to humility which is good ground for grace.

To commit a Crime is to kill the soul, but to despair is to fall into Hell. The truth of this old saying will be echoed by anyone who has ever tasted despair. Despair is not just painful. It is intolerable. The antidote is hope, or anything that gives pleasure and will encourage the vital elements of the body. Warm baths, rest, wine, music, friends, all the ordinary consolations are in order. But if the despair runs deep, more drastic measures are in order. Suicide is the logical conclusion of despair. Many people try to escape it via intense sensual pleasures, of which sex and alcohol especially recommend themselves. Here again is a precipitating point of escape mechanisms. But in the case of despair the senses are not only an escape from it, they also precipitate you into it.

The alternative to suicide and/or madness on the one hand, and to forced revelry on the other, is hope, the only real cure for despair. If the despair is deep the hope must be strong, which is to say that it must rest in God. This is the more essential the worse the mess people are in or the more melancholic their temperament.

It can be said categorically that people of pronounced melancholic temperament will only find consolation in God and *must* therefore have a strong religious life. Otherwise they will despair and their sorrow will itself lead to madness. Involutional melancholia has always been recognized as a distinct form of insanity, which tempts to suicide and is hard to cure. It is very bad for melancholic people to talk too much, and they should avoid any sort of analysis.

Opiates Are the Religion of the People

We are a nation of escapists. We run from our own despair, from the meaningless of our lives, from sorrow, from fear, from the spectacle of our own mediocrity.

It is on the whole a wise move. It is nature making one last effort at self-preservation. So it is wise not to remove the props, however unsteady, from under a man poised on the brink of despair, until you are prepared to support him otherwise.

Will you drown yourself in pleasure in disregard of the day of reckoning? Try sex or alcohol (not both; they are incompatible in the long run). The sins of the flesh will divert you for a while. Then what? Something may turn up to make it worthwhile to return to respectability. It won't be easy to return, but it will be possible up to a point. And if not, or if I can't return? Madness. If you live long enough and drink hard enough your brain will deteriorate. Lust may get you functionally. Or it, too, may destroy your mind organically through disease.

Perhaps it would be better just to keep too busy to think. Join committees like mad. Be an eager-beaver. Read everything. Go out every night. Never be alone. Never think a serious thought. But it's hard to keep up the pace. Something will happen that you will have to think about. Or you'll have a physical breakdown. Or more likely a nervous breakdown.

Opiates are the religion of the people.

Try oblivion if you're sure you never want to recover. It's done with drugs.

If none of the above suit you, or if they are too expensive or disgraceful, the thing for you is daydreaming. Doesn't cost a cent. Can be done under the very noses of a vigilant family. It gets progressively more interesting. As you become more adept at it, the pain of your circumstances eases. Who cannot invent a better world than this one? Maybe you will be able to cast off from reality entirely.

What Is Reality?

Most people are living in two unreal worlds. There is the ordinary humdrum world. It would be gross flattery to call this reality. It is unredeemed. Its values are all wrong. It does not consider God. It is the secularist nightmare. In it the millionaire's palace is as false as the slum tenement. As a matter of fact suicide comes easier amid material splendor, or on lovely sunny days. It is the contrast between one's aching heart and the riches and beauty which cannot assuage or satisfy that makes things especially intolerable. But to get back. There are tenements. There is almost universal ugliness. There is domestic strife, stupid jobs and all the rest. Only love can make it endurable, and only God can make it really real. The facts are always there: the irritation at the breakfast table, the fifty pounds overweight, the ten dollars a week, the spot on the carpet. But the world is a nightmare of meaninglessness without God, or without love (love is the most godlike thing among us, and whenever it reaches a selfless spiritual degree it has a power to transform things).

The other unreality is the world of the movies, the advertisements, the radio and the magazines. This is the world in which everything in the kitchen matches and everyone dresses like Hollywood stars. This is the world of tawdry glamour, of hypocrisy and pretense.

So with two unrealities already, why not a third? The advantage of the world of daydreams is that you yourself can be the central character, a sort of composite of all ideal qualities. Daydreaming absorbs the imagination, which should be busy supplying the intellect with data about daily life. That's why daydreamers are abstracted. You can daydream a lot before your imagination starts handing over daydream world data as the real stuff. But there is abundant opportunity for practice in the ordinary life. With many girls their work is an invitation to daydream, and their evenings are spent at the movies gathering new material. It can be laid down as a general rule that something is always going to be going on in the brain. Where people will not think, their imagination will take over.

Daydreamers are regularly classified as schizophrenics and almost certainly given shock treatments. What is the point in forcing persons by drastic means back into a grim unreality that they have been trying to escape from all their lives?

> The workingman of all his troubles,
> The social-worker rids.
> Freud relieves him of his soul,
> And Sanger takes his kids.

PART V. THE WAY OUT

We cannot repeat it too often. The world will do anything but reform itself. We'll spend a million dollars any day rather than make a radical change in our way of thinking. So long as we are committed to such a philosophy, we'll assuage our consciences with superficialities in regard to mental disease. We probably feel very virtuous now that we've lately stirred up a lot of indignation about the physical care of the spiritually tortured. But the physical structure of insane asylums is accidental to the problem of mental disease whereas the prevailing philosophy of psychiatrists is of the essence of the problem. Who has led a crusade against Freud? Who has campaigned for exorcists in asylums or for trained chaplains?

The fact that should be most obvious from this paper is that there is no hope for remedying the general condition of widespread mental breakdown without a spiritual transformation of society. If we don't reform we'll all be locked up, unless we are blown to bits first. If we keep on trying to wipe out venereal disease apart from morality, if we keep on trying to cure cancer without questioning the food industry, there just is no hope for us anyhow.

Having said that, there remains the problem of helping those who are the victims of our disordered society.

Relevance of Religion to Mental Disorders

Some indication has been given in this paper of the continual interweaving of religious considerations with those of mental health. We have barely touched on the stabilizing effect of objective "authoritarian" moral standards. We have discussed the matter of a troubled conscience and the therapeutic effects of absolution. We have mentioned the unbalancing propensities of sins of the flesh, and the mental torment of metaphysical uncertainty. For lack of space we have neglected until now any real mention of grace in this connection, although this is most important of all.

The synthesis that has to be made psychologically between religion and mental disorders centers about this question of grace, and it has not been made yet so far as we know. St. Thomas was not concerned with it, but elaborated a *rational* psychology which does not include the supernatural.

We usually think of mystical theology in connection with devout people well advanced in the spiritual life, and not in connection with neurotics and dipsomaniacs. Unconsciously we assume that progress toward God lies through the acquisition of natural virtue, forgetting that supernatural life is gratuitous and forever beyond our deserts, and forgetting also that the only disposing condition is humility.

It is the dipsomaniacs who have rediscovered in practice the approach to God through humility alone, although they don't know quite what to do with it. Natural despair is fertile ground for supernatural hope. Alcoholics Anonymous, who are drawn mostly from the spiritually underprivileged classes, work on this theory. They don't try the old tack of urging a drunk to make a man of himself. Instead they approach him at his humblest (just recovering from a disastrous bout) and urge him to admit his own impotence to reform and beg God to do for him what he cannot do for himself. It works, even among people who can't seem to go on from there theologically.

Why should it work, apart from the rather vague explanation that God is good? It works because those in a state of grace can, if they will allow it, shift over from a natural to a supernatural economy of operation. The supernatural gifts and virtues operate as habits paralleling our natural psychological equipment for human operation. Take a single example. Our control of the passions is accomplished partly through the natural virtue of temperance, which is markedly absent in habitual drunks and others snowed under by the sins of the flesh. Through humble and complete abandonment one predisposes oneself for a shift to the supernatural economy where virtues, including the virtue of temperance, operate in us through no direct effort on our part. It is rather as though a man were a puppet lying twisted in a heap, who consenting to be lifted up by God, is therefore raised up and untwisted in one process. Actually supernatural grace carries natural perfection in its wake. A neurotic who was converted to the Church and started going to daily Communion would feel the sanctifying and healing effects of grace at the same time, as though he were being at once lifted up and straightened out. He would feel as though he were being drawn upward to God for a long time in a spiral motion before proceeding in a straight line.

The shift from the natural to the supernatural economy is the only way out of bad breakdowns, personal and social. It is the "reaching for the stars in order to get out of the mire" technique. To use it means to offer a neurotic not a less trying life, or a less exacting goal, but to commission him to make over the world. Neurotics need to lose themselves in a great cause and complete dependence on God. We usually preoccupy them instead with their own mediocrity.

The Practical Problem

The practical problem in relation to functional mental disorders is that of how to combine spiritual assistance and psychiatric care. There are other problems of course: problems of money, physical care, etc., but this is the broad general problem to which the others are subordinate. It has three levels, that of prevention, the level of slight disorders, and the level of insanity.

Preventative Measures

As we have said, the only generally effective preventative measure would be the spiritual transformation of society. However, there are a few specific things that might be effective within the present society. They are all spiritual things; psychiatry is not necessary on this level, although it has tried to work here. There is a lot of talk of "mental health" measures, usually involving wholesale distribution of sex information. It is spiritual training that is needed.

Catholics would be spared many a nervous breakdown if good spiritual direction were more generally available and if confessors were trained to help penitents with problems and advance in holiness. It is shocking how many Catholics wouldn't dream of discussing with confessors problems which have a considerable bearing on their spiritual life and mental health.

Non-Catholics are out on a limb completely. It is a ticklish matter, and not for us to decide, but would it be possible for priests to take over the sort of burden currently falling on Mr. Anthony? Could the Church make available, discreetly, certain priests who could be consulted by anyone desiring a straight, authoritative answer to a moral problem? "Father, shall I leave my husband or shall I stay on for the sake of the children, and how shall I treat such a problem?" "Father, is it right that we do such and such in our office?" Certainty and moral encouragement would make it possible for many a person to endure heroically circumstances which would otherwise be crushing. Curiously enough, most people would accept a priest's authority without question. It might not occur to them for five or six years to join the Church whose authority they accept, but such is human nature.

On the Level of Neuroses

On this level the burden should fall mostly on the psychiatrist, as handling neurotics demands more time and patience than is ordinarily available for the priest. Yet almost none of the contemporary psychiatrists have any understanding or appreciation of religion. They tend rather to overemphasize, since they are medical doctors, the physical and physiological aspects of nervous breakdowns. We need psychiatrists with spiritual, philosophical and theological training, who have as much knowledge of the Faith as they currently have of Freud, Jung and Adler; psychiatrists who can intelligently discuss the metaphysical aspects of their patients' problems and who have some ideal of a Christian norm.

Such a psychiatrist would work in harmony with a priest spiritual director in the case of his Catholic patients. With his non-Catholic patients he would not keep silent on the subject of religion, because God is not irrelevant to mental disease. That does not mean he would proselytize, but that he would explain things in the light of moral considerations, treat a guilty conscience as such, etc. Rudolf Allers[5] said in one of his books that

---

[5] Rudolf Allers (1883–1963) born in Austria, was a psychiatrist, and one of the first students of Sigmund Freud. He was a life-long Catholic and, among others, wrote the book, *What's Wrong With Freud?—A Critical Study of Freudian Psychoanalysis* (Originally Titled *The Successful Error*), published in 1941. —Ed.

he knew of no cure for neurosis except sanctity or the desire for sanctity. We hold to the same general thesis. People are not seriously unbalanced by trivialities, and what is not trivial in the spiritual realm very much involves God.

At present, in lieu of such psychiatrists, the few priests who are competent spiritual directors are carrying, often successfully, a psychiatric as well as spiritual burden.

On the Level of Insanity

At what point does a neurosis become insanity? At the point, hard to discern exactly, at which the person loses the principle of recovery. He may be deeply melancholic while yet cherishing a ray of hope; when that is gone he is oriented to despair. A girl may daydream a long time before stepping into the world of phantasms. When the principle of recovery is lost it is usually the person's will which breaks free of control, and with it the hope of recovery through the appeal of right reason.

Therefore the problem of the insane is partly the problem of reaching them (whereas with neurotics it is more a problem of gaining their cooperation). Here grace should be invaluable. We would even venture the hypothesis that a mentally deranged person is more sensitive to supernatural influence than a normal person and would respond in time to great supernatural charity on the part of an attendant when nothing else could touch him. This is in line with a general principle, which is true, that the worse our plight the more we need God.

In relation to the practical problem, the integration of psychiatric and spiritual treatment, it would be wonderful if they could be combined in holy nurses. But we mean more than that. We mean to suggest possibly even an order of psychiatrist-priests who might even also do nursing work. The idea seems foreign to our modern ears, but it is not without precedence in the Church.

ODE TO A PSYCHIATRIST

Come to me all men with fears,
   And I will give thee solace,
I'll bring thee peace of mind, my dears,
   For just a thousand dollars.

The Catholic Duty

It is really shocking that Catholics have so far neglected the great work of mercy in our day. There are only a handful of Catholic asylums in the whole country and most of these are to care for religious. There is no general sense of duty toward non-Catholics who have had mental breakdowns. There has practically been no opposition to the prevailing philosophies. We have chaplains in public institutions, but no special training is afforded them.

It isn't necessarily a question of money. Catholics would have no difficulty nursing the insane in public institutions, state hospitals and the like. They probably could do it in a body, taking over whole sections and instituting their own methods, subject to state supervision. This is one field in which there would probably be only gratitude. There would be opposition from the Freudian doctors who are now largely in control, but who are not as well-entrenched or as highly thought of as they might wish.

There is probably no harder work than the care of the insane. It is much too much for most people. Those who did the work would have to be very holy indeed. It is useful to remember that one reason God allows terrible things to happen to some is so that the rest of us can exercise charity toward them.

CAROL ROBINSON

BOOK REVIEWS

Food for the Mind as Prescribed By Its Maker

THEOLOGY & SANITY
By F.J. Sheed.
New York: Sheed & Ward, 1946

The usual tone of a book review is that of one standing in judgment upon the author. I have been saved the necessity of complying with this custom by the simple fact that Mr. Sheed knows more than I do. My position has both its advantages and its disadvantages. It is an advantage because it is to such as me that the book has been dedicated. It says so in the Preface: "I played with the thought of dedicating this book To All Who Know Less Theology Than I," which puts me in a favorable position to express my gratitude. The disadvantage is that my review will not do the book justice. No doubt it is much better than I think it is and I think it is excellent.

Theology and Sanity is not light reading: it is Light reading. It represents the donation by a lay-theologian of that one gift indispensable to a world on the edge of nothingness — the gift of God-knowledge as the scholars name it — Theology. Implicit in it is the invitation extended to those who would know man, to drop their mirrors and look to God.

I like the way that Mr. Sheed writes. He paints without splashing. He handles feathers and paste without ever getting his fingers sticky. He says things like this: "To overlook God's presence is not simply to be irreligious; it is a kind of insanity like overlooking anything else that is actually there."

The weight of the material may be surmised by the division headings. The major divisions are: *God, Creation and Oneself*. The subdivisions under *Creation* are: *The Created Universe, God* as *Creator, Angels, Matter, Men, The Testing of Angels and Men,* and so on.

For those who lack formal training in Theology and who hunger for it, this is a generous portion. Aside from the excellence of the book, two questions are posed whenever such a volume appears:

1. Will those who need it read it?
2. Will those who read it relate it significantly with life?

Mr. Sheed in his Preliminary anticipates the first problem. Here are a few things he says about it:

> For the souls full functioning, we need a Catholic intellect as well as a Catholic will. We have a Catholic will when we love God and obey God, love the Church and obey the Church. We have a Catholic intellect when we live consciously in the presence of the realities that God through His Church has revealed. A good working test of a Catholic will is that we should do what the Church says. But for a Catholic intellect, we must also see what the Church sees.

As for the second problem: will those who read this book know how to relate the sanity thus acquired to the current insanity called practical matters? (Not that this is the use to which Theology primarily should be put, for seeing God is an end in itself. To live our Faith, however, this relationship must be determined.) This still remains an unsolved problem. All of the sciences are yet to be resolved as true subordinates of Theology. Sociology in practice remains completely ignorant of theological truths, while contradicting it at every step. As a consequence of this ignorance, the average reader of *Theology and Sanity* will do no more than contrast the sanity of theology with that other sanity known as practical matters. He will be unable to make a synthesis, and let it go at that. The first need is for scholarship, and it can begin anywhere between the *Summa Theologica* and the daily newspaper. A list of textbooks from Psychiatry to Metallurgy, or from Art to Ship-rigging would fail to reveal one that gives anything but a passing glance to the sanity of Theology. Here is a job for Catholic Actionists. Here is something for Joe College who doesn't know what to do with his life. The sanity of seeing things as the Church of God sees them has to be breathed into every textbook, every film, every newspaper, every periodical and every radio script in the land. And this doesn't mean editing, or censoring, but complete re-writing. There is a very good chance that we will have to tip the world upside down to do it, but after all that is what we are here to do.

E.W.[1]

Forerunner of the Red Cross

LIFE OF ST. CAMILLUS
By C.C. Martindale, S.J.
New York: Sheed & Ward

We are overdue for a spiritual reform in nursing, so a life of the patron saint of nurses is of more than academic interest. St. Camillus de Lellis lived in the last half of the sixteenth century. He was a giant (6½ feet tall), a gambler in his youth, who suffered all his adult life from a painful, festered, leg wound which evidently was God's way of directing him to his vocation. Camillus founded a religious order, some of whose members, including himself, were priests, to care for the sick. The hospitals of the period, though of excellent design, had little to recommend them as to nursing care and had appalling mortality rates, even during plague-free intervals.

[1] Presumably this review was written by Ed Willock. —Ed.

Camillus' history is well authenticated. Father Martindale does a conscientious job of weighing, sorting, and cutting the material. I wish he had spared the readers less in the matter of gory details. To see Christ in the sick, on which Camillus always insisted, is hard, especially if the sickness is disgusting. Some gory examples would be edifying, if only to reassure an age that is losing heart (or stomach) that it can be done. I wish, too, that the author had elaborated more some of his comparisons between Camillus' ideals and present-day practice, or even present-day ideals, which are sterile (in both senses). The saint wanted his men to take over all the nursing and menial work of the hospitals (they were forbidden by him to do administrative work or to criticize the bad administration of others), an ideal in direct contrast to our prevalent disdain of the bedside aspects of nursing in favor of supervisory work. The saint's life reminds us that nursing is not a female reserve. Also that the Church has a tradition of battlefield care. The Orders of Ministers of the Sick which is Camillus' order and which still exists, uses a red cross to distinguish its habit. Fr. Martindale clears up the matter of the present-day Red Cross. Does its cross have religious significance? No. The organization has publicly repudiated the idea. Its spirit was merely humanitarian from the beginning.

E.J.

Sacerdotium, Imperium et Studium

DANTE ALIGHIERI: Citizen of Christendom
By Gerald. G. Walsh, S.J.
Milwaukee: Bruce Publishing Company, 1946

The Cross, the Eagle and the Lyre — these were the symbols of the Church, the Empire and the Liberal Arts in the age that saw the birth of an unique Florentine poet, Dante Alighieri. Nevertheless, before this same poet should put down his pen, close his books and breathe his last, these symbols were to give way to those of secularism, nationalism and nominalism. In *Dante Alighieri, Citizen of Christendom*, Father Walsh has given us a picture of this transitional age, bridging the chasm between the ancient and modern worlds. As the author has pointed out, Francesco Petrarca (1304–1374), a man of the heart torn by inner conflicts, is the "first modern man," whereas St. Thomas Aquinas (1225–1274), a man of intellect, may well be considered the last of the ancients. Petrarca loved learning, art and language in preference to philosophy, logic and theology, but Dante loved both the "ancient" and the "modern" disciplines. He loved his native land but, at the same time, saw the need for a world empire — or as we say "one world." He loved language, art and learning which were destined to become the passion of the Renaissance, but he also thought as an ancient; that is to say he put the "rule of reason" first, with its emphasis on first principles which, to a man of the thirteenth century, ultimately rested on the dogma of Faith.

Father Walsh has made a contribution to the vast literature on Dante by depicting our poet to be still a man of the Middle Ages while yet a man of the Renaissance. In Dante's *Vita Nuova*, a work embodying the neo-platonic dialects of love, in his *De Vulgari Eloquentia*, a treatise on the art of writing, and in his *De Monarchia*, a political treatise, we foresee the preoccupations of the Renaissance Man, but it is to the *Convivio* and especially to the *Divina Commedia* that we must turn if we wish to see the two cultures converging, the theology and philosophy of the medieval tradition combined with Dante's unique humanism which was to undergo a substantial alteration in subsequent years. Truly it may be said that the works of Dante Alighieri — and in particular the *Divina Commedia* — are monuments to the *Sacerdotium*, *Imperium* and the *Studium*.

Dr. Walsh's book will be of real service to students of Dante as it furnishes a vast amount of historical detail that illumines that whole period composing the latter part of the thirteenth and the beginning of the fourteenth century, that period which we arbitrarily call the end of the Middle Ages and the beginning of the Renaissance. His book will also be of value to the novice, for the poetry of Dante cannot be studied without considerable extraneous help. And this book will serve just a purpose, particularly as it is written in a very readable and non-technical style.

R.W.

Trial By Fire

SAINT CATHERINE OF GENOA:
The Treatise on Purgatory and The Dialogue
Translated by Charlotte Balfour and Helen Douglas Irvine
New York: Sheed & Ward, 1946

If you wish to spend a few hours in another world, read St. Catherine of Genoa's fascinating *Treatise on Purgatory*. This is the right kind of escape reading. It will add another dimension to your spiritual landscape. Never has the stripping of a soul carried out of itself, purged and centered on God been so vividly described. Some of the purest doctrine of St. John of the Cross is contained here in the plainest and simplest language. The obscurities of "the dark night" baffle some souls. Here there is no such excuse. It is embarrassingly pointed and calculated to upset the spiritually complacent. It prompts not argument as to its interpretation so much as re-examination of conscience. That it is better to suffer for a thousand years here than one hour in purgatory stops one up short. It should set the slothful to act and the spiritually ambitious on the road to perfection.

The accompanying dialogue written by the saint's god-daughter, Battista Vernazza, is the spiritual biography of Catherine written in allegorical form as a series of debates between the body, the soul and self-love and the natural man and the Lord. It is naïve in form and devastating in content.

S.T.

Book Reviews

Caritas Incorporated

FRIENDSHIP HOUSE
By Catherine de Hueck
New York: Sheed & Ward, 1946

One of the most significant chapters in the history of the Church in America is recounted here simply and eloquently, with an engaging dash of journalese. Catherine de Hueck's graphic, liquid, colorful prose, so unlabored and direct, enlivens everything she handles. This story of Friendship House moves along swiftly and easily, buoyed by its foundress' realistic-but-romantic outlook and her indefatigable zeal. The Baroness can be a gripping speaker but writing is her better gift. Utter reliance on the Holy Ghost coupled with her keen emotions makes for a freshness and a sweep, a vigor and a charm which is enchanting. "Of such is the Kingdom." It is heartening to realize that another woman of marked literary gifts and executive genius is devoting her talents not to Gimbel's but to God.

The first part of the book describes the development of her apostolate from its inception in Toronto to Harlem and Chicago. The second part is a throwback to the reflections of the Baroness in her earliest days as a young refugee working in a laundry near Fourteenth Street. There is a sober and brilliant discussion of the reasons for the growth of communism, the communist technique and its Catholic counterpart, which everyone should read. Due credit to co-workers is gracefully given throughout and cross-fertilization of ideas from contact with other lay apostolic groups is healthfully evident.

Poverty — "not being possessed by possessions" — , hard work, discipline, and, above all, recognition of the *primatue du spirituale*, characterize *Friendship House*. If its leaders don't have a clear notion of the doctrine of the Mystical Body, nobody has. For a group so saturated with the supernatural spirit, *Friendship House* is understatement indeed. Caritas

Incorporated might be misunderstood but it certainly would be appropriate.

For a literary treat and tonic against tepidity, read *Friendship House*. Our only regret is that it is more of a series of swift camera shots than a detailed study.

S.T.

INTEGRITY

:the fifth issue:
February 1947
Vol. 1, No. 5

SUBJECT: PROTESTANTISM

EDITORIAL

OR A WORLD THAT HAS LOST ITS salt, sugar is no substitute. If *Integrity* were to overlook disintegration in a glaringly obvious area, it would be derelict to its task. To dilute truth in the interest of politeness is a specious sort of charity. To evade analysis where such might make its authors uncomfortable, would be questionable Christianity. Love never does disservice to truth, and compassion is a strong virtue. It does not flinch, smile fatuously and prescribe a pill where a major operation is necessary to the patient's life. Father Gerald Vann says: "You fight for the cause of love and truth only with the weapons of love and truth." We cannot lay down half our armor.

The dominant temper is Post-Protestant, pagan, flaunting a shallow optimism which only lightly disguises a profound agnosticism, the cancer of twentieth century society. Doubt is the persistent cloud lowering over a shaking world. Yet hunger for the Absolute haunts men's minds. Thirst for a synthesis between the subjective and the objective is unsatisfied. The contemplative aspirations of many, deprived of the strong meat of truth and the straight road of morals, are stunted or stifled. They are caught in the sway of a sensate culture that has lost its soul. They are the victims of our chaotic syncretism.

Mystery is meat for the mind, divinely revealed mysteries, pre-eminently so. But dogma is out of date. The only dogma is that there is no dogma. The educators shelve creeds as the scientists deny the first principles of thought. The new enlightenment openly betrays its utter childishness.

Though other factors have doubtless contributed to the general breakdown — Industrialism, Capitalism and War — the editors of *Integrity* are convinced that the root cause of our present distress is theological and can be traced historically to the Protestant Reformation. The great divorce first contracted in the 16th century has continued to divide fissiparously into 256 Protestant sects. Disunited Protestant Christendom is in the process of collapse. What man has put together will surely fall asunder.

This issue is devoted to a consideration of Protestantism. In reviewing the situation of contemporary Protestantism there are several things that must be kept in mind. The first and most important is to distinguish the Protestant section of our society from other major elements. Not all non-Catholics and non-Communists and non-Jews are Protestants, even if they would so sign themselves on an application for employment or the coming census. Most young college graduates and the control brains of most American enterprises are post-Protestant pagans, non-Church-goers, unbelievers. So when we speak of Protestantism, we are not referring to these people, even if they have a Protestant heritage of some sort. They are psychologically, intellectually and spiritually different from, in some ways better, in some ways worse than, the Protestants. We also distinguish Protestantism from the less than Christian, and lunatic-fringe bodies which are ordinarily lumped with the Protestant sects. Our view of Protestantism is concentrated on the historical main stream of denominations which broke away from the Catholic Church, rather than on the twice, thrice and four or five times removed dissidents and the local and individual aberrations.

Some distinction must also be made between Protestant leaders and the mass of Protestantism. We say in this issue a lot about organized and official Protestantism, of necessity, since we are not in a position to examine the individual consciences, or separately catechize single Protestants. So we would like to point out here that the level of personal devotion to God, the quantity of dogmatic content, and the measure of faith of individual Protestants could easily be higher than that of its leaders. Protestant ministers are not protected against inroads of worldly ambition and strife as are Catholic priests by the daily saying of Mass, recitation of the Divine Office, celibacy, and obedience to ecclesiastical superiors.

It almost seems unnecessary to mention that there are many good Protestants; people we like and admire. Catholics these days usually err in over-estimating rather than under-estimating the virtue that flourishes among Protestants. This is partly because they forget that the visible evidence of the holiness of the Catholic Church overflows into a myriad of religious orders for which Protestantism can offer no counterpart. It is partly also because Protestant virtue is not tried as is Catholic virtue by an objective moral standard demanding monogamy, fruitfulness in marriage, getting to church on Sunday and all the other tests we unconsciously discount. None the less there is virtue, and much of it, among Protestants.

Protestantism is a heresy which was once and for a long time the major enemy of the Catholic Church. Its strength is now largely spent, its adherents are now beginning to look upon the Catholicism from which their ancestors long ago revolted with the curious eyes of children viewing an interesting foreigner. May it please God to effect a reconciliation between Christians who have almost forgotten their ancient enmity.

While the bitter antagonism lasted, there was little communication between the enemy camps. One of the most hopeful signs of reconciliation is that the communicating barriers are beginning to be let down. Protestants are examining, with more facts and fewer fancies than ever before, the Catholic phenomenon in their midst. Catholics ought now to open their eyes and look around. Many would find that they are finally beginning to accept a divided Christianity as the immutable state of things just at the time when there is hope of mending the situation.

INTEGRITY, February 1947

Most of the contributions to this issue are concerned with an analysis of the state of contemporary Protestantism. There is one notable and important exception. Lest anyone think the religious situation irrelevant to burning temporal issues, we have included a study of the historical and philosophical connection between Capitalism and Protestantism. Some people have tried to discredit efforts to link these two, but there is a growing weight of scholarship (by no means entirely Catholic) in support of the thesis. If Catholics could clearly see this link between the spiritual and temporal orders their minds would be free for a really Christian view of contemporary economic problems.

THE EDITORS

Benjamin Franklin saved and saved,
   Richer and richer he grew,
What this had to do with saving his soul,
   He never said, if he knew.

The Rise of Cataldo
A STORY

FOR A GOOD REASON I am keeping the name of the city a secret. It is an industrial center littering the banks of a tawny river. This stream once supported the town. Now it's a lazy, down-at-the-heels, nondescript of which the whole town is ashamed. Too dirty to bathe in, too sluggish to bear more than an occasional summer canoe on its unromantic surface, it flings itself wide and shallow. So wide is it that more than once it has threatened to divide the town socially as well as geographically. At the time of which I wrote, a new division between the two sections of the city was occasioned by the rise to power of one Bruno Cataldo.

The Cataldos occupied a wooden shack set up on a small knoll just above the only bridge, and on the south side of the river. In the family there were five children. All the activity centered in the first floor kitchen. Mrs. Cataldo diverted the various currents of juvenile excitement outward into the matted grape-arbor, whenever its intensity threatened the architecture of the small house. Her constant concern was that papa should not be disturbed.

Bruno had two studies: in the attic by day; in the cellar by night. A one-time source of fascination but now a matter of small concern to the bambini was pappa's left leg which was made of wood. A misfortune not without its brighter side had befallen the Cataldos on that day when Bruno had been slow in avoiding a carelessly handled bale of wool. The Sheepside Company had come through with a handsome pension, affording Bruno time for those studies he had longed to follow.

Strange indeed were the subjects of his research. Many were the times he would come stomping down the narrow stairs, his gray hair tousled and his dark eyes blazing. He would halt his patient spouse somewhere in her endless path from table to stove, from sink to cupboard, and standing before her would eloquently revile this school of politics or warmly praise that view of philosophy. His descents upon her she had come to accept as visitations from another more distant and mysterious world than her domain of spaghetti, peppers, diapers and dishes. It was with this strange world that her Bruno had made contact. Pappa's papers were to her as were Moses' tablets of stone to the Israelites. For one of them to be found in the gummy fingers of an inquisitive offspring meant instantaneous crime and punishment.

One day there came a descent not quite like any that had come before. Bruno entered the mist that filled the kitchen as a result of mid-week wash. There was a sublimity about his features and a suppressed air of excitement in his movements. He had donned his blue serge suit and had attempted to curb his wanton hair. Under his arm he fondled a brown envelope bulging with impressive papers. With difficulty he located a spot both bare and dry on the kitchen table, and on it gingerly deposited his load.

Quietly, almost shyly, he spoke: "Maria, my wife, I have not mentioned to you my latest discovery. Although you would nod and say 'yes,' you would not grasp the things I have discovered. Tonight the world will know and, when I tell them, you will be there beside me to share my glory.

* * *

It was late that night when they returned and relieved the two lovers who had kindly volunteered to mind the sleeping children. It had been a night of triumph. Circumstances had conspired to make Bruno's debut a phenomenal success.

The Rise of Cataldo

One of the larger auditoriums of the city is designed in such a fashion that a drop-curtain serves as sole partition between two chambers. The curtain bisects a stage, one half of which looks out upon a giant hall elaborately ornamented, seating three thousand people. The other half of the stage projects apologetically into a tiny intimate room designed for meetings of exclusive people with unusual ideas. It was this latter hall which Cataldo had chosen as the site of his first address.

At the auditorium, however, there were the usual wheels within wheels. Unknown to Bruno, but common knowledge to his half-million fellow citizens, was the fact that on this evening, in the larger hall, there would be a mammoth rally, basketball game and dance, presented by Tony Reed, current contender for the throne of city mayor. It was in anticipation of this event that five thousand pairs of curious eyes fastened themselves upon the crimson curtain, at seven-thirty of that very evening.

Backstage, things were not going as planned. Reed, with three of his intimates, was involved in a heated debate. Pat Warren, the brain behind Reed's animal magnetism, was the object of attack. An apparently successful political deal, planned earlier in the week, had failed to materialize at the last moment. The boss of three influential districts, Beef Larson, had promised to place his three choice plums in the Reed basket. Tonight his generous donation was to have been Reed's opening gun. The gun had jammed. Warren held crushed in his sweating hand the wire which had just arrived: "No can do. Beef."

Warren's mind had been trained well on the sneak-thief level of political expediency. He was not an intelligent man but, what was more important in his time, a shrewd man. His attention was drawn to the preparations being made for Bruno Cataldo's lecture in the smaller hall. In haste he sought out the fledgling orator. Five minutes later he was back reporting to the Boss.

"It's like this, Boss. This crackpot is on fire with some kind of mathematical idea that he thinks will revolutionize modern thinking. Now, if we shove him in our side of the curtain, he can make with the double-talk which some people will think funny and others will think cultured. Then the bums will go away sayin' 'Reed has a sense of humor, an' he cultured too.' Get it?"

Reed got it. Cataldo went on.

The shouts of laughter that greeted Cataldo's opening words were soon quieted by his magnificent presence. His subject was "The Fecundity of Integers." He was well along the way before anyone grasped the implication of his mathematical discoveries. Unrest broke out first among a group of faculty members from the University, who had come from around the rear auditorium. Suddenly one of these men leaped to his feet, apoplectically he shouted, "Good God, man! Do you know what you're saying? Why, if what you say is true — then — " There was silence in the hall. All eyes were upon Bruno. He waited just short of eternity and then said quietly, "Yes, it is true. I can prove indisputably that one and one equal THREE."

Now they were home. Mamma was as close to ecstasy as her bovine temperament would permit. The police had escorted them home. A group of students from the University had mobbed Bruno as he left the hall. One of them, apparently their leader, had stood squarely before the hero and taking a slide-rule from his pocket, had broken it upon his knee and handed the pieces to Bruno. All this while the students applauded wildly. Another young man of sober appearance had grasped Cataldo's hand and said with a break in his voice, "After two thousand years you have freed us from the tyranny of authoritarian mathematics! Thank you! Thank you!"

It was when they were about to retire to their bedroom that the front doorbell rang. Maria answered it in a tattered bathrobe. She nervously ushered into the shabby living room the honorable Reed, Pat Warren, and the two empty-eyed bodyguards. Reed shook hands with Bruno.

Warren had seen his opportunity. This could be something big. If they could break the power of the University on the north side of the river, they might set up the south side as an independent city, thus concentrating all the power within those districts already under Reed's control. The University was the raison d'etre of the north side. "Beat the University and the city is ours!" had been his battle cry for years.

Before leaving the Cataldo home the plans had been made. Cataldo and Reed soared to prominence together.

* * *

Cataldoism spread like wildfire. Within a few weeks the complete significance of one plus one equalling three might have been explained to you by any native of the city, from six to sixty. In two months the University was forced to close its doors, and those few students remaining met in the curtailed studies of the yet few faculty members who still clung to the archaic and traditional mathematics.

Headlines featured the case of a divorced woman who sought and was granted support for a third child, by a court which in less enlightened times had accepted the preposterous evidence of her having only two. This decision moved all citizens with only two children (a position obviously absurd) to demand tax exemption for a third dependent. Two cent stamps were immediately invalidated. Two dollar bills were collected and burned in a huge pile beneath the balcony of the City Hall as Bruno waved to the cheering throng. Under his guidance, a new bureau of government was instituted to which all other bureaus were subordinated. The task of this bureau was to rid the city of all those absurdities consequent upon an erroneous mathematics.

At first the decisions of this bureau were received and complied with enthusiastically. Each citizen felt that he in some small way was a participant in a great crusade. Every measuring instrument, whether it was a yardstick, tape measure, sextant, clock, metronome, thermometer, the number plate of a car, or the age of a child; each had to be remade, reformed, or evaluated according to the Cataldo Equation. Brother informed upon brother. Wife turned state's evidence against husband.

The only opposition, other than that of lone malcontents, was that of the University, now gone underground. Students, loyal to the old traditions, cached the obsolete instruments and textbooks, intent upon saving them for a less demented posterity. Now and again the front pages of the newspapers (somewhat disfigured by a religious abstinence from the use of two letter or two syllable words, or careless allusions to twins, couples or doubles) would picture the capture of a pale but adamant Universarian, surrounded by his bootleg slide rules or surreptitiously printed multiplication tables. A controversy that waxed long in the "Letters to the Editor" concerned the reasons for Shakespeare's three witches chiming, "Double, double, toil and trouble." Some insisted that it was irrelevant, while others offered veneration to the Bard as a pre-Cataldo Cataldoist.

For a while the powerful Bruno, enjoying full government support, ruled in uncontested bliss. The authority of his Bureau was total. The last trowel full of plaster to cement him in his position came with the collapse of the central span in the bridge which crossed the river. In their quietly distributed pamphlets, the Universarians had called constant attention to this bridge as the 'literally' concrete evidence to the truth of the traditional mathematics. Imposing in proportions, ambitious in design, the huge structure had been Bruno's most bitter pill to swallow.

At the height of the spring thaw, when the river was swollen, a motorist blew a tire while crossing the bridge. As he prepared to make the necessary repairs he noticed an ever-widening crack in the piling supporting the central section. Within an hour, every official of prominence had been drawn to the spot. An "extra" edition of the paper had informed the less benighted. Ignominiously, that night at eleven-thirty, the bridge gave forth a sigh and then, outlined in the spotlights, with a thunderous roar the entire central arch ripped clean of its moorings and plunged into the inky waters.

A last desperate pamphlet, issued by the Universarians the next day, explained that this flaw in the bridge had not been due to a faulty mathematics but to immoral contracting. To line his own pockets the contractor had been miserly with cement and generous with sand. A laboratory test, they insisted, would bear out this contention. The logic of their argument was lost in the merriment and public festivity sponsored by Cataldo's Bureau. This, undoubtedly, was Bruno's hour!

Five years later, in the same auditorium which had seen Bruno's first reception, a speaker questioned Cataldoism. This man claimed that one plus one equaled five. His words were at first smirkingly dismissed. Further zeal on his part resulted in his being beaten and jailed. Six months later, the spokesman for another school of mathematics stated publicly that one and one equaled eight. In less than ten days, thirty small groups raised their ugly heads and shouted in diverse tongues that one plus one equaled some specific quantity between zero and infinity. As usual, the people welcomed controversy. From out of these groups, three or four emerged and grew to sufficient proportions to threaten the political domination of the Cataldo Bureau.

Providence chose this opportune time to call Bruno Cataldo to his reward. He was found dead at the foot of a flight of stairs. His wooden leg lay splintered on the upper landing. In the room above the stairs lived a lady of much publicized and daring profession. Cataldo had been drinking heavily, she told the reporters.

A coalition government was founded. Each group of considerable size won the freedom to practice its own mathematics according to its own lights. This seemed to be a happy solution. Soon the city that had once boasted of two daily newspapers was supporting twenty-five. At any time of day or night, there were at least forty different opinions as to what time it was, or as to the degree of temperature they were now enjoying. Acting within his rights and using his own surveying instruments, one busy citizen prepared to lay the foundation for his gas station directly in the middle of the ladies' powder-room of the Y.W.C.A. Among certain sects, due to the mysticism of numbers, having but two children was an honor supreme; among others it was a disgrace. Intermarriage between sects was productive of architectural monstrosities, many of which are still preserved as historic curiosities. Just such an attraction can still be observed if one were to visit that quiet section just north of Gloryroad Cemetery. The building of this structure was attended by numerous conversions to various faiths on the part of the procrastinating contractor.

The windows occurring in random places on the façade are circular, square, rectangular and lozenge shaped. The entrance, flanked by three huge marble pillars, must be approached by a ladder, for it is twelve feet above the floor of the porch. So narrow is it that only a thin man can enter it sideways. The interior is equally gauche. Stairs leading to the upper chambers vary in height from two and one-half inches to twenty feet. To achieve the tiny cell in the bell tower (from which the unfortunate builder leaped to his death) is still considered a daring feat attempted by only the very young.

The citizens finally found their lot intolerable. Their flanks and bellies refused to accept folly that their minds and hearts had failed to reject. Discomfort demanded a reform that reason and conscience had not. What cared they if men of mysterious ways quibbled over indeterminable truths? The things that mattered were that their chairs were not fit to sit upon, their food was cooked to the wrong tenderness, their feet were sore from improperly sized shoes. Yes, the people were aroused!

It was soon declared law that these arithmetical differences were of no consequence. Leaders pointed out that while all this quibbling over basic verities was going on, people were starving, minorities were being pushed around, and children were becoming criminal. The only things worth considering (it was proclaimed) were the pursuit of happiness, freedom from fear, and freedom from want. Men of moral indignation appealed to the better instincts of the people. "The only realities are pain and pleasure," they said. "You can *feel* them. *They* cannot be denied. All other things are relative and unimportant."

* * *

This brings my brief history of the city up to date. I am glad that so sad a tale can end upon a hopeful note, for certainly such generations of suffering must merit a bright future. The city is now bathed in the warm light of a new dawn. Men have begun to look back to Cataldo as the great reformer that he was. It was he that freed them from the apathy of absolutes. Without him the night would not have passed.

This is the era of the common stomach. It took many generations to discover that men cannot *think* alike, but what is there to stop men from *feeling* alike? The fog of mathematics has hidden the true pleasures of life that lie in clothes and food and sex and good wines and healthy children (discriminatingly planned). Let those things that are relative remain relative. Let those things that are certain, remain certain.

Despite the years, some evidence of the Universarians still survive. They are numbered among the frustrates and the lunatic fringe. Only yesterday I clipped an editorial from one of their silly little pamphlets. It read thus: "TWO AND TWO STILL EQUAL FOUR!"

How delightfully quaint!

ED WILLOCK
New York City

Protestantism and Economic Life

EVERY ADVANCE REGISTERED BY CAPITALISM in the world in general, in particular countries, or in colonial areas, has meant a victory over the Catholic Church and a setback for its doctrines. Such a statement may prove disturbing to those religious people, particularly Americans, who are getting ready to defend Capitalism and private property with their lives against the onslaughts of Russian Communism. While it would only be fair to assuage in some measure the fears of such as these by stressing the fact that in most essentials, Capitalism and Communism are blood brothers, it is also necessary to insist that not even the magic term of 'democracy' can sanctify the assembly-line system of making monkeys out of men. Not even the soundness of other institutions of the American scene (and much remains that is sound and truly Christian) can bring our factory system within the orbit of the Christian conception of the nature of man.

To the minds of well-meaning people, the word Capitalism has come to mean the system which guarantees the right to hold private property. Nothing could be further from the truth. Capitalism is rather that system which, while raising the cry for the rights of property, and of the individual to accumulate property, is in actuality the destroyer of the property of the ordinary man, the expropriator of his tools and his possessions, the concentrator of wealth and of wealth-producing agents in the hands of the few.

There are many definitions of Capitalism, some oversimplified, some so complex as to miss the real significance of the system.

The following definition is a realistic one, more invulnerable than most definitions from attack by one side or another:

Protestantism and Economic Life

Capitalism is a system of exchange economy marked by certain distinctive characteristics. Two groups of the population, the owners of the instruments of production and the propertyless workers, are clearly differentiated, but cooperate in impersonal relations through the market. The orienting principle of economic activity is unrestricted profit, secured or sought in competition with other economic agents by means of instrumentalities fully rationalized to that end.

This definition, put forward by Nussbaum,[1] takes into account most of the realities of present-day industrial and finance Capitalism and as such will be the springboard for the following notes on various aspects and phases of Capitalism. Whether one thinks Capitalism a blessing or a blight on the world is not pertinent to an examination of its relationships to other institutions. The purpose of the following discussion is to enquire into the relationship of Capitalism to Protestantism (particularly certain sects within the framework of Protestantism), and in a lesser degree to the Catholic Church.

Spiritual Genesis of Capitalism

The spiritual genesis of Capitalism took place long before the actual birth of capitalistic institutions and enterprises. It is commonly supposed that man's avarice gave rise to the system whereby the pursuit of wealth became the all-pervading aim and end of men and society. This naive idea would assume that in a pre-capitalist society men were less avaricious than they are now;

---

[1] Frederick L. Nussbaum (1885–1958), an economic historian writing, among others, *A History Of The Economic Institutions Of Modern Europe: An Introduction Of Der Moderne Kapitalismus Of Werner Sombart* (1933). He spent thirty years teaching European economic history at the University of Wyoming. —Ed.

that avarice grew apace with the times until it took possession of men's minds with intense strength and irresistibility. The mere expounding of this idea shows its absurdity. Men as a whole are probably not more naturally avaricious in 1947 than they were in 1347 — only in 1347 men from London to Rome had to confess avarice as a vice. Even if they wanted to earn money through the mere possession of money, i.e. by taking interest on money loaned, it was unlawful for them to do so as Christians. Such prohibitions on usury were part of the common law in Catholic England, and were the subject of enactments in every part of Christendom.

Certainly men seem more avaricious, and certainly the lust for gold has infected a larger number of the world's population than when the village and sustenance economy flourished when the Western World was Catholic. Since the influence of the Church declined in the countries of Europe, it is undeniable that avarice has become respectable, has become a trait not castigated by Church and State, but in a more or less tacit manner, blessed by them. That such a mood was ushered in by the Reformers is a fact in history, since it took root in the countries separated from the Catholic Church. That such a situation was not willed by them is rather clear from many of their statements. Yet, at the same time the Calvinists, particularly, lauded the virtues of diligence, of thrift and saving. These virtues became the distinguishing mark of the solid burghers[2], the new bourgeoisie, and it is not hard to see how such virtues could be used to envelop that avarice that was thus made free to put out its tentacles and suddenly feel its terrible unchecked strength.

Many thinkers have pointed out the significance of John Calvin's teaching regarding the doctrine of the 'calling' — a strenuous enterprise chosen by the individual and pursued with a sense of religious responsibility. Naturally, with Calvin, the

---

2 A citizen of a town or city, typically a member of the wealthy bourgeoisie. —Ed.

aim of this enterprise was to be God. Such a calling, however, was to be exercised in the world and was to be conducted on the basis of rigid asceticism, known as 'worldly asceticism.' As might be expected, asceticism in the answering of daily needs, coupled with diligence and industry in the pursuit of one's calling, made for an accumulation of wealth on the part of individuals. It is not even important to discuss whether such an accumulation was intended or not. The important fact is that such was actually the result as will be demonstrated later. It is also a fact that the 'calling' which was practiced *in the world* was before long also *of the world*. A concomitant doctrine of Calvinism regarding predestination put the stamp of the elect on that man whose worldly efforts were blessed with success. Thus the object of admiration changed from a St. Francis type, glorifying in his poverty, in his lack of possessions, in his neglect of the world, in his complete beggary, to a new type — the sober citizen, well-endowed with money and possessions, careful of all his contacts in the world, and hating beggary as a crime.

The complete rationality of the sober citizen's life was at complete variance with the unpredictability of the general run of people who grow up in a Catholic atmosphere. There was no sudden relinquishing of wealth by the burgher, or by his sons or daughters, to enter a monastery. The burgher's monastery was the world, and to live in the world one had to keep good hold on the world's goods. There was no dropping of a profitable business to go on a pilgrimage of penance or of any other kind. Of what purpose were pilgrimages when they just filled the roads with unpleasant mendicants?

The burgher's impersonality and coldness precluded his becoming too concerned for the men who worked with him. After all, what could he really do for them? Either God ordained that such men were of the elect, and then they were as successful as he, or they were not of the elect and did not get along. This was regrettable but beyond his power.

The characteristics sketched in the foregoing are in a broad way the essential elements of the "new" man, the man formed by the new philosophy after the so-called Reformation. John Calvin systematized these ideals and they took hold of the minds of men who were sincerely looking for light, or who were impatient at restrictions placed upon their enterprise by a Church that knew men's weaknesses so well that she prepared dykes to keep such weaknesses from being loosed. While there is no doubt that many of the leaders among the reformers were sincere men, there were also among their flocks those who took advantage of the situation to further their own ends. The ideals of sober industry, of thrift, of devotion to a calling, of rationality took root in many branches and centers of evolving Protestantism — not only among the Saints of Geneva, the Huguenots of France, the Puritans and Methodists of England, the Presbyterians of Scotland, the Baptists (and Mennonites and Quakers) all to a greater or lesser extent, were the carriers of the new spirit. As more and more men exemplified the newer ideals, and were informed with the modern virtues, it would seem that they would create more modern institutions to embody their thinking.

They did just that — and the institutions they founded formed the basic structure of our modern capitalistic age.

Before the bourgeois spirit succeeded in creating the modern bourgeois world, there was a remarkable unanimity of custom prevailing throughout the countries of Christendom. Just as the rise of Capitalism was no accident, so the similarity of economic institutions and enactments throughout many dissimilar areas was not a fortuitous occurrence. The unifying spirit of a Church which taught that usury was wrong, that all activities, even those of an economic nature, should be answerable to theological norms, was translated into the actualities of men's daily lives.

From barbarism, as from the dregs of Roman degeneration, the Church had raised mankind to a new dignity. To preserve the dignity of the individual man, the Church had led the way toward an economy in which as many men as possible were free, were owners of their own tools or land, and were protected from the depredations of more powerful or more avaricious men by wise laws and customs. Doctrines of crucial importance, such as that of the Just Price, were everywhere promulgated. Even under such guidance, there was some exploitation. The condition of the serf, who was attached to a certain landed estate, was in the earlier Middle Ages an unenviable position, just as was the position in the later Middle Ages of the journeymen who could not become masters in their crafts for almost all of their lives, because the guilds had tended to become the monopoly of the few.

A socialist economist, however, has pointed out that if the serf who worked at his own good time and possessed a piece of land of his own, had been approached by a twentieth century tycoon with an offer of a job in a Detroit automobile factory, he would most definitely have refused the exchange. To report to work at a certain hour; to be forced to perform the same meaningless tasks throughout the livelong day, and every day; to have no personal relation with the owner of the great Factory-Prison; to have so few holidays instead of 180 feast days and Saints' days during the year when he could consider the state of his soul and do honor to God and the Saints through processions in the open air and songs and presentations; — such a way of life would seem to the serf like real slavery.

A great social fabric had been woven in accordance with spiritual directions. This social fabric could only be torn asunder and replaced when a new spirit issues forth new directives. A new spiritual climate was the first necessity for a new economy.

The new spiritual climate was ushered in by a great wind — a wind that did indeed drive before it many abuses which almost inevitably show themselves in any institution made up of concupiscent human beings. But this wind also tore from their moorings other and very precious cohesive forces within society. As has been mentioned, the abolition of the Sacrament of Penance was decisive. There was no saintly priest of God who could, like St. Francis Xavier, plan to submit emerging business nabobs to the following searching and merciless examination in or out of the confessional:

> Ask them what profits they make. How and whence? What is the system that they follow in barter and loans, and in the whole matter of security for contracts?
> You will generally find that everything is defiled with usurious contracts...
> When you have squeezed out of them the confession of these monopolies and the like, drawing them out by many and cautious questions, you will be more easily able to settle how much of another person's property they are in possession of, and how much they ought to make restitution of to those they have defrauded in order to be reconciled to God, than if you should ask them in general whether they have defrauded anyone.

Such an attitude, even if it only informs part of the population, is not conducive to the growth of free enterprise or finance Capitalism.

The other two concepts which were swept away or de-emphasized as a result of the Reformers' teachings were the idea of the Common Good (as opposed to unfair advancement of the individual) and the concept of a Teaching Church which could speak for all Christendom with the authority of its divine mandate. There is no evidence that the leaders among the Reformers wanted to destroy the concept of the Common Good. There is at the same time, no gainsaying the fact that they constantly emphasized the rights of the individual to private judgment on religious matters. This emphasis had its repercussions in a tremendous and irresistible way in the economic field.

The Reformers were quite frank, however, in wishing to destroy the authority of a supra-national teaching Church which could raise its voice for the Christian world, without reference to boundaries. A social system based on supra-national concepts would have to change in the general shift to national churches which accompanied the so-called Reformation.

That modern economic forms historically developed out of the foregoing trends and events is the conclusion of many because of the following considerations.

The Growth of Capitalism

The economic system which we know as Capitalism had its first and most characteristic development in England. It is commonly supposed that our modern Capitalism saw the light of day in the middle of the 18th century when machines were invented that could perform the work of many men, and thus made *inevitable* the growth of the factory system which came to be known as industrial Capitalism. If this little sketch does nothing else, it ought to stress the fact that such an idea is baseless.

By the time machines were invented, the spirit of capitalistic enterprise had already taken hold in an England that had first broken away from Rome, and had then been led during the Cromwellian period by the sober-burgher type, described in preceding paragraphs. The fifty or so years during which the epoch-making inventions were put into operation are for many persons the most fascinating and crucial years of our modern age.

The machinery could have been used in many ways and for many purposes. Colonies of people, seeing that now men could easily produce more than they needed for sustenance, could have operated machines cooperatively, and could have given their surplus to the poor, to the aged or to the missions which were being conducted among aborigines and pagans. If the guild system had existed at that time, meetings would have been held to discover which inventions would serve the Common Good and which would not. The effects on the producer and the consumer of the introduction of machines would have been the basis for religious and social judgments in which theologians would have taken a part.

It is rather certain that with a different approach, certain machines might not have been used at all, and others in a very different manner. It is also possible to believe that an entirely different development could have been expected from the development of such industrial aides as the steam engine, the spinning jenny and the flying shuttle if they had been projected into a different spiritual climate than that of Protestant England.

As it was, they were immediately put at the service of capitalistically-minded, Protestant, businessmen. This class of businessmen were in spirit and in blood, the descendants of those who had been given a real stake in life at the time of the dissolution of the Catholic monasteries. As Belloc points out, "Every single man who sat in Parliament for a country required his price for voting the dissolution of the monasteries; every single man received it."[3] Out of this group came many Puritans. The lands and possessions of Oliver Cromwell, for example, were secured for him by an ancestor who achieved his share of Church lands at the time of the confiscation.

In England during the mercantilist period, the rising burghers went into business as a calling. They became the entrepreneurs who made money from money, who became rich by foreign enterprises and by the work of other men. When large, more expensive machines were invented, it was only the men of this calibre who had the money and the enterprise to make use of them. It was then that the death blow was dealt to

3 *The Servile State* — Ed.

those small English proprietors who had survived the Statute of Frauds by means of which so many independent English peasants were deprived of their small holdings and made into cotters or rural proletariats. Independent craftsmen, artisans, tradesmen joined the small proprietor in journeying to the environment of the tall smokestack to become what has been termed, "factory-fodder." The English slums were a terrifying spectacle new to the world, with consequences to family life which have marked capitalism consistently. The poor were dispossessed and the rich grew richer. This was unrestrained competition; this was progress. Karl Marx has described the Merrie England of capitalism. Gradually, the exploitation of English labor was somewhat curbed, but the uncontrolled expansion which gives the essential nature of true capitalism found other men to use for gain. The "lesser breeds outside the law" in colonial areas were forced into the discipline of capitalistic enterprise. Into India, Africa, North America went the missionaries of both Business and Trade. As Marx put it — the capitalists of England "began drinking the blood out of the skulls of the slain" in colonial areas. Protestantism had given rise to the enterprising mentality; the spirit of enterprise now pushed Protestantism to a place on the periphery of life. It was in such an atmosphere that Adam Smith's *Wealth of Nations* could be taken so seriously.

In Holland, where Calvinism took firm root, a similar pattern emerged, except that the Dutch distinguished themselves as manipulators of money exchange in a very special manner. The importance of Holland as an international money market and as a focal point of Capitalism was increased by the great number of Jews who took refuge there upon their lamentable expulsion from Spain, and by the number of French Huguenots who fled there after the Revocation of the Edict of Nantes. The Huguenots were the Protestant minority in France, who in leaving that country, took with them just about all the business know-how of their period. The Catholic majority of the French nation, while subtle of intellect and brilliant in discourse, never achieved the leadership in business affairs attained by the enterprising Huguenots. It was generally accepted as a truth that: "There is a kind of natural ineptness in the Popish religion to business, whereas on the contrary among the Reformed, the greater their zeal, the greater their inclination to trade and industry, as holding idleness unlawful."

This evidence is culled from a tract of a Protestant pamphleteer of 1671. The natural ineptness was not traced, as it could have been, to the fact that Catholic teaching held that business, in its constant temptation to avarice, acquisitiveness and worldliness, was perilous to the soul of man.

It is often stated that the enterprising spirit of Capitalism is intensified and activated among minority groups, and therefore there is no relation between Capitalism and Protestantism as such, but rather between Capitalism and those Protestants who formed minority groups. Certain superficially convincing arguments can be given for this thesis, which advances a thought that a minority must be more avaricious and diligent than the majority in order to survive. However, this thesis should also work the other way. When Catholic minorities find themselves within a Protestant majority, they too should exhibit capitalistic traits. Studies were made of Catholic enclaves in Germany and it was found that on the basis of actual tax records, Catholics had less wealth than Protestants. Further, the Catholic part of the population neither chose the education that would prepare them for business, nor did they enter industry or business in general. It has never been claimed that there is an affinity between Lutheranism and Capitalism, but at least there is not a strong antipathy. Again, the Catholic minority of Holland, though put to grievous disabilities, never even tried to challenge the business acumen of the leaders of business and industry who belong to the Reformed Church. The Irish Catholic minorities in England and Scotland have never shown the tendency to excel in capitalistic exploitation that such a theory would lead us to expect from a small group that has had such a struggle to live and survive. As a matter of fact, in their own prodigal way, the Catholic group in England have been lavishing their hard-earned surplus not on building banks or factories but on churches and even cathedrals. No more anti-capitalistic activity could possibly be imagined. Such people, little educated as some of them may be, chose to search after "the good life rather than goods."

Another unexplained phenomenon is that the system of industrial and finance Capitalism which took root in England and spread from there to the United States, never took real root in countries of predominantly Catholic culture. The visitor to a country like Spain or Portugal, where among ordinary people older habits of thought exist, is amazed at the lack of acquisitiveness among them. Of course, an enterprising class has sprung up in both countries now, but still in Portugal, the riches of the port wine trade are exploited by English merchants. The Portuguese producer still clings to pre-capitalistic forms of making the wine. The exploitation of land laborers in Spain is a fascinating study for someone who wants to consult ownership records. In 1834, Liberalism, with all its connotations of modernism and anti-clericalism, managed to seize the twelve million acres of Church lands. True, this was an awful lot of land for the Church to have — but it must be remembered that the Church was the Social Security for the Spanish masses. Even hostile critics admit that these lands were used in the main for social ends. What happened in England at the Reformation, happened in Spain in 1834. The liberals voted the expropriation of the lands and then had their pick of choice lots at nominal costs. These lands were then no longer used for social purposes at all, but in so far as the liberals could harness the Spanish masses, they used them for the production of wealth for themselves. The liberals, now capitalistic land-owners, arranged titles for themselves under a corrupt monarchy, and hatched the problems of the land and the rural proletariat that were fought out almost exactly one hundred years later.

Even in the colonial expansion, the Iberian nations showed no real capitalistic pattern. The remark of the Conquistador that he had a "disease of the heart that only gold could cure" is often quoted. But the tremendous social experiments of the Catholic monks among the native populations are hardly ever recounted. As well as their duty to curb the acquisitiveness of the Spanish Conquistadors, the monks counted it their obligation to protect the Indians, and later the Negroes, by positive measures, including the *hospitals* (community and training centers) of the Spanish monks, and the *reductions* (cooperative colonies) of the Portuguese Father Viera in Brazil and other Jesuits in Paraguay. The present-day Indian population of Latin America, numerous and integrated into national life, bears testimony to the monks' success in tempering the greed of the Conquistadors. Where are the North American hordes? And what is the condition of the remnant that remains?

It was not that the Iberian nations had access to less wealth or natural resources or even skill than the Dutch, French or English nations. It was just that the Catholic mentality did not use them capitalistically. Perhaps the most striking example of this is the use of the immense amounts of gold and silver mined in the new world and brought to Spain and Portugal. A great deal of this gold and silver can be seen in the towns and cities of the Iberian Peninsula. It was used to make altars to show the Lord by action as well as word that everything really belonged to Him — and more particularly those things which the world held most precious. When the Jewish populations of Spain and Portugal were forced to leave because of an intolerant order of the monarchs, much of the remainder of the gold and silver went with them since the Jews had been the traditional moneylenders to the Kings of Spain at Toledo and to the nobles of Portugal. The same gold and silver was transported to Holland, where it entered commerce and was used capitalistically to promote loans and overseas enterprises.

It is a part of the history of our country that the Puritans settled in New England and established their theocracy in freedom. These strong and enterprising men gave a tone to the life of that area and to that of other areas where they settled in later times. The United States became the largest country to be formed in the very time when industrial Capitalism was getting under way, and to be settled by a business-minded colony. It is hardly surprising that our country has become the strongest industrial and financial bastion of world economy. Eduard Heimann[4] has pointed out that the leaders of American industry, the Rockefellers and the Fords, are indeed Calvinists whose business is a calling. However, there were many cultural patterns and spirits active in the integration of the American system, and there are many areas of its economy, and many examples of its institutions that are hardly affected by the impersonality of finance Capitalism. I would refer to the many small businesses and trades run by independent workers — often by the foreign born; to the number of people who, though wage-slaves in factories, still are not completely dispossessed since they own their own home; to the completely admirable system of State Agricultural Schools and County Agents serving the smaller farmer in his independent domain.

Nevertheless, American finance Capitalism is busy with the exploitation of South American labor and thus will cause many crises in the near future. It is also busy about its own destruction.

---

4 Eduard Heimann (1889–1967) was a German economist and social philosopher influenced by Paul Tillich and Martin Buber. This particular reference may come from his book *History of Economic Doctrines: An Introduction to Economic Theory* published in 1945. — Ed.

The Crisis

Factories, like concentration camps, don't just grow; don't just happen. They proceed from the mind of man. An attempt has been made to indicate that there has been, historically, an affinity between Capitalism and Protestantism. The obverse of this is that there has been a continuous antipathy between Catholicism and Capitalism. At the present moment, when Capitalism is clearly in a crisis, the Catholic Church, particularly in the United States, has made an uneasy alliance with Capitalism, and seems to aspire to be the repository of the bourgeois spirit. But such an aspiration will not of course be fulfilled since it is only a vocal minority who move along this trend, while the majority of Catholics are, as usual, not in the directing end of capitalistic enterprises but rather the workmen, the laborers and the farmers. Rather than by any widespread teaching on the part of its leaders, it is the inertia of the Church, and the weight of her great body of social doctrine, that has kept alive among the great masses of Catholic people the anti-capitalistic mentality that goes along with agrarianism, belief in poverty, a sense of the wrongness of impersonality and the usury in the affairs of men.

Even a simple Catholic clerk in the Reeves corner grocery store would catch the evil basis of Henry Ford's dictum "to work together it is not necessary that men should love each other." The grocery clerk would know that the impersonality of business is un-Christian and that it is necessary to love those about us, even those who work with us.

It must make us pause, however, to see England, the first country to embrace Capitalism, publicly repudiating it in its institutions. Capitalism, then, is admittedly a failure in our day in its very home and earliest bastion. What then of the spirit, of the ideals, from which the institutions of Capitalism sprang? They too are under fire — they too have disintegrated along with their fruits.

Undoubtedly then, Capitalism is on its way out, its principles, even that of the sober burgher, discredited. Men are everywhere talking bleakly of what system will come, or will be imposed upon them next. Socialism and Communism, carrying in themselves many of the faults of the system they hope to supplant, are gaining adherents among confused, hopeless, and hungry men. Here and there are evidences of new economic beginnings with more Christian roots. One thing only is certain: the economic direction of the future will reflect and embody the, as yet undecided, spiritual direction mankind is going to take.

JEREM O'SULLIVAN-BARRA
New York

BIBLIOGRAPHY on Protestantism, Capitalism and Catholicism

Nussbaum, Frederick — *A History of the Economic Institutions of Modern Europe*

Weber, Max — *General Economic History* (translated by Knight)

The Protestant Ethic and the Rise of Capitalism

Tawney, R. H. — *The Acquisitive Society*

Religion and the Rise of Capitalism

Belloc, Hilaire — *The Servile State*

The Restoration of Property

Fanfani, Amintore — *Protestantism, Capitalism and Catholicism*

Toynbee, Arnold — *The Industrial Revolution*

Behold in awe, oh saintly boor,
 The social grace of the paramour,
At the evening feast, mid the heat of noon,
 The usurer uses the proper spoon.

The following statistics, frequently quoted, were compiled as a result of a questionnaire addressed to a group of American Protestants.

The denominations represented were 20, including Methodists, Presbyterians, Baptists, and Congregationalists.

Of those questioned, 700 replied.

The two groups were a) acting clergymen and b) students for the ministry.

The results were as follows:

DOCTRINES AFFIRMED	CLERGY	STUDENTS
1) Belief in original sin	67%	13%
2) Baptism is necessary	35%	14%
3) It is necessary to belong to a church	41%	16%
4) Christ is Divine	76%	—*
5) Christ rose from the dead	82%	—*
6) God is omnipotent	—*	64%
7) God has wrought miracles	—*	24%
8) Christ's death was the one act which made possible the forgiveness of man's sins	—*	29%

Only 9% of the students believe that there is a devil, probably the key to the problem.

* Questions not asked.

Contemporary American Protestantism

IS AMERICA PROTESTANT?

The usual answer to a question of this sort is given statistically, and it proves practically nothing. There were, at the time of the 1936 census (notoriously unreliable in this regard) 31,000,000 avowed Protestants in the United States, as against 20,000,000 Catholics and 70,000,000 unchurched. The Protestants comprised over 250 sects, quite a number of which can be considered "Christian" only by stretching the imagination.

A better index to the times is gained from the personal sampling of the spiritual atmosphere of the newsstands, hotels, churches, suburbs, movies, radio and by taking careful note of what has happened to hometown friends and college classmates. The vitality of a civilization is spiritual, and spiritual temper cannot be reduced to statistics. On this basis then, of a clue here, and clue there, plus our own powers of discernment, the following appears to be the situation.

The period of Protestant ascendancy was finished a generation ago. The country is now in the grip of no intense spiritual force, nor is there any all-over general direction in which we are heading. An uncommon number of our present leaders get their vitality from a residual Protestantism, but are not themselves Protestant and are not passing on their heritage. Just as the country has for a long time been feeding the cities its own best vitality, so has the traditional Protestant home, steeped in Bible reading, been providing men and women of strong character. Often the two sources of vitality coincided. Rural America has now been drained of vitality. The traditional Protestant homelife was progressively abandoned by the laity, then the ministers, and now even the missionaries. Dorothy Thompson, Henry Luce, Robert Hutchins, and many other prominent figures (note that they are articulate America, not America fatted on mercantile profits) came from ministers' and missionaries' homes. Does anyone expect that a childhood of Superman and progressive schools will produce citizens of like caliber?

Anyhow, we are now coasting along on a residual strength, which is not being renewed, or even acknowledged. We are living in a post-Protestant age, turning barbarian. We are in a moment of indecision, waiting for a new source of vitality, ready otherwise to retrogress rapidly. Two strong forces are coming up, from sharply opposed directions: Catholicism and Atheistic Communism. It seems unlikely that Protestantism, modernized and mild as it is, will prove a serious contender for tomorrow's America, but we shall examine the potentialities in this regard presently. The average man of today is a neo-pagan, frustrated in his directionlessness. Some are being converted to Catholicism. Some are falling prey to Communism. In between is a large area of neurosis and alcoholism, laying waste much of our country's best blood and natural gifts.

Why the loss of Protestant supremacy? It is useless to look to external conditions for its present weakness, for it had a clear field in the building up of America. Protestantism must either have inadvertently pulled its house down on top of itself (as, for instance, in its unfortunate and now lamented support of secular education) or be suffering from internal disorders. Let us first examine the internal malady.

DISEASES OF PROTESTANTISM: SENILITY

The 400th anniversary of Luther's death was commemorated last year. It is four centuries then, since the Reformation breach in Christendom, a schism which broke the floodgates which might have held back the rising tide of uncontrolled humanism and commercialism. It has taken 400 years for the unleashed forces to run their course to the breakdown of

Western Civilization. 400 years to undermine the mental ability, the health, the hope, the peace, the happiness, the common morality of man. 400 years to destroy the beauty of the face of the earth, to upset the balance of fertility in the soil, nearly to exhaust the natural resources of the earth. 400 years to pervert knowledge to the total service of destruction. 400 years to go from an ideal of self-discipline to an unashamed commercial exploitation of the passions. 400 years to twist men's minds to an acceptance of the perversions of birth control, homosexuality, abortion and euthanasia. 400 years from an ordered society with respect for authority to a hideous alternation of pressure-group democracy and fanatic dictatorship. 400 years from a civilization built and permeated by the Church to a monstrous scientific barbarism untouched by Christ. In that 400 years what has happened to the branch which broke off from the vine? Has it withered yet? Nearly. It is certainly senile, and the best measure of its senility is the prevalence of religious indifferentism. Future ages, if any, will look with horror upon the time when men by the millions disregarded God, when schools and courts and hospitals and jails and insane asylums and day nurseries neglected to pay homage to God. They will read that the more or less established religion "played" to almost empty houses, while thousands upon thousands of men gathered to watch nine men play baseball. They will learn that whole sections of newspapers recorded the minutia of money trading while little or no space was given to religion. They may even learn that men sank so low mentally and spiritually as to try to identify, in a muddled sort of fellowship, creeds not only diverse but contradictory.

DISEASES OF PROTESTANTISM: DISINTEGRATION

Protestantism keeps falling apart, subdividing like an amoeba. Everytime someone is displeased he can, and he often does, start a new sect. There are now some 250, without the process' having

HUMPTY DUMPTY SAT ON A WALL—

been stemmed. The reunion effort of the Federal Council of Churches does not check the disease, but merely arranges for cooperation among the diseased parts. The disease itself is of the essence of Protestantism, rooted in its rejection of authority. It was a serious and terrible thing for the original reformers to break the unity of Christendom and reject the rightful authority of the Church. After that, however, Protestantism had no ground on which to object to further fissure. It is like marriage. If you stand on the ground that it is indissoluble and allow no divorce, you have a tenable position. If you deny the indissolubility, you undermine the whole structure of marriage and inevitably let yourself in for a string of divorces. The only way to stop the disintegrating process and its unlovely consequences is to return to the initial tenable position. This Protestantism is still reluctant to do, both in the matter of itself and its views on marriage.

Protestantism clung to the "right of private judgment," as they call it, which is really an indirect way of saying that there is no objective truth. It is consistently foreign to the Protestant temper to search for a truth external to the individual and binding on all men. Instead the tendency is to search one's own mind to determine the credibility of a doctrine. This may explain why the word "humility," which to a Catholic suggests an ever so desirable virtue,

—HUMPTY DUMPTY HAD A GREAT FALL.

has a distasteful, servile connotation in common American parlance. The rejection of authority and the lack of humility is a Protestant characteristic which has been engrafted on the American temper. Our country was populated, someone has said, not just by Protestants but by Protestants who couldn't get along with other Protestants. Once here, the disgruntled or avaricious could always proceed westward. Over a period of several hundred years this tendency has produced its exemplar in the rugged individualist of recent unlamented memory. You couldn't make a society out of him, so he is at length disappearing. His progeny are much less splendid. They are just plain undisciplined in every way.

If protest against authority (and chiefly, of course, against papal authority) is of the essence of Protestantism, one ought not to wonder at the present hew and cry against the rising tide of Catholicism. The ordinary non-Catholic citizen responds instinctively and unreasoningly with a shudder to the prospect of authority, especially when it is called "authoritarianism."

But men get tired of following their own rule, just as children get tired of doing as they please. Anyone with half an eye can see that the United States is spoiling for strong, unhesitant, leadership. In the political field the danger of dictatorship lies in the mood of the people rather than in the strong-armed tactics of ... of whom? The miracle is that no one has yet set upon such easy prey.

In the religious sphere, official Protestantism is making one last barrage attack against the Church which, having authority, has stood firm on the same ground since the breach. Some of it is hysterical. Most of it is pelting with marshmallows. In the spirit of reconciliation Protestants and other non-Catholics keep making friendly overtures to the Church, involving slight compromises. Unbend a little on birth control, concede a few points on mixed marriages (by contrast the Anglican Archbishop of York is lately getting scrupulous in reverse on the matter of mixed marriages. Is the tide of their usual effect turning, or is it a revenge move?). But most of all we are besought one way and another to admit that one religion is as good as another. Were it not for our obstinacy in this regard, all Christians (and Jews, Buddhists and others) could join in a splendid spiritual fellowship.

With so much genuine good will on both sides, and so little personal enmity, now that vast rivers of water have run under the bridge, it is just possible that the obdurate position of the true Church may suddenly be seen for what it is, and that the Protestants may begin to appreciate the magnificent strength with which Catholicism has held to the fullness of truth which alone can restore society. They may even look up and see the Church's outstretched arms of welcome.

Their alternative is to return to the tyranny of petty authority. "Jesus, I was certain," said Rev. Dr. Harry Emerson Fosdick in his farewell address to the Riverside congregation, "would not be in the least intent on such a ritual detail (as baptism by immersion)... and I had decided that I would never be a minister of a church where all Christians, devoted to our Lord, could not freely enter on equal terms with what form of baptism — or none — their Christian heritage made sacred to them." How do you know, Dr. Fosdick? By what authority do you presume to read God's mind?

DISEASES OF PROTESTANTISM: SELF-CONTRADICTION

Eventual self-contradiction is the invariable mark of heresy. The true Church preserves all the intensities of Christianity in delicate balance. Heresy, by denying some truths, or exaggerating some at the expense of the others, destroys the balance, so that its adherents become extremists in one direction, and then swing to the opposite extreme by way of reaction, always without finding the stabilizing center. This process is very clearly marked in Protestantism, the more so now that the process has run its course in a half-dozen different aspects. Protestantism has swung from the gloomy despair of Calvinism (man, being especially corrupted by original sin, cannot please God) to the presumption of liberalism and modernism (there never was any original sin, there is no Hell, and if there is a Heaven I shall certainly arrive there without effort.) It is starting to swing now from an exaggerated confidence in the temporal order and man's reason to an exaggerated and phoney mysticism. Its morality has ranged all the way from "no fun on Sunday" to the solemn and sentimental endorsement of euthanasia. It has swung from an excessive individualism into the yawning Russian jaws of collectivism. This pendulum swing accounts for the phenomenon which attracted Chesterton to the Church: Protestantism alternately criticizes the Catholic Church on diametrically opposite grounds; now for being too other-worldly, now for being too this-worldly. But the Catholic Church hasn't moved from dead center. It is her critics who are revolving.

Two major reversals warrant particular attention:

FAITH AND GOOD WORKS

It pleased Martin Luther to declare good works useless for salvation, even though he had to discredit St. James' Epistle to do so. The effect of his doctrine of salvation by faith alone was a local and immediate abandonment of charitable works; indirectly, and with other contributing factors (such as the greed of the political arm) it meant the virtual wiping out of the works of mercy in the Protestant countries of the western hemisphere. Nothing is more disguised and misrepresented in our textbooks than this appalling fact. There was, under a united Catholic Europe, a magnificent network of good works, ranging from universities to orphan asylums, from hospitals to burial societies. They were operated by the Church, not the state, and were mostly under the auspices of religious orders. They were manned by thousands and thousands of nuns and monks leading heroic, dedicated lives of piety and poverty. In one Protestant country after another the properties belonging to the charities were usurped, that is, stolen, by politicians for ignoble reasons, and the lot of the poor and the weak was reduced to intolerable, unalleviated misery. Protestantism lost the Catholic idea of works of mercy, that Christ was to be seen in our weak brothers. It has never recovered that idea, although the pendulum has now swung over to social service Christianity. The change began with pharisaical, patronizing philanthropy, which still faintly lingers in our society. The rich helped the poor without impoverishing themselves; pried into the lives of those whose benefactors (and often exploiters) they were, judged and managed, and tried to make the poor clean like themselves.

Now the whole of Protestantism is permeated with the spirit of good works. Faith is irrelevant and salvation unimportant. Never mind if poor Mr. X goes to Heaven or Hell, the important thing is to get his teeth fixed. Who cares about the morality of abortion; it is economically advisable. This social service Protestantism is usually now just social service, and never mind the Protestantism. The child it bore had repudiated its mother. But within Protestantism the social service spirit is still rife. When sincere, earnest Protestants want to intensify the practice of their religion, they do not go on retreats or make corporate acts of faith; they go down to the Italian section of town and help empty the garbage. They form colonies of college students to build houses for mine workers, or groups to do occupational therapy in mental hospitals. This is even, and especially, true of the Quakers whose attraction is usually reputed to be their emphasis on the contemplative.

We associate Communism with Russia, but it had its birth in Protestant Europe and gathered momentum from the absence of good works in a society bred on salvation by faith alone. In a sense Communism, social security legislation and the curious material messianism of some of the United National committees, represent a final, extra-religious exaggeration of the emphasis on good works apart from faith.

Now the pendulum is trying to reverse itself again, but the effort is deceased and diffuse. The emphasis is no longer chiefly on the temporal welfare of people but on their "emotional" welfare, with Freudianism and sentimentality muddling around in everything.

THE BIBLE

The Protestant somersault in regard to scripture is a sad commentary on the waywardness of dissidents. The Bible is the inspired word of God, completely true but neither the sole nor the primary authority for Christianity. Protestants having left the Church (which is the supreme authority), were more or less forced to regard the Bible as the sole and comprehensive religious guide. Since the Bible is not easily interpreted, they were further reduced to specifying the literal meaning as a criterion (after some convenient changes in the original text had been made by the reformers).

Bible literalists still plentifully exist in America. The control movement of Protestantism, however, has swung over to a denial not only of the authority, but even of the *authenticity* of the Bible. They derive their position from some 19th century German scholars, the "higher critics," who questioned traditional dates and texts. Although the most credible scholars among the higher critics came to eat most of their own words in favor of the traditional teachings, Protestants seem not to have heard of this. Even, and especially, in the major Protestant seminaries (which have been liberalized) a view of the Bible is taught which entirely discredits it. It goes like this: the gospel of John is of late date and not apostolic. The other three, synoptic, gospels are all variations of an original manuscript, possibly Mark, plus some other sayings. Mark is the most authentic gospel. It contains no account of the Virgin Birth (which is anyhow common religious folklore) which therefore never took place. The end, which treats of the Resurrection, is a later interpolation in the text. Christ died in agony and despair. The miracles were exaggerations, lies, epileptic fits; anyhow, not miracles. Christ didn't think himself divine; it was pinned on him later. Judas was a well-meaning zealot whose plans went awry. Etc. It is essentially the same account of Our Savior which is found in the Jewish Encyclopedia.

Incredible though it may seem, this sort of stuff is not only taught, but is even considered edifying. "How much more inspiring Christianity is, now that it is shorn of its superstitious coating," is the sort of double-talk by which it is justified. This is similar to another common trick of speech, wherein one first denies that men have souls and then talks about their sacred personalities. The students with better minds, those who can follow through a premise to its conclusion, understandably resign from Protestantism to join Alcoholics Anonymous.

It is well to keep this scriptural aberration in mind when considering Protestant plans to restore the teaching of religion to secular colleges. Unless Protestantism suffers a change of heart, this is what they are going to be handing out. Wellesley College has been teaching this sort of "religion" for years in a required course, without conspicuous increase in student piety.

DISEASES OF PROTESTANTISM: THE THEOLOGICAL VOID

A galaxy of churches, millions of members, wealth incalculable, good will in abundance, the blessings of the political wing, and every other material and social advantage cannot perpetuate Protestantism in a theological void. If Protestantism doesn't believe in anything, it isn't anything. Creeds are of the essence of religions. Liberal Protestantism has abandoned creeds. The result is sound and fury signifying nothing. Protestantism is always expending a lot of money and effort to start something which tomorrow will still be there but will not still be Protestant. It will be secular. Protestants are now fearful of the threat of secularism, but they brought it upon themselves. There is hardly a one of what are now the "best" colleges: Harvard, Wellesley, Yale, etc. which is not of pious Protestant formation, and usually for the training of ministers. Now they are secular. What is Presbyterian about the Presbyterian Medical Center in New York? Nothing. The universities and hospitals founded at great expense by the Protestant missionaries in the Far East were almost immediately secularized. Protestants keep pouring missionaries and money into China and Japan, but with very little *Protestant* effect.

This all stems from theological deficiencies. One of its most pathetic manifestations is due to the absence of *moral* theology. Modern irreligious psychiatry is threatening to fill this void. For instance, Protestant chaplains in state mental hospitals (often admirable men) are actually learning from psychiatrists how to administer spiritually to the patients.

It is curious to the point of absurdity, how strenuously Protestants avoid theological criteria. The current upheaval in the Episcopal Church is illustrative. This Church, which encompasses within itself all shades and degrees of personal belief, is considering whether or not to merge with the Presbyterian Church. One can search the accounts of the debate in vain for the slightest inquiry as to whether Presbyterianism or Episcopalianism, if either, is *true*. A very daring person might bring up the question of the validity of orders, but theology is verboten.

Protestantism is formally split into fundamentalism and modernism, representing (characteristically) two untenable positions at opposite extremes. The fundamentalists are Bible literalists who accept the major Christian dogmas with an exaggerated emphasis on Christ's imminent second coming. Their adherents are mostly from the lower middle classes. Fundamentalism produced the good living, good willing, sincere and believing Protestant that Catholics have in mind when they talk about how certain it is that Protestants will go to Heaven. How many of these typical, sincere Christians with a grossly over-simplified religion remain? They are said to be legion in the south; yet closer investigation reveals that southern churches are strong on social life, but not conspicuous for the piety of their members. Then there is the Negro, who lent his own particular dignity and grace to a shorn Christianity. The rapidity with which the Negro is being de-Christianized is scandalous, and not pertinent to this discussion. The third great repository of middle-class Protestantism is in the middle-west, where simple goodness and godly talk is hard-pressed by the radio, movies and "an ever-increasing standard of living." Many of the new sects are lunatic-fringe offshoots of fundamentalism.

Let us now observe what has happened to the modernist, liberal wing of Protestantism. Dr. Fosdick exemplifies it in his own career. He is a Baptist minister who had to give up his Fifth Avenue pastorate in the twenties because, chiefly under the influence of the current evolutionary doctrines, he could not believe fundamentalist dogmas. Rockefeller built him the imposing Riverside Church, where he could preach as he pleased. In this church, adjacent to International House, the Union Theological Seminary and Columbia University, Fosdick developed to its fullest the liberal positionless position. The liberals seemed at first to have chosen the part of reason and science. The irony is that they ended up with sentimentality and double-talk. They are prey to every passing secular aberration, hastily readjusting their tenets to the latest findings of this and that. The capitulation of liberal Protestant leadership and pseudo-science is complete and abject. They deny the divinity of Christ, more or less deny immortality, hold no objective moral standards, concede divorce, recommend birth control (indeed, sponsor it) and now endorse euthanasia (at least, some of the prominent ones, including Fosdick, have done so).

The liberals control organizational Protestantism. They rule the seminaries, control the Federal Council of Churches, get written about in the papers, run the leading Protestant magazines, and occupy the city pulpits. Do they also have a majority following? Quite likely not. It sounds silly, but they may well be self-appointed shepherds with precious few sheep. For one thing, as we pointed out, their followers tend logically to drift altogether away from religion.

A word about the sacraments. Liberal Protestants are thoroughly unsacramental. They have dispensed with the two sacraments which Protestantism in general did retain for some time; matrimony, no longer considered binding, and baptism. Some sort of baptismal rite is usually performed in liberal churches, but it is regarded as merely symbolic, and therefore is invalid. To "join" a liberal Protestant church you need only signify your belief in Jesus Christ, not specifying what you believe about Him.

WILL THERE BE A PROTESTANT RESURGENCE?

We cannot pretend to measure accurately the residual vitality of Protestantism, but we shall indicate some of the places where it is to be found.

The respectable, conservative, monied element of American life is still nominally Protestant, but it is not true that they still hold the reins of our national life. Leadership has fallen to propagandists and labor leaders, the lower classes, the poorly educated and the mercantile owners. Few if any of these groups are Protestant. So the upper-middle class affiliation is not the asset it might at first appear to be.

A better gauge of Protestant strength is the spiritual strength of its members. How is that determined? It is not necessarily reflected in the leaders or in the official publications; there are no religious orders to flower from it. The best place to look is among the rather old, or among the young laity and clergy. And here and there you find it; an isolated man or woman of saintly character, an occasional godly family. Among the young you find groups forming to do works of mercy, to go to the missions, to restore rural community life, or to think out religious problems. The Christian Students League has considerable vitality. The more conspicuous Youth for Christ movement we would be inclined to disregard. It puts on a good show, but it is a bit on the hysterical side for accomplishing permanent results. Protestantism is subject to revivalist waves which always catch up men's goodness and desires for religion, without being able to sustain them. The Oxford Group was evidence of this.

To sustain such vitality as remains in Protestantism there must be theological food; else it is sheer emotionalism. It is true, as we said before, that Protestant theology in America is conspicuous by its absence. This is not true of Europe where there is renewed interest in theology. One movement, which has followers in this country, is backwards to neo-orthodoxy. Here and there you will find people who have returned to the original Calvinist or Lutheran position (some Lutheran sects have never departed from the teachings of their founder and stand apart from the usual Protestant federations). Then there are contemporary European theologians who are attracting a lot of attention, but whose influence in this country is still limited to the intense groups: earnest young lay people and theological students. Brunner[1] is one such. He is straining toward a theology which will synthesize religion and life. Most famous, however, is Karl Barth who holds to a position of exaggerated supernaturalism. He catches Protestants on their

---

1   Heinrich Emil Brunner (1889–1966) was a Swiss Reformed theologian who, along with Karl Barth, was part of the neo-orthodox or dialectical theology movement within Protestantism.   — Ed.

pendulum swing back to the supernatural and the mystical. The same tendency accounts for the attraction of the young to the Quakers, some of whose leaders have borrowed heavily, and quite indiscriminately, from mystics, Catholic and pagan. They are rediscovering the potentialities of prayer, silence, solicitude, and the inner life in general. There is also in most of the Protestant sects a groping for a return to the sacramental life. Especially marked is the renewed emphasis on the Lord's Supper, long reduced to symbolism and grape juice (of course without powers of consecration). There is a sort of liturgical movement in process too; a renewed interest in good Church music, including Gregorian chant, and a borrowing of ritual from the Episcopalians and the Orthodox.

Ritually speaking, the upward movement is most pronounced among the high Episcopalians (who decline to call themselves Protestants at all, but consider that they are one of the three Catholic branches of Christianity[2] — the third is the Orthodox Church. *Time*, whose managing editor is Episcopalian, has lately taken a dogmatic stance on this point for his magazine usage). They smother in incense, have elaborate and very beautiful services, increasingly favor clerical celibacy, and stress the sacraments. They hold (contrary to the opinion of the Holy See) that their orders are valid. Devout Episcopalians receive "communion" every morning.

There is a less lovely variety, of a sort, within Protestantism which consists in residual hatred of the Catholic Church. This provides a rallying point (it is, after all, the common element in historical Protestantism) for diverse elements. It is very outspoken where it exists, but on an hysterical, low intellectual level. We are not referring to the fulminations of the Jehovah Witnesses, who can hardly be classed as Protestants, but of such

---

[2] The so-called "Branch Theory" of ecclesiology as formulated first by High Anglicans in the 19th century — Ed.

people as Bishop Oxnam.[3] These people see horrible portents in Myron C. Taylor's[4] mission to the Vatican. Among other Protestants, outspoken antagonism is not very common. There is a vestigial, instinctive, horror of Catholicism fairly common, but usually beneath the surface. There is a growing good will of the "some of my best friends are Catholic" sort. It is impossible to estimate how much of an anti-Catholic conflagration could be started in a crisis.

These, then, are the main reservoirs of Protestant strength. They do not seem strong enough to effect a resurgence from within. It seems as though Protestantism is losing more ground than it gains. There remains to be considered whether or not its life may be prolonged artificially from outside, notably through the support of some strong political force.

PROTESTANTISM AND COMMUNISM

Nothing is too absurd for it to happen in this age of drastic changes and strange bedfellows. It might conceivably suit Communism to effect a resurgence of American Protestantism for its own ends; and it might be able to do so. The muddled minds of liberal Protestants would be opening enough.

We do not say that this will happen, nor even that it has begun; but only that it might happen, and that there are some evidences of a beginning here and there. The strongest indication of the possibility, however, lies in the general situation of the world today. This is a time of growing absolutism in which there are two strong forces and a handful of weakfish factors. Protestantism is weak as compared both with Catholicism, which stands like a rock in her 2,000 year old position; and as

---

3   Garfield Bromley Oxnam (1891–1963) was a social reformer and bishop of the Methodist Episcopal Church. — Ed.

4   Myron C. Taylor (1874 – 1959), an American industrialist who served as the US ambassador to the Holy See from 1940 to 1950. His appointment was condemned by many Protestants as incompatible with the American idea of the separation of Church and State. — Ed.

compared with Communism, which drives relentlessly from the opposite pole. It is weak not so much materially as in the sense of wishy-washy; weak in the sense of being diluted or fragmentary Christianity. How can it hold out in the face of these forces? If it stands by its original position of protest against Catholicism, it may well find itself in the Communist camp.

What are the signs? There is the "Red Dean" in England. There is the conspicuous presence of the Russian Orthodox clergy at solemn Episcopal functions; a clergy under strong pressure from the Kremlin. There is the protest against Myron C. Taylor, which is at least useful to Russia. There is the militant immorality of the liberals with their birth control, euthanasia and abortion. There is the tendency of the clergy of affiliated Protestant churches to busy themselves with political and international issues, in which they could easily be duped.

The hysterical anti-Catholic element in Protestantism hugs the Communist partly line, but whether inadvertently or advisedly is not clear. Not only is this true of *The Protestant*, which is not quite a reputable magazine, but also, for instance of *The Churchman*, an Episcopalian magazine which is lay and not official, but in sufficiently good standing to give a dinner for Eisenhower at the Waldorf-Astoria. *The Churchman* has lately run a series on the Stepinac trials, written by the Yugoslav Ambassador. It took a pro-Wallace stand on the cabinet upheaval. It devotes much of each issue to tirades against the Catholic Church.

WILL PROTESTANTISM RE-UNITE WITH ROME?

Anything can happen today, but reunion seems very unlikely. We pray for it in the Church Unity Octave and this is probably the most effective single measure that can be taken. What separates Catholics and Protestants now is almost a matter of temperament; something which can be healed by prayer or by common suffering, by mutual love or by explanation (rather than debate). Certainly individual Protestants are much nearer, and much more receptive to Catholicism, than in all the long past history of bitter schism.

However, in point of fact, those who are finding their way home to the Catholic Church are post-Protestants who have gone through a period of doubt and suffering. The trend is not so much from Protestantism directly. The one exception is in the case of the High Anglican Church where there have been group conversions, and might conceivably be a mass conversion.

There is something besides ignorance which keeps Protestants from becoming Catholics. There are now quite a number of educated Protestants who have a fairly accurate idea of Catholicism (except that they do not see the Church as Christ), and view it with repugnance. Union Theological Seminary in New York (Liberal Protestant) has an excellent collection of Catholic books for instance. But Protestants can read Max Weber's indictment of the concept of a "worldly calling" without considering it unflattering. They can look on the civilization which they have largely made, and like it. They are still scandalized by dirt (more than sin), and poverty, and beggars, and Latin Americans who would rather sit in the sun than work on an assembly line, and nuns who "waste" their lives in contemplation, and wives who have more babies than they can afford, and bingo which looks so much like gambling and so little like banking. Worst of all, they continue to glorify the search for truth at the expense of finding the truth, so shutting themselves off from the joy, and humility, of certainty.

Perhaps this explains why our world has come to such a pass. The worst punishment men can suffer is that which they bring upon themselves by preferring their own to God's way.

CAROL ROBINSON

Calvin Cox is doing research
   On the Hagiology of the Lower Church.
He isn't very busy,
   Is he?

Why I am Not a Catholic

We wanted to know how the Catholic Church looks to Protestants, and we thought the best way to find out was to ask them. The views given below are printed exactly as written for us, and are representative, not of the Protestant masses, but of thinking, deliberate, articulate Protestants of diverse affiliation.

A PRESBYTERIAN THEOLOGICAL STUDENT IN A BAPTIST SEMINARY.

I feel that I owe much to my Catholic friends. And I believe the Catholic Church serves our world well in many ways. I have found intellectual stimulation from some of its writers, spiritual devotion in many of its adherents, and consecrated service to God and mankind in many of its members. But still I am not wholly attracted to the Church and I do not feel altogether uncomfortable with the label of "Protestant" or one who protests against the Catholic Church. I believe as did the early Protestants that every man may be his own priest — if he chooses. My knowledge of Catholic doctrine, however, is not sufficient to undertake a discussion of the Protestant point of view on doctrinal matters and therefore I shall confine myself to some of the things which I have myself experienced and which incidentally, I believe, are not unrelated to matters of Catholic dogma.

Recently a young couple came to me for advice concerning the wisdom of a marriage between them. The young lady was Catholic and the young man a Protestant. He, of course, had been free to go to the Catholic church of the young lady and to speak to the priest, but she was forbidden the privilege of speaking to a Protestant minister or attending a service in the church of her friend. The unfairness of this struck me as well as the lack of confidence which the Church placed in the ability of the young lady to choose and choose wisely for herself. I believe that too often in practice the Catholic Church holds to too low a view of human nature and does not give its communicants sufficient responsibility and trust.

A related difficulty, I believe, is inherent in the attitude which many Catholics I have known take that they are satisfied they have the one and ONLY true way to God and his kingdom. There is, I affirm, no monopoly on the wisdom of the earth nor the wisdom of the divine either in the Church or out of it. The Catholic training I have observed tends in some cases to lull one into the belief that all theological difficulties are solved by the Church. There is too much dogmatism in it and too little room for questioning and new light on old problems. The old answers are too often substituted for fresh inquiry and fresh answers.

Another thing which has troubled me amongst many of the Catholics I have known and observed in this country and in Mexico when I was there is the tendency to be absorbed in a religion of ritual. For me, religion is only half begun if praise to God and attendance at His church has been performed, and the Catholics I have admired most are the ones who I believe have realized this too. They are the ones who have gone out to serve the poor, the sick, and the uneducated, or to try to live more wholesome lives wherever they might be. A serious danger, I think, always lurks nearby when men come to celebrate their religion together that they may come to elevate a particular form above all others, or that having been to Mass or said their prayers or sung their hymns to feel that they have satisfied the Lord.

There is too great a willingness amongst Catholics and Catholic leaders to compromise with the powers of the world. One reads of the defense of gambling or bingo games. Certainly all would agree that conscientious objection is a very uncompromising position for a Christian to take whether they agreed with that stand or not. Amongst the conscientious objectors in America in the recent war, I observed Catholics were very few in number in proportion to the size of the Church in America.

I believe also that one gains much by experience and that a clergy set apart from the experiences of married life cannot serve their people as well as they otherwise might.

I suppose in the final analysis the reason I am not a Catholic is because I have been born and brought up a Protestant. If then this be true, the objections which I have raised above are merely things which I deplore in the Catholic Church and which I might hope could be changed so that the world would be served by a healthier, more courageous, and more consecrated Christian institution.

A LIBERAL PROTESTANT PROFESSOR IN ONE OF OUR GREAT SECULAR UNIVERSITIES.

The gracious courtesy extended to me with the request that I answer this question in complete frankness would remind me, if reminder were necessary, that writing as a Christian I am also writing for a group of fellow Christians. Will you be patient with me, then, if in the interests of that mutual understanding among Christians which the staggering tasks of our time demand, I write things that may at first seem distasteful?

After an early training that had induced a strong Protestant loyalty, I came presently, through the course of my university teaching, to reconsider these convictions and to believe that the differences of Catholics and Protestants were more formal than essential. Then about this time I chanced to be a fellow traveler with a group of Catholic priests from American metropolitan parishes on a voyage to the Mediterranean. On the Sunday morning when we slipped out of the harbor of Marseille, I fell in with one of them, attended Mass for the first time, and afterwards walked round and round the deck with him in earnest religious discussion. My mood was most pacific; I sought to establish that in the deeper things of faith we were in full agreement. But I found myself blocked at every point by my genial instructor. I spoke of the Mass: "Now you mean that the wafer and the wine are only symbols; the devout worshipper through them participates spiritually in the saving work of Christ?" "No, no," he replied, "I mean that they are the actual body and blood of Christ." Nonplussed, I tried another line; I spoke of forgiveness. "You mean that when the sinner has truly repented you tell him that God has forgiven him?" "Not at all," the priest answered, "I feel that in myself I have the power to forgive sins." The first statement struck my Protestant consciousness as superstition, the second as presumption. However, I made no comment, and our chat ended on a cordial note. But out of it there came for me a realization of the greatness of Protestantism. I now saw, as I had not before, its unique position as an affirmation of the spiritual essence of true religion.

A few days later, as I came up from dinner I found three of the priests resting against the rail in the gentle air of a spring evening in the Levant. Once again our talk turned immediately to our religious faith. They were pleasant men — except one, who was consistently offensive. He impressed me as a person who had never done serious religious thinking; secure behind the high walls of his church's dogmas, he had accepted and then reiterated stock answers without having himself ever come to grips with the problems of personal faith. I do not recall at this distance details of our talk; we ranged far and wide over miracles, Bible text and authority, foundations of Christian faith, and the like. But we found little agreement. Yet the occasion was a turning point in my experience. Out of the deficiencies and inhibitions of the priests' thinking, I saw, as in a flash of illumination, the historic significance of the Protestant Reformation. One of the great strands running through history has been what we may call the struggle for the freedom of the human soul; freedom from political oppressors, from economic destitution, from ignorance and superstition, and not least from the sort of religion that enslaves rather than uplifts. Protestantism, I now saw, is but the latest and greatest affirmation of man's inherent right, as man, to be free and to seek and find truth without let or hindrance — greatest, because it is but a re-affirmation of "the liberty wherewith Christ hath made us free."

Presently it dawned on me that I had always known these things. I had learned them in my boyhood, then later ignored them. And so the striking situation had come about that ignorance had made me kindly toward Catholicism, but the return of knowledge had brought recoil and a realization,, now deep based, of the greatness of Protestantism.

Through the succeeding years, I have learned much on the subject, some of it from priests, some from other Catholics whom I have come to admire deeply. I have realized more fully, too, the weakness of some Protestant practice and the confusion of much Protestant thinking. Nonetheless, the two insights received from Catholic priests on shipboard have deepened with the deepening experience of life. Steadily I have recognized more clearly the epochal importance of Protestantism in cleansing Christianity of lower elements that had attached themselves through a thousand years, and in pointing religious devotion to the deep realities of our Christian faith. And I have seen, too, how Protestantism stands as a great bulwark of human freedom. The Catholic doctrine of the Church, resulting as it does in claims of unique knowledge and authority and a privileged place in society and the state, constitutes an acute social menace. But Protestantism repudiates all this; it sees all men alike as but humble seekers for the truth of God; in His truth alone resides real authority.

There are, I well know, millions of devout Catholics, born into the church they love deeply, for whom no course is possible but to find their religious satisfactions there and to hope for their church's growth in its expression of truth. But I am a Protestant, heir of a glorious heritage reaching back across all the Christian centuries and far beyond wherever men have in sincerity sought God. For me to turn my back on this heritage and to consider the possibility of becoming a Catholic would be to sin against the light which God gave to my fathers, and which he gives to me to walk by.

INTEGRITY, February 1947

A PRESBYTERIAN MINISTER'S DAUGHTER ACTIVE IN RELIGIOUS AFFAIRS.

I have been asked to tell why I am not a Catholic. To go back to first causes, I was born a Protestant. However, during my college days, I was administered about equal doses of Protestantism and Catholicism and a much larger dose of agnosticism. Since I emerged a Protestant, I should have my reasons.

I do have. And there is nothing unusual about them. They are traditional and trite to the last degree. For the sake of brevity I will state them baldly. The first is that I do not accept the Catholic *jure divino* theory by which the Pope has authority in all matters of doctrine, discipline and worship. Another is that I do not believe I need a mediator. I believe that I can repent and be forgiven without the offices of a priest.

The Catholic Church, granted its premises, has, I realize, a rational apology for the tenets with which I have just expressed disagreement. And I will defend unequivocally my Catholic brother's right to a free exercise of conscience. I do not, for that matter, see eye to eye with the Southern Baptist, the Quaker or the Unitarian, to mention a few, or with every Presbyterian. I do not expect to.

I am at times disturbed by the feeling that while I as a Presbyterian regard the Catholic and the Southern Baptist and all Christians in spite of our differences as my equals before God, with like opportunity for salvation, the Catholic does not so regard me. He is not a heretic in my eyes. I am in his.

The late Dr. William Adams Brown of Union Theological Seminary in his book *Toward a United Church*, posthumously published by Scribners, makes this statement:

> It belongs to the very genius of the Roman Church that it can brook no rival, and any discussion of points of difference which assumes that the disputants stand on equal ground is ruled out from the start.

This brings us to a third reason why I am not a Catholic. It is because I do not believe that any church has the inner track. There are many Catholics who are better Christians than I but I do not believe it is because they are Catholic.

I could mention other points of variance, but I think these are the basic ones. One thing remains to be said, that while these reasons are sufficient to keep me a "Non-Catholic," they do not persuade me to forget that all Christians, Catholic and Non-Catholic, profess a common creed.

A QUAKER

Now as for my writing why I am not a Roman Catholic, what good would that do anyone except perhaps myself. Heredity is a factor; my political philosophy which deplores hierarchical structure which is so prominent in Roman Catholic Church polity, and which displays often a spiritual imperialism which I deplore; a deep attraction to the corporate mystical experience which I find in the silent Quaker worship; a deep desire to abolish the clergy that all may understand their responsibility as priests for worshipping God; less historical sense than most people that consequently makes me value the presence of Christ here and now — more than the vehicle or pipes through which the external tradition has been sent; and a feeling that Roman Catholicism is the victim of its bigness.

Yet when I have said all of this I should want to add that I am profoundly thankful to what I have received via this vehicle; that I acknowledge those who find God through it as far better men than I; that I know it has been the nurse of saints and mystics and that today it stands as a great transcendental witness to the fact that this world and this civilization are not all and that there is a redeeming presence operative upon it, which it neglects only at its peril. As for the mass, I find it nearer to being a service of worship where in prayer and in a corporate act of elevation I donate myself anew to God and experience his act of donation for me than anywhere else except in the silent assemblies of the Quakers. In the sense that all life is one and that the inner and the outer must be joined in apostolic acts of charity yet still with a sense that being precedes doing, again I find myself in particular unity with your paper's position and with the Catholic Worker.

What I long for is a wave of Franciscan passion that will sweep across our sin-pinched, cold hearts and open them again laying on us our unlimited liability for our brothers and our privilege to be joyous sons of God.

* * *

We asked several very vocal anti-Catholics to contribute to this symposium, but with unaccustomed reticence they declined. We therefore present their position as gleaned from public utterances:

The Catholic Church is at once a Church and State and therefore represents a singular threat to democracy. It is authoritarian and fascist. While taking advantage of the religious tolerance to be found in America, the Catholic Church would not reciprocate in tolerance toward Protestants were it to gain ascendancy in this country.

Particularly intolerable is the persistent Catholic claim to have the only truth, and to refuse to cooperate with non-Catholics.

The Catholic Church is cruel to allow women to suffer from the physical and financial woes of endless childbearing; and incurable cancer cases to suffer the pain of their hopeless disease, when modern science has made possible relief in both cases.

VARIOUS ANONYMOUS CONTRIBUTORS

BOOK REVIEWS

The Presence of Presences

TRUE DEVOTION TO THE BLESSED SACRAMENT
Pustet Press

Devotion, which is an act of the virtue of religion, is a promptness in the will to dedicate itself to the service of God and the things of God. A devotion merits the addition *true*, when it most adequately responds to the object of the devotion. This explains the title, at first glance somewhat presumptuous, of the work on the Blessed Sacrament under review. The author, who prefers to remain anonymous as a tribute to the humble and obscure Dominican friar, Father Joseph Damian Pendergast who first introduced her to this devotion, has with great accuracy and real piety presented the full magnificence of Eucharistic doctrine and suggested a devotion that will most perfectly measure up to the reality of Christ's Sacramental Presence in all the tabernacles of the world.

What is new in this devotion? Nothing that is not very old. Inspired by the renewed emphasis on the doctrine of the Mystical Body of Christ, this devotion focuses attention on the fact of Christ's Sacramental Presence in the tabernacles of the world. In every one of them Christ is praying and working for the salvation of souls, Catholic and non-Catholic, that reside under the jurisdiction of each tabernacle. In response to such a reality, the truly devout soul unites itself to Christ in all these tabernacles; with one simple prayer, it petitions Christ for all souls that come under the influence of His Sacramental Presence.

There is something new about this work that should be noted. Most frequently, books on special devotions tend to emphasize the devotion they are concerned with to the exclusion of others; at least they do not attempt to show the relation of the special devotion to other devotions of the Christian life. A *true* devotion, however, cannot be exclusive. The author of this work on true devotion to the Blessed Sacrament has understood this and has carefully explained its relation to devotion to the Holy Ghost and to the Blessed Virgin.

We earnestly recommend this work to all readers of *Integrity*. The basis of Christian integrity must always be devotion to God and the things of God — true devotion to Mary, to Christ, especially in His Sacramental Presence, and to the Spirit of Truth, the Holy Ghost.

J.V.C.

Catholicism Down Under

AUSTRALIA: THE CATHOLIC CHAPTER
By James G. Murtagh
Sheed & Ward

Australians and Irishmen will appreciate this book especially. It is a pain-staking, well-documented account of the Catholic contribution to the growth of Australia, and it does not omit to trace the careers of the more colorful Irish figures involved. Others than Australians and Irishmen will be interested chiefly to contrast the position of the Faith there with its position here, especially in view of the economic situation. After early, and unsuccessful, efforts to build an economic system on small agricultural free holdings, Australia fell prey to capitalism and its abuses. Things happened faster in Australia than here. The country is now considerably socialized and highly unionized (they have a statute to the 8-hour day). All along the Church was involved, usually through vigorous bishops. There was an interesting controversy as to whether the socialization process was that which the popes were warning against. The presumption was (the same thing now going on in England) that this was a different socialism, somehow harmonious with the faith. One wonders.

Book Reviews

Significantly, the strongest American influence on contemporary Australian Catholic social thought is, according to the author, that of Dorothy Day and Peter Maurin. There is an Australian *Catholic Worker*, and it is refusing to accept an economic goal which does not include a plan for redistribution of property into small holdings.

     C.J. (CAROL JACKSON ROBINSON?)

A Telescopic Survey

MAJOR TRENDS IN AMERICAN CHURCH HISTORY
By Francis X. Curran, S.J.
America Press

Sometimes the history of the Church in the United States is written apologetically, the author inadvertently giving the impression that it was a comedy of errors. Such an author is so lost in the welter of historical detail or so beclouded by an unconscious attitude of Protestant supremacy that he cannot see the blinding light of the Mystical Body of Christ. All thanks to Father Curran for having the simplicity and learning to coordinate our Catholic and Protestant religious backgrounds so that it synthesizes with the Faith. In this book, Protestantism is seen for what it is: a heresy with a troublesome present and an inglorious and intolerant past. Throughout, one senses the tremendous power, confidence, holiness and growing strength of the Catholic Church. All this is done not as a distortion of history, but as a restoration of true historical sense. The book is straightforward, dispassionate, charitable and precise. It is short (less than 200 pages) and so cannot qualify as a major historical work. It is more like an essay, but one which might well form the basis of a more detailed study.

     P.M. (PETER MICHAELS?)

INTEGRITY, February 1947

Eclecticism

THE CHRISTIAN HERITAGE IN AMERICA
By George Hedley
MacMillan

A series of sermons given at Mills College on the different Protestant denominations, the Catholic Church, the Orthodox Church and Judaism. Much less substantial than other recent Protestant reviews of the religious situation, it is overlaid by the cosy, eclectic philosophy of benign indifferentism.

C.J.

Solid Reading

THE GREAT RELIGIONS OF THE MODERN WORLD
Edited by Edward J. Jurji
Princeton University Press

A ready reference manual on the basic theological positions of Confucianism, Taoism, Hinduism, Buddhism, Shintoism, Islam, Judaism, Eastern Orthodoxy, Roman Catholicism and Protestantism by representative scholars in each field.

S.T.T.

Centrifugal Christianity

RELIGION IN AMERICA
By Willard L. Sperry
MacMillan

For the benefit of an English audience, Willard Sperry, Congregationalist and Dean of the Divinity School at Harvard, has written a remarkably readable, balanced book about the growth of religion in the United States with a Protestant emphasis. His genial scholarship and scrupulous honesty are noteworthy. Pertinent quotes abound, for the book is packed with shrewd commentary. It is diffuse and complex because the subject does not lend itself to clear-cut analysis or sharp focus, at least from a liberal Protestant point of view. The one chapter on Catholicism was borrowed almost entirely from Theodore Maynard's *The Story of American Catholicism*, regrettably, for Sperry's independent views would be welcome. At the end of this chapter, he levels two criticisms at contemporary American Catholicism – activism and over-patriotism. Are we guilty? To note that there is a contemplative resurgence among Protestants and to remark that it is lacking among Catholics shows that Dean Sperry's contact with representative Catholics has indeed been slight.

The chapters on American Theology, Religious Education and Church Union call for careful scrutiny. In the last, George Tyrell's specious justification of schism is cited. But the author admits towards the end of his discussion: "We habitually think of it (Church Union) as an ideal not yet realized, not as a past fact long lost and now to be recovered." But like all of his confreres, Dean Sperry is mistaken as to the means.

S.I.

Whatever the judgment,
  Whether cursed or blessed,
Be sure you accept it
  Properly dressed.

O God, Who dost correct what has gone astray and gatherest together what is scattered, and keepest what Thou hast gathered together, we beseech Thee in Thy mercy to pour down upon Christian people the grace of union with Thee, that putting aside disunion and attaching themselves to the true shepherd of Thy Church, they may be able to render Thee due service.

(Collect from the Votive Mass
for the Removal of Schism)

This is a Madvertisement*

BITTEN INTO A FRESH, DELICIOUS REAM OF CLEANSING TISSUE?

No? Then you have never tasted WHEEEE-T BRED! WHEEEE-T BRED (pronounced wheat bread) is colorless, odorless, and tasteless. It is as light as a feather. After eating a slice (or half a loaf for that matter) of WHEEEE-T BRED, you feel as though you have not eaten at all. And you haven't!

KILL THAT GERM!

Our ten thousand window bakery is death on germs, especially wheat germs! Carefully, hygienically, our master bakers grind, bleach, boil, scald, in TWENTY different ways the wheat fresh from the fields.

Then, with equal care, we inject into the fluffy dough a bouncing, lively shot of vitamin Z, so that we can advertise on the wrapper that WHEEEE-T BRED is nutritious.

ONE SLICE OF WHEEEE-T BRED is equal in nutritive content to:

(1) A half cup of scrapings from the bottom of a badly burned cake.
(2) Two WHEEEE-T BRED wrappers.
(3) The fuzz from one peach.
(4) Oh, almost anything.

Wheat is the staff of life, but try and get it from us!

Editor's note: We have been fortunate in finding an ad-writer who is mad. The form his madness takes is an absolute passion for truth. Since he is out of work, we have consented to run his stuff from time to time.

INTEGRITY

"GO! THE MASS IS FINISHED."

: the sixth issue :
March 1947   Vol.1, No.6
SUBJECT: LET'S GET TO WORK!

EDITORIAL

E ARE MEMBERS OF A Church Militant. The outcome of the battle is measured in souls either in Heaven or Hell. The final score we will not know until a time when editing a magazine will be the least of our worries. We can, however, while still earthbound, sense the direction in which the battle is moving. This we can do more or less by estimating which is in the ascendancy, Good or Evil. Is Christ being made more manifest in the affairs of men, or less? To whom are the activities of society directed, to God or to Mammon? To what degree are directives of the Church being ignored, to what extent are they being obeyed? Since this knowledge must be at best intuitive, it is liable to be a truer judgment the closer we are to that borderline where Religion meets Life. The spearhead of the Church's thrust is the laity. In the home, the forum, the laboratory, and the workshop, the spiritual either clashes or weds with the material. This is the battleground for which the Mass is a preparation. Behind us, tempering our weapons, welding hilt to blade, are the ministers administering and the cloistered praying. The question of the day is: "How goes the battle?"

Here in the United States, it appears that we have reached a stalemate, and to a great extent, since the solution to the world's temporal problems waits upon the political direction of this country, a stalemate here retards the apostolate the world over. The disease from which the world suffers is at the stage of crisis. An injection of potent Christianity at this moment might stave off complete collapse. This potency is within the Church in more than sufficient quantity. It is not being administered. The need is urgent! Why do we hesitate?

For our purpose here, the laity can be roughly divided into two groups. Let us call one group the eager beavers, and the other, the blushing violets. The eager beavers are those men and women who have successfully separated their religion and their careers so that at no place do they overlap. Thus at any one time you will find them eagerly attending to either the needs of their souls or the needs of their bodies. They are frightfully concerned about each, but never simultaneously. A bit of religion found in their daily affairs would be extracted with tweezers as a foreign ingredient. With equal care they keep their religious moments unadulterated by temporal considerations. As a consequence, if you were to broach the subject of God's Providence, they would immediately shift over to their *religious* shortwave, out-of-town, foreign broadcast circuit. Were this sort of thing to come in on their local station circuit, the wave-lengths dedicated to practical affairs, it would only be considered static, and be filtered out.

There is one thing that would make this divorce impossible in the lives of the eager beavers, and that thing is contemplation. No one knows that better than them. It is in the avoidance of such a catastrophe that we find a third category in their lives. This is the time devoted to doing *anything* but thinking. It is the answer to the question, "What are we going to do tonight?" This urge to do *anything* but contemplate reaches its heights on Saturday night, and Sunday afternoon, the two periods in the week traditionally set apart by the Church as periods for contemplation! Saturday night is the Vigil; Sunday is the Sabbath.

And then there are the blushing violets. These are the Catholics to whom it is obvious that Monday morning is a poor continuation of a week that began with "I will go unto the altar of God, to God Who giveth joy to my youth." They can see the great divorce between the nobility of the Faith, and the petty matters of trade and commerce to which their time-clocked lives are dedicated. Not unlike the eager beavers, they too live for their hours of leisure. They spend these hours either in a speed-up program of religious devotions, or in arguing, discussing or debating with other blushing violets on the subject of what they should do with their leisure time.

The habits of both these groups conform to some degree with the habits of a pagan society for whom the end of work is leisure. They are willing to turn away from the main problem of our day, which is not where you go on Saturday night, or to what devotion you devote your Wednesday evenings, but... how do you WORK? You see, if every Catholic were to devote his leisure to preparing for his work, relating to his Faith to the way he spends his days, then the problem would stand out in black and white. He would see first of all that the end of his work is not his to decide. As he inquired further, he would see that the company for whom he works, when it set the end of his work for him, directed it to profit, not to God and the common good. It would be then, when these questions arise first in his thoughts, that he would come to grips with the enemy that is stalemating the apostolate. He would see all this seething activity of our daily lives as a huge tornado spinning and, at its center, the soul of man sitting in immobility. Then he would wonder if it is possible to counteract with a leisure-time apostolate the evil that precedes the blowing of the five-o'clock whistle.

The full efficacy of grace and the enlightenment of the Holy Ghost will fail to be made manifest if we hesitate to examine the fundamental premises which decide the ends and nature of our daily work. We must first decide if Industrial Capitalism, or State Socialism, or Communism, are compatible *in practice* with Christian living. Of these three, our immediate attention must be centered upon the first, for it is the mores of a Capitalistic society that encompass us now. Let us not be misled by what its advocates say of Industrial Capitalism, but put it to the test of daily experience. Capitalism has prospered on the reputation of being an amoral or indifferent economic system caring neither whether there is or is not a God. Let us remember that this system traffics in bread and in the lives of men, and these things cannot be done without considerations of justice and charity, and the final End of all Who is God.

We believe that the design for the future social order, and the steps to be taken toward achieving it, pre-exist in the mind of Almighty God. Today's call to Catholic Action should lead us to seek to know what part we must play in bringing this new order about. To do this we must become enamoured of the Word that He has spoken, and disenchant ourselves from the Bigness and multiplicity of our present social structure. The spell must be broken soon, or it will be too late. A certain limit can be reached, and beyond that lies retribution. We have done nothing to escape the fate of Europe.

In this issue of *Integrity,* we are presenting some principles and some projects which may indicate for some men the steps to be taken. We have asked ourselves these questions: Suppose that men did believe that Christianity is not only the way to Heaven but a way to work? ... Suppose that men decided that they would set about making over the social order without asking the Capitalist's "by your leave," but just went ahead as though all that mattered was that it was the obvious and most prudent thing to do? ... Suppose, in other words, that they did not wait to look to the Kingdom of Heaven and its justice until they had made their pile, but rather let the satisfaction of all their needs follow as a consequent act of God's mercy? To imagine this we had to presuppose men who are first moved by Faith, then common sense, and then experience. We had to presuppose men who still retain the first principle of their own motion, men who can act without being *employed*. We had to presuppose men who believe that their right and ability to redeem and restore flows from their membership in Christ, the Redeemer and Restorer.

We dare not envision the consequences or the eventual society which would emerge if every man were to look inward to the Holy Ghost and make charity the first principle in his work. We are certain, however, that it would be a society ennobled in its toil and joyful in its pain. We are equally certain that if this is not done, and in this generation, the breakdown will soon be complete. The choice before us is not between a perfect and less perfect way of life. The choice is either the cold comfort of a life-boat and the promise of a new landfall, or a last luxurious hour in the steam-heated bowels of a sinking liner.

There is one other fact that we must remember. We, as writers, have neither the right nor the ability to direct the consciences of our readers. That is why we only point out the principles from which activity should flow. What any one person should do, he alone can determine. We do not insinuate for a moment that any apostolate is unworthy of consideration, and we are very much aware that for many the apostolate must be worked out within the confines of the present system. Any apostolate, to be fruitful however, cannot fail to examine the basic structure of society, even though it is not his, but someone else's apostolate, to set the framework for a new and better order. Each man must seek out his own calling prudently and patiently in prayer, in seeing, in judging, in acting.

The work will be started by a few, and it is to these few that we direct our message. The complete uncertainty of our educators, the flounderings of our statesmen should urge us to greater zeal. Only we can act with assurance. We have nothing to lose except Hell, and everything to gain for all eternity. The work is Christ's to do and we are His instruments. The Church stands by to strengthen us with the Bread of Christ and the Wisdom of Mary. What a magnificent place this world could be if we would but "magnify the Lord"!

THE EDITORS

INTEGRITY, March 1947

A man is not great in the wealth that he makes,
  Or the number of servants he uses,
But great is his day, regardless of pay,
  Who serves in the way that God chooses.

Making Concupiscence Pay

IT HAS TAKEN ME MORE THAN NINE YEARS since graduating from a Catholic college to evolve a complete philosophy of work including a philosophy of manual labor; more than nine years to evolve a philosophy of poverty; more than nine years to fight through the conviction that Christianity is a way for every manifestation of life, including the economic manifestation. (Do you remember how St. Paul referred to Our Lord's teaching as "this way"?); more than nine years to realize that the modern world is completely lacking in a sense of social sin, simply because we Catholics don't know what's going on, and don't seem to care to find out; more than nine years to realize that, although the good will and charity of my educators is something I can never forget, Catholic education is failing lamentably because we do not know all these things at Commencement.

But let me tell you about my pilgrimage for the right work, a pilgrimage that progressed into less and less pay, and more and more manual labor. The stops on the pilgrimage were: clerk in an insurance adjustment bureau; clerk in an advertising research agency; clerk in a rubber company office; sales clerk in a department store; social worker for a Catholic children's home; boarding-out department; two months of domestic and farm labor combined on a farm in Arkansas; five months in the greenhouses of a florist just within the New York City Limits, transplanting chrysanthemums by the thousand; three and a half months in the Women's Land Army, as a "hired man" on a New York State dairy and subsistence farm (I was not yet a C.O.); and almost eight months working three hours a day in the kitchen, laundry and nursery of the Franciscan Missionaries of Mary temporary shelter for children. My first two jobs quit me, after a year of each; the rest I quit. My first disagreement with present day jobs was from the standpoint of creativeness, and thus I began to look for a job in advertising copy. Then I found that I could not cooperate with most modern jobs because I found their ends immoral. Then I began to realize that the modern world is completely lacking in a sense of social sin and is consequently fast losing all sense of personal holiness.

Intuitively many Catholic and other Christian consciences, entering the business world, react violently to a mystique which they sense to be evil; however, they cannot give conclusive reasons for their revulsion, and suffer much by a terrible feeling of being pulled apart. It took me many years to be able to give reasons for what I knew, at least in part, intuitively in the beginning. My own college has been notable in refusing to include business training in its curriculum; however, most of the girls take business courses afterwards and get jobs as advertising copywriters, receptionists, secretaries, etc. But it is with anguish that I see that many Catholic colleges — Fordham, Manhattan, Notre Dame, and Holy Cross are examples — have incorporated business training into their education.

FACING THE DILEMMA

I say that I note with anguish. True it is that Catholic Actionists face a dilemma in this regard; their future course will be simplified if they realize that the essential spirit of Industrial-Capitalism is so opposed to the Christian ethos that such strange bed-fellows are each dedicated to the destruction of the other.

If one were to put in a few words, in modern economic lingo, the basic philosophy of Industrial-Capitalism, one would have to state two premises: "Make Concupiscence Pay" and "I am not my brother's keeper."

To illustrate the first, let me tell you an incident. The *American Way,* you will admit, is to do as much work as possible in order to make as much money as possible, and to keep it in circulation, and thus keep people working. Let us turn to the South American Way, which had some of our leading industrialists, Catholics at that, tearing their hair in frustration. This story assumes in my mind the quality and insight of a legend.

An American industrial enterprise, owning a great part of South America, including cotton mills, banks, guano fertilizer deposits, plantations (one would think our Holy Father had never mentioned small ownership), decided to raise the wages of a group of native laborers, thus magnanimously to distribute some of their profits. Was it whispered by their detractors that the great enterprise was afraid of unionization, and besides that one of their branches was selling washing machines, or some such? It was. That is beside the point at the moment but the fact is that the laborers were offered a substantial increase for their five-day week, so that they received as much for four days' work as they formerly had for five. What did they do? Did they rush out in joy and gratitude to buy labor-saving devices that they had lacked so long? They did not. They merely decided to save labor and cut down their working week to four days. They used the most ancient, inexpensive, and thorough of all labor-saving devices — not working. There they sit in the sun, a hopelessly backward people, like the man who said "Don't rush me, Boss. I'll work cheaper." Another thing which infuriates their employers is that during siesta time they simply stop working and wander up into their mountain villages.

That's another way of saying that a little bit of land gives one a great deal of independence. Perhaps that's what Jefferson meant when he said, "When we lose our nation of small farmers we shall lose our democracy." Well we've lost our nation of small farmers. Let us remember also that in a country like ours, without private property, the unions are the only thing that they have given the working man a voice in regard to his work, even if so far it has not been a Christian enough voice.

THREATENED BY VIRTUE

This frustration of the Capitalists in the face of a people who do not consider it the highest good to make a lot of money with which to buy things they have not before needed is not surprising. What is surprising is that we Christians do not think, or will not see, that there is a real and intolerant tension between the Industrial-Capitalist way of life and asceticism of any kind, whether it is the asceticism of Chinese "cheap labor" (Do you remember the fuss over that?), living on less because they had to charge less in order to get any business at all; or the asceticism of St. Francis of Assisi and the *Curé d'Ars*. and the Catholic Worker Movement, living on less so that others may have more, and also that the heart may be free to love God; or the asceticism of the South Americans, living on less because they didn't find the game worth the candle.

However, American advertising, via radio, movies, press, and billboards, will soon put an end to this fantastic notion that time — time to pray, or to play with one's children, or to see the sunset — is more important than the things that money can buy — American advertising with its avowed purpose of inducing people to buy "what they don't need, what they don't want, and what they can't afford to buy." If we are to keep our *American Way*, they must be tempted. Let us put an end to this St. John of the Cross notion that the progressive aim of the Christian is the annihilation of worldly desire.

Now just as the Christian mystique is exactly the annihilation of desire for the things of this world, in order to give love room, the Capitalist mystique comes very near to the deification of desire. Denis de Rougement writes: "All pagan religions deify desire." It's not sufficient to prove that something very like the deification of desire is necessary to support our present economic framework, and conversely that Capitalism is a pagan religion. For if you were to suddenly forbid the manufacture of a whole group of non-essentials such as three-quarters of women's clothing, pulp for advertising, cosmetics, bric a brac[1], jewelry, men's ties, you would suddenly have a lot of men out of work, but at the same time you would have the same and an adequate amount of food being produced. That certainly means that a lot of farmers are overworked. The immediate problem would be how to get the food to the moneyless unemployed (leaving aside of course the simple economics of charity, which would be simply to give it to them. Capitalism, which is *essentially* hostile to charity, slaughtered the pigs and burned the wheat and is now letting the potatoes rot while the world starves. It is interesting to note that the thing which really puts Capitalism in a sweat is the danger of an upsurge of Christian charity. They really are mutually exclusive. The Folly of the Cross which is Christian charity can and must refuse to be crippled any longer by this mystique which puts self before the other). This impasse was exactly what happened during the depression. So that our prosperity, or rather our employment, does depend on the manufacture of luxuries, those things which we as Christians are supposed to do without. Witness the ad which appeared during the war: "We're spoiled, Thank God. That's the American Way." It's a bad climate for saints.

The annihilation of worldly desire and the deification of worldly desire, under a camouflage of words like "standard of living" and "the American Way," are trying to be reconciled by our Catholic educational system, with disastrous results. We have tried to convince ourselves that these things are given us by God to enjoy. This might be so if they were not produced at the price of grinding down "the faces of the poor," and if the exhortation to Christian joy were the exhortation to pleasure.

Joy is not pleasure; it sometimes includes it, but, if not hostile, it is at least independent of it and is, in the saints, often coupled with pain. Joy is to get up on a wintry morning and to go to Mass, having conquered the natural man's pleasure in his warm bed and room. It is literally true that the air-foam mattress people

---

[1] Small decorative objects of various types and of no great value — Ed.

and the coal and radiator people would prefer that you have nothing to do with it. Joy is to rise glorified after the Crucifixion.

This is the Christian mystique, and St. Valentine's Day, tomorrow, typifies it. For strangely enough the patron of love is a martyr; martyrdom, you must admit, is in the nature of an unpleasant experience while filled with Christian joy. The Communion of the Mass has these words of Our Lord: "If any man would come after Me, let him deny himself..." But the point is that the Cross (am I trite?) is essential to Christianity, for which Holy Mother Church arranges the coming gracious season of Lent. That's why you cannot be a Christian without the denial of concupiscence. At the same time you cannot keep your job nowadays without making concupiscence pay.

For industrialists know that it is highly profitable to shower the public with superfluities. In other words they are making rather a good thing out of inciting people to want things, first the people at home, then the people in foreign countries (they call it opening foreign markets). In other words, they are just as interested in having us believe "Blessed are ye rich," as Christ is in having us believe "Blessed are ye poor." The Catholic Church up until the coming of Humanism, the Protestant Reformation, and the Industrial Revolution, used all her vast influence to cool those fires of concupiscence which resulted from Original Sin. Industrial-Capitalism fans those fires to a vast conflagration. How is it that Catholics think they can make peace with such an ally?

Let me remark in passing that these same industrialists cannot help but make a good thing out of war, which opens new markets through destruction, and the making of implements of destruction. There is really an alternative to the "Boom and Bust" cycle, — the "Boom and Bombs" cycle.

The diabolical cunning of the whole thing is that, in order to obtain the necessities of life, the majority of working men have to make the non-necessities of life, which corrupts other people, and, in time, themselves. The diabolical tragedy of the whole thing is that the clergy naively expect them to cooperate in such a system, and then in family life to practice Christianity. Birth control is an inevitable result of Industrial-Capitalism, both because passion and desire are increased through advertising and industrial exploitation, to a point where Christian discipline is impossible and pain or privation unbearable, and because Industrial-Capitalism pays the same wages to the married man as to the single man. The married man begins to act with foresight. He refuses to have a family.

VIRTUE PAYS OFF

Now once you have established your end (let me stress again with Industrial-Capitalism it is to make concupiscence pay), and shrouded it in mystery by making your enterprise sufficiently big, even world-wide, Christian virtue can do great service in scrupulously carrying out the means. That is why employers, as I discovered, prefer Catholic graduates, as long as they are not inquisitive. It is ironical that the dean of one of our well-known Catholic colleges recently remarked that employers prefer Catholic employees because they have to confess theft in confession. Obedience, honesty, and punctuality are well appreciated by banks and insurance companies especially, for usury requires accuracy. What have we Christians to do with interest which is dubiously earned? Is it not even a lesser thing then we might do when we ask for capital back on a loan? Do not we belong to the dispensation that was exhorted to "lend to him from whom you expect nothing in return"?

A scrupulous honesty about the means is necessary if modern exploiters, both of men at home and "lesser breeds without the law," are to achieve their hidden, nefarious ends. Hence the preference for Catholic employees. The employers are in perfect agreement with St. Alphonse Mary de Ligouri's vow never to waste a moment's time. After all, time is money. How morally outraged they are when a teller absconds with the funds! We must have honor among thieves and a house divided against itself shall fall. What! cheat the cheaters! One is reminded of the old rhyme, written about the historic theft of the lands from the people. (How about restitution?)

> They prosecute the man or woman,
> Who steals the goose from off the common,
> But turn the greater villain loose,
> Who steals the common from the goose.

Let me take the opportunity here to explode two myths: the myth of controls and the myth of labor-saving machinery. As to the first, I am, and always have been, a proletarian, owning nothing but my working ability. My father was too — an Irish-born immigrant, a taxi driver who eventually owned his own cab. In that, he almost left the proletarian class by becoming an owner. There is a good friend of ours, still a taxi driver, and an owner, who is finding it increasingly hard to compete against the company-owned cabs. An owner does not cheat himself, but the cab companies, taking in sixty percent of returns and paying the driver forty percent, employ spotters to see that the taxi drivers are turning their flags down on calls. It's the same thing with the OPA, rent controls spotters in industry etc. The minute you get away from the small owner, peasant proprietor, subsistence farmer, call it what you will, you automatically bring in a weighty system of controls, records, bureaucracy, which eventually collapses into dictatorship, probably preceded by revolution.

As to labor-saving machinery I hear you say "Would you have us go back to striking flint?" There is no doubt that there have been good machines invented, such as the home sewing machine. There is also no doubt that the majority of machines were invented not to serve but to make profits and that they have been and are making profits out of the exploitation of the common man. There is again no doubt that all the time and more gained from the making of labor-saving devices has been used for the making of luxuries, and that the common man has worked harder since their advent than ever before. Now at the peak of the age of labor-saving inventions, offices and factories are ablaze into the night.

As I stated before, there are two basic premises to the practice of Industrial-Capitalism: "Make Concupiscence Pay" and "I am not my brother's keeper." Even if you disagree with everything I have said before, or consider it not too serious, it is on the failure to support our brothers that Capitalism stands irrevocably condemned. The facts attest to this failure and the philosophy makes it inevitable.

All the faults of the Industrial-Capitalist system are incidental to the main fault: that modern work is immorally ordered to profits rather than to service. This may seem a small thing to you, and that things might be righted by using the profits for charity, but what that simple statement implies is a fundamental reversal of the whole Christian ethos. For pursuit of profits really means dedication to self, whereas pursuit of service means dedication to "the other," the other being God and God in "the neighbor." Now it is no small thing to motivate your life by daily choosing self to "the other." It is that small detail which will settle the rather vital question of Heaven or Hell. It is by the practice of the works of mercy or the non-practice of the works of mercy, all relating to "the other," that we shall stand condemned or saved.

DIFFERENCE OF OPINION

The Manchester School of Economics, which promulgated the creed of our present economic order, stated that the peace and order of society, the common good, would flow from unrestrained competition in economic life, or each one seeking his own good. No one ever told me in economics class that this is a reversal of the doctrine of Jesus Christ: "He that saveth his life shall lose it, and he that loseth his life for My sake shall find it to life everlasting." St. Thomas wrote: "Peace ceases when each one seeks what is his own." We have sought our own, ceaselessly and ruthlessly, and as always happens in that case, we have effected individual and collective Hell. "It is by this roundabout way *through the other* that the self rises into being a person... beyond its own happiness."

But in what way have we neglected "the other," you may ask. Partly through promoting his eternal damnation by fanning the fire of his concupiscence, but mostly by the most horrible exploitations of native and rural populations, what Kipling calls "lesser breeds without the law." Most of the time the workers are ignorant, and are kept ignorant by an unscrupulous few, of the most terrible crimes against our distant brethren, the producers of the raw materials from which our industrial products are made. These are the rubber workers, the tobacco growers, the coal miners ("blood on our coal"), the Cuban sugar workers, American tenant farmers and sharecroppers (seven of our family of ten burned to death in a miserable New Jersey hovel last year, women and children in the southwest harvest the bean crop at night with the lamps on their foreheads), the keepers of the pigs in the mammoth Secaucus, New Jersey pigyards. (One of these last died with us recently down here at the Catholic Worker -- back to the Sacraments, thank God, after 30 years' neglect. He used to work for six months, collect his pay, then get the stink out of his nostrils with Bowery whiskey, standing across from the Catholic Worker, cursing. Victims of our system, Peter Maurin calls them. Round about us they drown the misery and the betrayal in whiskey or whatever they can get. Peter has also said that "labor is not a commodity to be bought and sold across a counter.")

But what of the rubber companies? Let us take these as an example because I worked for one, and I know that the majority of their employees is Catholic. Most of us want or have cars and I believe that makes us the keepers of all those who have anything to do with the rubber, from the raw product to the tire. I know now, although I did not know it then, that rubber companies are involved in the manufacture of contraceptives. That is only half the story. Let André Gide speak for the rubber workers of

Africa. He speaks of two very young rubber agents who, he says, "seem to be honest."

"Let them have no illusions: their honesty will do them harm. The company will necessarily prefer agents who bring to their coffers more than can be brought in *honestly*."

Further on, Gide says that another agent told him, "that he employs the natives to work at rubber for a wage of twenty-five francs a month, plus one franc's worth of rations every Saturday; otherwise they are neither fed nor lodged, and of course the rubber they bring in is not paid for. They are what is called 'volunteer laborers,' who prefer even this lamentable situation to being requisitioned by the administration. This terrifies them to such an extent that they desert their villages and hide in inaccessible places in the bush. They have another dodge for escaping from forced labor (this was said laughing) and that is to get blennorrhea. The rascals know the administration doesn't take such cases; and it's easy to find women who will give it to them."

When rubber workers prefer venereal disease to working for industrialist enterprise, we may have some idea of what the industrialist enterprise is.

Human wreckage and sin. "There must needs be scandals, but woe to him by whom the scandal cometh."

And what of the deserts left by the business-growing of wheat, and the cavities, bigger than those left by bombs, left by strip mining of coal? A young sailor, born in Newfoundland, was in to the Catholic Worker yesterday. He spoke of the reckless despoliation of timber up there, in order to make pulp for Canadian and United States' newspapers (in order that Lord & Taylor can make a whole page for a glove ad). Meanwhile the housing shortage is acute. What theology, what ethics can justify such things?

Jacques Maritain has said: "The first need of our time is an intellectual need . . . a need of intellectual clarity. Good will is not so obviously wanting as good sense." From another point of view, the deepest need of our time is a mystical need, a need of what Father Vann calls "the dimension of worship." We would make our work worshipful then, truly the love of God and neighbor made visible. There is so much real work to be done, so many poor, so many sick, so many insane. "I was sick, and in prison, and you visited Me not." There is no time to make money. St. Thomas said there is something mean about trade, of its very nature. Finance is one step lower.

We might remember then what bleakness, what ugliness, we have forced upon the common man, what beauty we have taken away from him. I sometimes think that the Garden of Eden could not have been much more beautiful than the countryside and the Christian village. There are so many things that I remember from the country (the times I have been privileged to go) that still fall on my memory like a benediction. The mystery of life in animals, the wheeling of the swallows in front of the wagon as we gathered in the hay, the damp forget-me-nots in the brooks, the flash of color as a red-winged blackbird took flight, the hoot of an owl at night (which made me thankful to be in my bed), going out in the dawn to milk, the smell of a wood fire. There is no doubt, too, that such work tends more toward contemplation. Remember how often the Blessed Mother has appeared to shepherds and shepherdesses. We have yet to hear of an apparition in the Ford plant.

IRENE MARY NAUGHTON
New York,
Feast of the Apparition of the Blessed Virgin
at Lourdes, 1947

My daddy was a laborer,
   And, good Lord, so were you.
But now that I have my Degree,
   Must I get dirty too?

To Be Specific...

ADVERSE CRITICISM OF THE PRESENT SOCIAL order has been abundantly widespread, for which may God be thanked. I refuse to admit that there has been too much, but, at the same time, it is true that there has not been enough consideration of a positive program of action. For that reason I am devoting the best part of this article to a summary of some steps that might be taken to restore the social order to Christ. Before doing so, a few preliminary remarks must be made so as to help clarify my specifications and prevent misunderstanding.

First we must realize that the world has gone on for a long time without Christ and, indeed, as Our Holy Father has said, "against Christ." Secondly, we must recall the statements of Our Lord, "Without me you can do nothing." So, even if the affairs of the world were not familiar to us, we would suspect the worst. For those who are aware of what is going on, it is immediately obvious that without Christ we have done exactly nothing.

The work of restoring all things to Christ (which is the accurate way of saying "putting everything in its *right* place,") naturally falls upon those who are members of Christ, specifically Confirmed Catholics. There are others upon whom the burden falls, but it is from this class that much is to be expected, for it is only they who are properly equipped to bring such a social change about. The scope of the work is tremendous. It involves every phase of living. It must go on everywhere. It demands the total effort of every Catholic.

Although the reform is fundamentally a spiritual one, the occasion for the spiritual reform is the work of reforming the social order. In other words, the way we are to work out our salvation these days is by reforming the social order. This is the work assigned to the laity by the Church herself.

To Be Specific...

The greatest obstacle to the reform of the social order is that Catholics have fallen victims to the same disease for which they alone possess the cure. The antidote to this insidious poison is sanctifying grace and the wisdom of the Church. The Church *sees* the plague and the method of restoration. She dispenses the graces which give us the ability to bring the restoration about.

Before acting we must orient ourselves and see where Catholics stand in the present disorder. The average Catholic layman at his daily work participates in an economic system the end of which is determined by someone other than himself. Now, by carrying his convictions into his work, and acting zealously in consequence of a mature spiritual life, the best he can hope to achieve at any time in the near future is some slight conversion or reform of a minor victim or minor symptom of the entire system. I do not underestimate such a conquest, nor the heroism required to bring it about. I do not imply that it is an unworthy endeavor. I do, however, question that it is the best we can do. If it is not the best we can do, then in conscience we should try another method. There is small justification for busying ourselves with improving the conversational habits or working conditions of our fellow workers if it lies within our power to displace the entire system of which they are (sometimes happily) the victims. It seems utterly ridiculous to shave down the apostolate to fit a whole which is ever widening. A careful look at the foundations of our society (which are the family and the consciences of men) indicates that total collapse is not far away. The most conservative groups have given up trying to salvage a sinking ship, and are at this very moment provisioning each his own life boat. It is to this day of reckoning that the apostolate should look, adopting a technique in which revolution is implicit, for you may be certain we shall either lead or else be the victims of an inevitable crystallization of the present reaction.

Two things stand in the way of our evaluating these problems in the proper light. One of these is our failure to appreciate the dreadful evil of an economic system geared for profit as its final end. The other is our failure to see that the work we do must be chosen in the light of salvation, and our efforts be God-inspired, and directed to the common good. Whatever the work is that we are doing, there is a particular work we should be doing, for as God creates and sustains us, He does so for a purpose not unrelated to our work. For the most of men, the only vision they have of the justice and mercy of God is that which they see reflected in the good works of Christians. These men, seeing the same solicitousness for worldly goods among practicing Catholics that characterizes today's pagans, a solicitousness that relegates the work of social reform to the category of a part time activity, will receive from us a stone, when they have asked for bread.

It is in the light of the above arguments that I will proceed to point out various works that cry out to be done. The needs of his neighbor should indicate and inspire the work of the Christian. To seek the good of our neighbor and the common good of all is truly to "seek ye the Kingdom of Heaven and its justice . . ." What a shame if our failure to do so were from doubt of Christ's assurance: " . . . and all these things will be added unto you."

Every field of work stands in need of restoration. I have chosen four categories: politics, science, propaganda, and housing. Politics, science, and propaganda will be considered briefly, mentioning only general faults and general cures. I have reserved most of my space for a plan of parochial housing, since this might well be the vehicle for achieving great strides towards a better social order.

POLITICS

This field today is one in which the harvest will be slow in ripening. The reason for this is that political health, especially in a democracy, cannot exceed, and must wait upon, the health of the small units of which the body politic is comprised. There is an immediate need for men of faith to bring the field of national and international as well as local politics within the long and merciful arm of God. Since the need exists, then to fulfill it some men have been called. This calling demands the utmost in heroic patience. A man strong in knowledge of God's Providence, fortified by the Sacraments, seeing in his work a stewardship of the highest order, can sow in patience, undeterred from his task by the corruptibility of his constituents and fellow statesman. He had best free himself from the need of human respect at the start. Good statesmanship is applauded only by posterity. If he is the man for the job, then he will find himself content when he is alone with God. His reward will be in heaven.

He cannot depend upon the political machinery now in use. This machinery has as its purpose the separating of the wheat from the cockle, and it is the wheat which is first retired to private life. His appeal must be directly to the people. His delight in the cause of right must be contagious. Frugality of living and a willingness to sacrifice every ambition rather than betray his convictions will free him from the stigma of graft, and must be his primary instruments for winning the good will of the people. If he is to display any partiality, it should be to those who are most in need. He must see as the end of society the cultivation of the *good man,* not merely the *good citizen.* Law must be made to assure the widest possible distribution of *productive* property. The good of the family, not that of the corporation, must be made the yardstick for measuring economic progress. The money-growers must be reduced to their proper stature in society, being given the alternative of choosing a contributive function or else being penalized.

The aspirations of men of ideals to political office will continue to be frustrated as long as Catholics divorce a sense of morality from their right of franchise, as they have so scandalously done in the past. Until they can see in the statesman something more admirable than a Robin Hood with the animal magnetism, and look for men of the caliber of Thomas More or Edward the Confessor, this calling of the individual man of

God to public office will go unanswered. The voter must come to respect the statesman who can subserve the interests of pressure groups to the dominant good of the commonweal, even if the voter himself is part of such a group. The cause will also be served if the man already in politics who finds these standards too high would take this to indicate that he is too small for the job, and gravitate to some humbler place more in proportion to his stature. Nowadays in politics the last should be first and the first last.

SCIENCE

The academic study of the natural order in its relation to the supernatural order, and the application of resultant discoveries to the temporal and spiritual well-being of man, is a field to which the Holy Ghost calls many men. Science, thanks to the blindness of materialism and the puffed-up pride of the intellectually curious, is virgin territory for the man who is pure of heart and sound of intellect. Marked only by a prodigious collection of unrelated information which has been erroneously termed "progress," modern science has failed in that very purpose for which it should exist: the organization of the knowledge of God as He is observed in His creatures. Although a certain logical relation of fact to fact has been achieved within the narrow limits of each scientific category (a gigantic task considering the vast wealth of information so recently brought to light), the relation between categories is obscure, and little or no attempt has been made to relate empirical knowledge with common sense and Faith. All of nature has its roots in God. To know one thing about Him is to know a million things about His Creation. Hence theology is the light by which the book of life is read. Denying this, the modern practicing scientist fails in many spheres where the medieval peasant and midwife were successful.

On more than one occasion the Holy Father has called upon men to enter the field of the rational sciences. This has been mistaken in some quarters as an indication that we must outdo the materialist in his search for phenomenological data. The result is only to increase the number of scavengers. Lost in a maze of cyclotrons, seismographs, and bacteria incubators, the Catholic scientist is as liable to forget what he went out to seek as his pagan brother. Our stock in trade is Revealed Truth, which the modern ignores, and common sense, which the modern denies. Entering the field of the rational sciences equipped with these superior tools, we shall see things which will enlighten the Gentiles in their own backyards. We shall level the hills and fill the valleys raised by the omni-scientist in his fruitless excavations and proceed directly to the heart of the problem, and Christ will come behind us administering, soothing, healing, and bringing to perfection.

Men who are called to this work must first study theology and in all their tasks remember that proper human knowledge (since they are human) is philosophic, and proper Christian knowledge (since they are Christians) is theological. Since their responsibility as Christians precedes their responsibility as men, and their responsibility as men precedes their responsibility as scientists — they must justify their scientific conclusions in relation to philosophy and theology. Then, whether their work is academic or clinical, they must adopt techniques consonant with the nature of man as revealed by his Maker. To do this would be to renew the face of the earth.

PROPAGANDA

Social reform is impossible without propaganda. Since a Christian reform is directed at the very root of society, and is itself rooted in the Word of God, it implies radical changes in every sphere of oral and written thought. Everything must be propaganda for the truth. Poetry is needed, and plays, and music. Radio scripts, puppet shows, folk dances, scenarios, sculpture, posters, cartoons, sermons, inquiries, novels, histories, text-books, trade journals, daily newspapers, curricula, and new Gregorian melodies are needed. Choral groups, orators, singers, writers, artists, dancers, and actors are needed.

Again, as in the case of science, the need is not to augment the field of secular activities. The excuse for these ventures is not to run in competition with existing pagan institutions. The need above all is *not* to present the Catholic view. There is no such thing as a Catholic view. To the degree that we suppose the ideas of the Church to be a *view,* to that degree have we fallen for the Protestant heresy — that every opinion is worthy of respect. There is only one opinion worthy of respect, and that is the *right* one. It is to the end of spreading the truth that Christ our Lord founded the Church. By this is not meant a mere set of principles or groups or laws. The Truth is a Person, Who is the Holy Ghost.

Thus the man called to the field of propaganda for which he has the talent, if he is truly a tabernacle for the Holy Ghost, will be inspired to say, or sing, or act, or draw to the greater honor and glory of God. There is no necessary art too lowly or too humble which is not transformed if it is directed to this End. In writing a letter, or speaking on a national network, we can bear testimony to the truth that is in us. Whether the truth be factual, as in the reporting of news, or implied in the writing of a poem, or explicit in the teaching of doctrine, there is yet but one Truth to be revealed.

Much of our God-given talent is being wasted today in the cause of that spurious phenomenon called advertising. The immorality of this institution is not so much that it appeals to our lowest instincts or that its end is profit; but worse than this, it is rendering to creatures the honor due only to God. Men who might in another age raise their voices or dip their brushes to image for the edification of mankind the glories of God, today spend these talents to encourage smoking, washing, eating, and drinking not for our pleasure but for the profits of their masters. Advertising today is the art of The Lie.

Men have seldom before thirsted so vainly for the Truth. God has called many of us to the task of quenching that thirst. And the call is an adventuresome one, for as we empty our minds to the ignorant, the Holy Ghost will fill us, again and again. The instrument of the artist will move with a facility never before suspected if the artist himself be moved. Pick your weapons, men, and get to it!

PAROCHIAL HOUSING

From coast to coast there is a frightful housing shortage that must be met. The family and marriage, already in a precarious position, might find in this shortage and its resulting strain, the last straw. We all know how bad it is. Talking about the causes will not help matters. Something must be done — but fast!

The obviousness of this need might be a providential sign pointing the way to a better, more Christian social order. The house is a roof over a family. The family is the root of society. Perhaps in solving the problem of the house, society itself may be preserved.

In every city parish there is sufficient wealth, talent, energy, and know-how distributed among its parishioners, which, if organized, could solve the housing shortage in a parochial way. Some men are familiar with finance, others with construction. Some men have the skill of hand, others have the capital for initial expenses. There are men with initiative to lead, men with persuasive powers to arouse and sustain enthusiasm. There are men who have studied our present system of economics who are spoiling for the chance to show the world that the honor and glory of God and a desire to serve the common good are incentives that can drive men to great heights. There are priests who lie awake at night wondering how they can restore a sense of community to their parishes, or praying that their parishes may be made smaller so that they might have more personal contact with each parishioner. There are liturgists who want to see a family Mass. There are social apostles who long to see the Church transplanted to the country. And then there are the families crowded together to a point beyond bearing. There is the sin of birth control. Perhaps parochial planning is the answer.

The Christian family cannot long survive without a Christian community, for the family will always be dependent upon the community. It is to bring such a community about, that the parochial housing organization must aspire.

This housing project would be a long range venture requiring an apostolate deeply rooted in the spiritual. Unlike the municipal projects we see about us, it would have as its end not merely the relief from slums or overcrowdedness, but would aim at creating new economic communities which would serve as microcosmic parts of a future organic society. New homes within the geographical parish would only act as poor rivals to the projects erected by the state. For those who have had experience with them, it is obvious that such housing developments for the proletariat are usually worse than the slums they displace. Proletarianization becomes a psychological as well as economic condition when perpetuated in brick and cement. Such institutions are the first infiltration of totalitarian techniques.

The site of a parochial housing project must be on the land, providing room for gardens, and the housing of productive tools. It should be in a rural or semi-rural area as near to the parish as is possible. Thus the large city parish would conceive and nurture a new parish on the land. Across the bridge, families could move outward, with the least amount of estrangement or confusion, to surroundings best suited to their needs. At no time during the transition would the family be placed in a position of insecurity since its well being would always be incorporated in the common good of the whole parish, rather would its sense of security be strengthened by evidence of enthusiasm for a common cause.

Each parish would have its own unique problems to solve, but there would be some problems common to all. Let us anticipate a few.

To Be Specific...

1) The supernatural motive must be stressed in every way. Daily mass and Communion should become a part of the lives of those who first respond to the appeal. A weekly novena service to the patron saint in petition for guidance and Divine favor might be started. Then a Sunday high Mass could be held for this special intention. Lay leaders should be spiritually formed so that their words and works might serve as inspiration to the others.

2) The work in its organization and execution must be strictly a lay activity. Instead of an additional job for the priest it should be apostolic extension of his work into the parish. On the other hand, the opposite evil of lay trusteeship must be avoided. In other words, both the priest and the layman must each stick to his own last. If this is understood from the beginning, things should proceed smoothly.

3) No one should be imported from outside the parish until an exhaustive search has proved fruitless. To do otherwise would serve to weaken the parochial aspect and impede the community growth. Persuading those reluctant to cooperate would thus become a special apostolate of its own.

4) Personal sacrifice for the common good must be stressed. All waste or wanton use of wealth or materials must be avoided. It is in the nature of things that perfection proceeds from adversity and the eventual strength of the new parish will not be served if sacrifice is not at its foundation.

5) A good deal of study, debate, and conference must attend each step of the way. For that purpose it might be best to have two councils, one public and the other private. The public council should be a family affair attended by a husband and wife. To this end the young people should make an apostolate of baby-sitting. As a result of these meetings the wife will understand what the husband is doing and thus may accept the necessary sacrifices he must make for the common cause. The private meeting will be for the settling of particular problems, and will probably be made up of committee heads.

6) Financing should be through the use of credit unions and private donations. Bazaars, lawn parties, lotteries, etc. should be avoided. These methods of extortion presuppose a reluctance to give, and if this reluctance is not overcome the whole project will fail. On the other hand, patronization must be prevented. Let no one give with strings attached, leaving the spending of the money to the discretion of those specially chosen for the job.

7) Raw materials will be hard to get, but no more difficult than it would be for a commercial contractor. And here is a warning: should any commercial person involve himself in the affair (and it is hoped that such persons will) let him leave commercial methods behind. Black market buying, competitive bidding between parishioners, graft, and special privileges would ruin the whole project overnight. It is of the essence of this plan that all of the work be done within the group. Nothing should be contracted out unless absolutely necessary, and certainly it must not be contracted out to a fellow parishioner. Eventually a federation of these projects, national in scope, might provide a clearing house for the exchange of intelligence and raw materials which might be lacking to any one parish.

8) The site of the new village should be rural or semi-rural and within commuting distance of the mother parish. All the work must be done by parishioners themselves. Just wages to meet their needs should be meted out to the workers. Young men without dependents might be willing to accept a frugal wage while adding each week to the procurement of a deed for a small holding.

9) The homes should be designed for permanent use and to accommodate large families. There should be land with each house to provide a garden. In addition, there should be a common pasture and some woodland.[2]

---

2 As soon as there are permanent residents, facilities for saying Mass must be installed. Later a church and school. Perhaps a religious order with similar ideals could be invited to share the community and run the school.

10) Private ownership of homes and gardens and common ownership of large tools (electric plants, refrigeration lockers, plows, horses, etc.) should be the goal.

This is only a brief summary of the complex problem. It will require many heads and many hands, but more than that it will need men of vision not intent upon their own aggrandizement but willing to labor in the cause of the common good. The results will do more than satisfy man's need for a house, rather it will bring into being that phenomenon so strange to our times, a community. And it might very well be that kind of community that once evoked the remarks of pagans of another age, "See those Christians, how they love one another."

ED WILLOCK

LAMENT OF AN AGING TYCOON

With tired eyes he watched the crowd,
   As it moved about in the street below him.
"So many people to do," he sighed,
   "And so little time in which to do them."

ALL OF THE TEMPORAL AND SPIRITUAL
OF ALL OF THE PEOPLE

"A JOB? SURE! W

Song For Those In Search of Riches

Judas doodled dollar signs,
Graphed the rise and fall
Of elemental metals
On his hard heart's wall.

Shrewd, he purchased silver stock,
Traded Truth and Light…
But then he went and hanged himself
One silver startled night.

Silver stroked his silent hands,
Silver hushed and white,
And the noose about his neck
Was silver silver tight!

THOMAS J. BEARY

I'd Rather Be a Menial
IN THE HOUSE OF THE LORD, THAN TO DWELL AMONG PRINCES

THE PSALMIST HAS EXPRESSED EXACTLY THE longing of today's idealist, caught up in huge commercial financial and military enterprises, when all he wants is to spend himself, however humbly, for a great cause. He'd rather be a buck private in a conflict which really is a crusade than be a major general in a trade war. He'd rather tend the fires of a modest concern making good soap to supply local human needs than to be on the board of directors of the international soap cartel. He'd rather sweep the floors of the Vatican than be managing director of Radio City. It isn't that serving God necessarily involves waste of talents or gross self-abnegation (indeed, usually quite the reverse), but just that serving God is so much more delightful than serving Mammon that all other factors involved pale by consequence. It's just that the *end* of our work is primary. It overshadows the means and conditions and remuneration. Its dignity is our dignity; its goodness is our goodness. It measures our stature.

WHAT CONSTITUTES A GOOD ACT

The morality of an act is determined chiefly by its end. This theological principle offers the clue to the understanding of the moral problems of our time relating to our life work. It can be applied to the military, to show that the lack of great purpose in our modern wars has robbed soldiers of heroic stature. It can be applied to politics to show that statesmen have lost dignity and honor because expediency has replaced the ideal of the common good. We shall apply it to economics. We shall show, presently, that our economic system as a whole is directed toward money-making and not God as a final end, and that this fact degrades all the millions of us who are caught up in the system.

An act can be considered in respect of its natural species or in respect of its moral species. When considered in respect of its natural species, morality is accidental (so the act of typewriting a page is not a moral act as such. Morality comes in accidentally, as in what it is that is being typed on the page or — to a much lesser extent — as to how accurate the typing is). Conversely, when an act is considered in respect of its moral species, as in spreading truth or untruth, the natural species (whether the matter is typed, mimeographed or printed) is accidental. Now it is not an arbitrary matter whether you regard things according to their natural or their moral species. We are obliged to regard them according to their moral species because we are human beings and, as such, moral creatures. There are no acts in the concrete which are not morally good or bad. There are no typists typing blank pages. They all have something on them, and that something determines, largely, the morality of the act of typing.

From this distinction between natural and moral species it is immediately clear that in our society most of us have our eyes riveted on the natural species of acts. We train to be typists, accountants, file clerks, salesmen. The morality of our future work will be determined chiefly by what we type, what we account for, what we file, what we sell. It is understood by us that this crucial matter of WHAT is to be determined, not by us, but by our future employers. If the WHAT is evil, untrue, trivial or unworthy, our work is going to be bad, or stupid, or both,[1] while an

---

[1] It is possible to separate our ends from the ends our employers have in mind, providing we cooperate only materially, and that the operation we perform is not bad in itself, and there is a good and serious reason for our staying in that job. So a man in a menial capacity can work *in order to support his family*, or a Jocist in like capacity can work *to do an apostolate among his fellow-workers*. However, you cannot in practice nowadays will as your end to provide people with shoes if you are in the employ of a shoe manufacturer who wills as his end to make money, because you will find all the messages are geared to his end and you will be impotent to carry out the implications of your desire.

Furthermore, wherever there is material cooperation you cannot sanctify yourself wholeheartedly through your work, but almost in spite of it.

increase of accuracy, punctuality, efficiency and speed on our part can only aggravate the trouble.

There are other factors involved in the determination of the morality of acts. Almost as important as the end is the question of the means. A good end does not justify bad means. But if the end is bad no means whatsoever can justify it. Often enough, but not always, bad means are the result of a bad end (as when a mechanic fixes your car poorly because he wants the money you will have to pay for periodic repairs).

The *means* of modern work have been thoroughly explored by such keen thinkers as Eric Gill and Dorothy Day. The monotony, frustration, waste, regimentation, and impersonality of modern work have been brought to light. Many people say that industrial capitalism must be condemned on this score, because the nature of the work destroys human personality. No doubt these grounds are sufficient to condemn it, but it would be more sound to shift the attack to the end, maintaining that the system must be abandoned (progressively, of course, to prevent worse suffering) because it is not ordered to God. By striving to order the ends of the economic system to God instead of to Mammon, the nature of the work itself will be transformed. On the contrary, concentration on the means will not rectify the end and consequently will not make what is bad good. Craft production (which would transform the means) can be ordained to Mammon too; indeed (because it is a better way of making things) the few crafts that are left are just this under our present economy. Only the rich have hand-made shoes, custom-made dresses and suits, hand-hammered silverware and Rolls-Royces.

Much less important than the *means* is the matter of the *conditions* of work: such things as nice washrooms. Conditions have an accidental relationship to the problem of the morality of acts and therefore of our work. They seriously affect the morality only if they are very bad. Really serious overcrowding of offices, very dirty washrooms and exceedingly long hours can make otherwise good jobs bad. But that we can tolerate a lot of deficiency in regard to conditions is obvious from the sacrifices we make for things we really want. We gather in crowds for Mass, dispense entirely with washrooms on camping vacations, and the whole family works eighteen hours a day to run a small Italian grocery store; all good things. What is happening today is that *magnificent conditions* are being offered as a camouflage for the indignity, the immorality, and the monotony of our work. The more regimented office and factory work is, the more magnificent the washrooms; the more meaningless the work, the more necessary it is to dangle the leisure state in front of us; the less a stenographer has to use her head, the more gadgets she will find on her typewriter. What we need is not a three-hour day of meaninglessness, followed by cocktails and culture, but an eighteen-hour day building a new world founded in Christ. We are spoiling for a great release of energy, not for idle corruption under the southern sun.

The *remuneration* also has a sort of accidental relationship to work (actually it is almost irrelevant, but this is too big a subject to discuss here), and becomes important only through gross abuse. We could be handsomely paid and still be slaves, as is evident now that many industries and businesses do pay handsomely. Through disregard of the entirety of what the Holy Fathers said in their encyclicals, and through uncritical admiration of secular trade unions, we have failed to notice that we neglected to effect the peaceful revolution the popes had in mind. It was their idea that men were to band together to get some breathing space, some little leisure and some excess cash *eventually to buy productive property and escape from the system*. Where workmen have obtained the leisure and the cash they have settled down to an ever-increasing standard of living. What they needed also, and did not get, was a spiritual revolution. They were formally caught up helplessly in a system ordered to Mammon. Now they are themselves ordered to Mammon.

THE END JUSTIFIES THE MEANNESS

Let us make it quite clear. The industrial and financial capitalistic system of which we are almost all a part has concentrated our whole economy into one highly intricate and interdependent whole, ordered to Mammon. Mammon is just another word for money. Money is the final end, the ultimate criterion, the measure of everything.

At the center of the system are the banks. We like to think that banks are primarily places for the safe-keeping of money. It would be more accurate to think of them as establishments for making loans at interest. Because these loans are not necessarily, or even primarily productive loans, it would also be quite accurate to call bankers "usurers,"[2] although it would make them much less acceptable socially.

Just off-center is the stock exchange, which likes to pose as a beneficent organization which provides the capital to launch worthwhile industrial enterprises. Like the banks, the stock exchange is mixed up with usury, but not always, and there are also other accounts against it. It increasingly resembles a large-scale gambling establishment, as one broker in New York recently was so obtuse as to say quite flatly. An increasing number of "investors" behave like people playing the numbers racket. These facts are discreditable, but perhaps not as discreditable as the highly respected conduct of the "conservative" brokers who have practically eliminated the risk of investment (risk is inherent in a productive loan). To have come through a general depression without financial loss (as they often boast of doing) is like coming fatted through famine.

Manufacturing (this is by and large) is a matter of concentrating machines and machine workers under the control of a

---

[2] St. Thomas' and Aristotle's definition of usury is any interest at all taken on an unproductive loan (one which does not bring about an increase of natural wealth) and its condemnation is rooted in the true nature of money, that it does not fructify. If usury is permitted, by a normal process the wealth of a society will accumulate in the hands of the usurer. This accounts for the enormous power of the banks.

certain organization for the end of enriching the owners thereof. Now this is important: the thing that is produced (let it be shoes or sheets or sleds) is, in our system, the *by-product* of manufacturing. The *end* is profit. It should be the other way around. A man should be a producer of sheets for the human need of sheets, and his living be incidental, be in the nature of a reward for, this production. It is because money is the last end that we have large factories and concentration of Industry. Take shoes, for instance. The machinery used to make shoes (all rented, incidentally, from a monopoly company) is rather simple, and needs only a few men. A shoe factory contains over and over again the same unit, whereas each unit could be better separately owned and decentralized. The only reason for duplication is so that *one* man or *one* group of men can grow fat on very many men's labor.

The money goal also accounts for this frequent phenomenon: that a given company makes highly diverse products. If the Dromedary Company only furnished us with dates we might have some romantic notion that they were date men, devoted for generations to the skillful cultivation and careful transportation of this exotic food. But when they also sell us gingerbread we begin to suspect that they are trafficking in anything that is profitable. We cannot avoid this accusation in a case of companies like General Foods. Indeed, it is taken for granted and considered honorable. The thing is that when you take your eye off the product itself (which really could hold your interest) you think in terms of mechanization and organization; and once you have an organization and all sorts of equipment and trained salesman and reduced advertising rates and accumulating capital, you might as well branch out. So R. H. Macy, the most over-swollen of department stores, sells cows and cars and airplanes now, although it started out to sell dry goods, and there is no real reason, on our present principles, why it should not take over all the retail distribution of goods in the United States and even in the world. There is no natural limit to the desire to make money.

The National Association of Manufacturers would not exist in a rational, Christian society. It is composed of a group of factory owners whose aim is to make money by the use of machines and the labor of other men. They have a common problem because they have a common interest: money-making. In a rational, vocational, functional society not ordered to profit, but to the common good, and ultimately to God, you would have associations of cobblers, of linen weavers, of watchmakers and winemakers. These groups would readily have common problems and not just a common greed.

Advertising is not an embellishment of our system, it is an integral part of it, a natural though monstrous growth on the parent stem. The advertising profession began within living memory. It started at a time when men's normal needs (that is, the needs of men who could pay to have them filled — nobody cares about the needs of poor or destitute men) were largely satisfied, and its function was (and is) to create new needs for the enrichment of merchants and manufacturers.

Radio is an interesting example of Capitalism's unselfish interest in the advancement of scientific discovery. When it first came to light that men could transmit sound by radio waves nobody was interested, because it did not seem to be an invention from which profit could be derived. Only after radio's advertising potentialities came into view did men's interest quicken. It would be edifying to know how many useful inventions have been suppressed, how many patents bought up in order to ensure their *disuse*, in an economy which pretends to foster science.

Financial Capitalism has made money out of money (more accurately, out of credit). Industrial Capitalism has made money out of our needs, real and artificial. But our system went further. With truly remarkable ingenuity we have devised ways of profiting by men's deaths and misfortunes. Insurance is the prime example, with life insurance especially interesting. It should be seen as an inverse work of mercy. How can a life insurance company claim to exist in the interests of widows and children (its clients) while foreclosing mortgages on thousands of other widows and children (as was done during the depression)! How can it claim to be solicitous on behalf of those who die prematurely when the very people to whom insurance is denied are those who seem likely to die prematurely? The natural Christian instinct in the matter would have been to form a society, rooted in charity, to take care of the most needy. Were charity fluid in society it would not be necessary for everyone to insure against every eventuality of God's Providence.

Hospitalization plans follow along the same charity-less pattern, the same mercenary ideal cloaked in beneficence. They are non-profit organizations which exist that hospitals may get their bills paid — in advance. As in insurance, the system works by getting the healthy to pay the bills of the sick; not as charity (which would be meritorious) but as self-interest (in which there is no virtue, unless worldly prudence is a virtue). It is interesting to trace the course of these schemes. As in life insurance, they avoid taking on those who are in imminent need of their services. Usually they start on a group basis, taking a given number of people from a certain office where average health can be presumed. However, there is a renewal privilege clause on an individual basis. What happened was that the unhealthy renewed the insurance, the healthy often let it lapse (and reasonably enough, for hospitalization should be a very rare occurrence in a man's life). So the rates went up. What is interesting to note is that this and other things are calculated to destroy the charity of the one outstandingly Christian institution left amongst us, the hospital.

Lastly, in this brief survey, the whole publishing field bears sad testimony to the ordering of society to Mammon. Within comparatively recent memory nearly all our magazine and book Publications have turned from editorial criteria (worn thin to be sure, from loss of respect for objective truth) to financial criteria and standards. Now writers write for money and editors buy what will sell, and it is only occasionally that this turns out to be something true and useful.

THE PRESENT SITUATION

Capitalism is not in its youth but in its senescence. One consequence of this is that we cannot presume much discrepancy to exist between the Capitalistic system and those involved in it. The greed which characterized the leaders of early Capitalism is now universal and respectable. Americans by the millions take it for granted that all other considerations defer to the profit motive, that everything is to be measured in money. Furthermore, our educational system has been diverted from the pursuit of truth to the preparation for money-making. This is even true (one is sometimes tempted to say especially true) of Catholic schools. That is a chief reason why the Church is frustrated in Her proper work of today, the making over of the temporal order. Catholic colleges are not pouring our learned Sir Galahads; they are belching forth aspiring business men and career girls, with a side course of apologetics. It is almost hopeless to look among them for men and women to lead us out of the money markets. Saddest of all is the spectacle of nuns who have dedicated their lives to the service of God, founding and staffing shiny new business schools with accelerated courses, so they can pop innocent, fresh young Catholic girls into the steel catacombs of insurance companies and banks. Surely they know not what they do. There is a whole world to be made over, and we keep providing grist for the Capitalist mill.

THE PRIMACY OF THE SPIRITUAL

Anyhow, what matters it now if the system *is* finished. So are we. We are all ordered to Mammon too. Therefore it first behooves us to reorient our own selves. *Nothing* can be made better now without better people. An increase in holiness will not of itself rectify things, but it is the prerequisite. By an increase in holiness we mean a turning again to God as the end, and not a continuation of worldly ends accompanied by an increase in devotional piety. If God is to be preferred above all things *then* we will break the chains that bind us to the ever-increasing standard of living, to our $300 radios, our sensitivity to the pulse of fashion, our cult of pleasure, our lust after new automobiles and our worship of glamour and pretension. This will be the sign of a spiritual revival in our time, a turning to asceticism and penance. It is our *only* hope, and there is no real sign of its beginning anywhere. One reason may be because we entertain false hopes of saving ourselves otherwise.

Within a materialistic framework, what could we possibly hope to achieve? The trade unions are excellent examples of the failure of reform where it remains within the material order. After all the effort and sacrifice they expended against cupidity, they have arrived in a like state. It is doubtful if their material condition has permanently improved, considering the change in the value of money, the frequent incidence of strikes, and the possibility of a new depression. They have substituted collective insecurity for individual insecurity. Furthermore, although we like to pretend otherwise, it is doubtful if the spiritual condition of the workman has improved either. It is better to be ground down by greed than to be greedy. The labor unions might have been the vehicle of our economic salvation. They have failed for not having been godly.

Or, take another example: socialism. Socialism is what Capitalism turns into, left to itself. It is only more of the same thing; just as materialistic, but even more concentrated, even more regimented, even more dull, and hopeless. It is just another palliative in the material order.

In this vale of tears good does not ordinarily grow out of evil, unless it is God who draws it out. Let all Christians beware of falling for schemes by which indifference is supposed to work itself out into good. They say, for instance, that the advent of electrical power (which is adapted to small unit use) will more or less automatically decentralize industry, allow us to finally live in the country and make things locally. But we lived in the country and made things locally to begin with. We only centralized, and urbanized, and industrialized, and mechanized and materialized, out of love of money. The only thing that can save us is to despise money.

If anyone doubts that it is cupidity which perpetuates our system, let him imagine the mortal effect which would result from a change of heart. A wave of penance and mortification would ruin advertising. But advertising is integral to the system, and production would largely collapse if it failed. Again, widespread dependence on God's Providence, or practice of fraternal charity would ruin insurance companies, and considering that their financial entanglements are colossal, there is no doubt but that repercussions would be heard throughout the land. How terrible, you say? No, that would not be terrible. What is terrible is that we have an economy which could not stand up under the genuine practice of Christianity. A penitential movement so widespread as to effect these collapses suddenly is so unlikely, and would be so wonderful, so pleasing to God, that we wouldn't have to worry about laws of economics during the interim period of adjustment. We might be fed manna, who knows?

However, reform, if reform there is to be, is more likely to be gradual. There are beginnings everywhere, but to our mind the movements appear to bog down because they do not see their temporal goals clearly enough in the light of their final end. Catholic Action is committed to restoring all things in Christ but many engaged in it seem not yet to have realized how radical a restoration is necessary in the economic order.

THE NEW ORDER

If God is the final end, what are the proximate ends which must be considered? The proper goal of economics as a whole is *the prosperity of all the people.* Clearly Capitalism sharply violates this principle by enriching some at the expense of others. Hence it comes about that men will produce luxuries, which can be made profitable through advertising, while millions are starving for lack of enough to eat. In reorienting the economic order we must first, therefore, lend our energy to a vital project rather than aspiring to get in on a new field on the ground floor. One of the most naturally gifted young Catholic men we know is planning to establish a helicopter service, and he wants to apply all the papal principles to his relations with his employees. He would do better to apply Catholic principles to his choice of occupation. There is, as yet, no crying demand for helicopters. We seem to have heard that there *is* for housing, for statesmen of integrity, for someone to facilitate the return of industrial workers to organic farming. You cannot justify going into the sachet business where there are not enough people growing potatoes. You ought not to take up straightening of teeth when there is no one to fill cavities. Catholics cannot justifiably gravitate toward the sidelines where there is a major battle for a new world to be fought.

An appalling number of us are doing nothing really useful. We are transporting back and forth across the country, goods which would be better made locally. We are filing minutiae, or adding up figures which will be cleverly misrepresented on the annual statement. We are retouching photographs of $8.98 dresses, counting the number of women who pass a corner in tan stockings, indexing foolish books, recording batting averages and making copies in triplicate of interoffice memoranda.

So for many of us, the problem is not how to Christianize the work we are in, but how to get enough courage to think our way out of our jobs. It isn't easy to reason the ground out from under you, especially if you have put in several years of graduate work and have professional standing. That is why an almost heroic sanctity is needed, and a great trust in God's Providence.

PARTICULAR ENDS

All legitimate economic projects have distinctive proximate ends from which a whole set of principles of operation can be derived. This is the field in which Catholics should make detailed studies, especially Catholic Action groups. It is complex and technical to make these studies, but it is not difficult or vague; the principles all fall in line once you get started. Courage is needed, and heroic objectivity. It is not usually a question of minor repairs. Here we will give only a brief indication of the framework of such inquiries. They cannot be made exhaustively anyhow except by the people actively engaged in the field. *The Professions* have as their proximate ends the works of justice and mercy. While most of them are corrupt and deteriorated at the moment, the Christian framework is still visible.

Production of basic human necessities is where the drastic change is necessary, because here is the heart of industrialism. In this category we include the making of shoes, dresses, sheets, houses and other necessities. The general criterion is the *right making of things.* The product has become a by-product; let it become the end. Clothes rightly made are custom-made and not subject to fluctuation of fashion, nor shoddily made. Things rightly made are made to last, to fit, to nourish, to be suitable, to be beautiful, etc. If any inquiry such as this is pursued, it will likely turn out that most necessary things are better eventually made by craft-type production, combined with refinements made possible by the increase of scientific knowledge. It is very hard to make things by craft skill in an economy ordered to large-scale manufacturing, just as it is very difficult to serve as a small shop-owner in an era of mammoth department stores; but if giant department stores are economic monstrosities, then we must try to start a movement in the other direction. It will gain momentum as it goes along. It is a question as to whether things are done according to God or not. If they are not, as now, we just cannot decide to put up with them; morality is involved. We have got to order our ends toward God somehow. If it takes ingenuity, then we have to become ingenious. If it involves hardship, then we must brace ourselves for hardships; if it needs mass movements, then we must have mass movements.

People are disheartened when they begin to suspect that we have to change the whole manner of making things. Actually, the fact that most things are better made in comparatively small units will probably be our salvation. It is true that it is better to have shoddy shoes machine-made than to go barefoot. But if we stimulate young men who wish to be cobblers to drop out of industrialism and start supplying local needs on small scale, then when the shoe factories collapse (as they will) we shall still be shod. The whole idea is to build up, with small beginnings everywhere, an economy which can take over when industrialization collapses. As Christians who understand what is going on, we have a duty to build for the future. There are plenty of others who will perpetuate the present system as long as we need it. The Jocist idea of cooperating materially in Capitalistic enterprise, in order to save souls by a personal apostolate there, is quite another matter. There are two sides to the apostolate; the spiritual leavening, and the reordering of the institutions of society to God. Some people are called more to one than to the other. Let leaders infiltrate into the factories by all means; but let them also send out a stream of rejuvenated people to make new beginnings.

Transportation Units such as automobiles and airplanes are not strictly basic human needs, so whereas they should be well made, it is legitimate to work toward making few of them if that seems to be the common good. They are not good in themselves (except materially) but according to the use to which they are put. Planes have so far overwhelmingly served the use of war and commercial exploitation; whereas automobiles have made it possible for men to live far from their places of work and recreation, and have also served good uses. It is true that these things, and telephones, typewriters and the rest, are necessary under our present economy, and especially in view of international unrest. The chances are that an ordered society would make only moderate use of them and that it might be more practical to make them then in semi-skilled fashion. It would be worth looking into whether the Rolls-Royce might not be a more economical vehicle in the long run than the Ford.

Catholics should realize that they are perfectly entitled to use automobiles, airplanes, typewriters, power presses and all the rest of things which are materially good, even if they should be plotting to do away with them eventually. St. Augustine could not exonerate Rome from the evil involved in her conquests. Yet God used a united, peaceful Roman Empire in which to become Incarnate, the Roman highways on which to spread the Gospel; and Rome itself as Peter's See. The boycott idea must be of non-Catholic origin, because it can rarely be used in a healthy way. We are not meant so much to withdraw from society as to walk unscathed in the midst of evil. This does not mean that we should perpetuate, or even prop up disordered things which can be put to good use. No matter what happens, God is not frustrated. And it is our duty to promote what is good with all our strength.

Agriculture is the field in which the manner of operation is most clearly indicated by God's natural laws. The present mechanized commercial farming will have us all starving if it continues much longer. The key to proper farming is that it should be *organic,* operating in regard to the balance and rhythm of nature. It will be difficult to reorientate farming, but not because it is impossible to find out the rules. We need to apply the real rules, and we need many more farmers.

* * *

The need of more people on the land is just one of the many indications of the fact that most of us cannot begin to restore society where we are, but must first find our proper places in it. A machine-worker in a shoe factory is not necessarily a frustrated cobbler; he might be meant by God to be a farmer or a newspaper editor.

So in a way the first problem is to straighten out our own ends. The beginning is a divine discontent: "I'd rather be a menial in the house of the Lord, than to dwell among princes."

CAROL ROBINSON

"Ours Not To See The Triumph of the Truth"

There is a cathedral to be built; the plan
Is great and long to be fulfilled. A man
Will dream it and conceive the spire.
His zeal will blaze in passioned fruitful fire
And he will rise and start to clear the ground
Quietly. Some workmen will be found
To help him. When his genius-hand
Has failed, another will have come to stand
In his proud place. Thereafter, each man's son
Will seize the work his father has begun.
Each one, blessed in his birth-right task,
Will bend his strength to it, nor ever ask
Who thought the thing. A smaller part
Of the whole grandeur will be in each heart.
Some will be sculptors, and their lives will sing
In saintly marble, and the noble fling
Of arches; while the cruder craftsmen free
The earth-embedded stone, and pile the masonry.
They will fall in silence, in a prayerful hour
Of labor. They will not see the tower
Who visioned it. A few will die
Crushed by the loose-hung rock, and buried, lie
In their own wall's shade. The noble ones who dare
The breathless scaffolding will know the fair
Blue heights; and if their feet should cease
To be secure — theirs, then, the martyr's peace.

When it is done, the dreamers will be gone.
Only the dream will live. Some queenly dawn
Will find the finished temple standing high
Perfect and proud and beautiful against the sky.

ELIZABETH ODELL

Calvary Canticle

Dear Son, what love has done to Thee,
Thy nail-kissed hands, Thy sanguine brow,
Thy kingly head, not crownless now —
Oh blessed wood, Thy throne to be!

And oh, exalted hill to hold
The jewel — Thee, Thy royalty —
Oh cradle of the holy tree
For what these arms did once enfold!

I prayed Thou might protected live
From Thy own greatness (loneliness
To be a Prince). That harsh caress
Of God upon Thee I ungive.

Wert then my Son? My mystery
Not motherhood, not suffering,
Not joy of Thee, no sorrow-thing,
But Thou whom I did make, made me!

My silence — let loud earth applaud
I-still-of-words. The sealed heart
Lets Thee speak, keeps Thy voice apart,
My God, my Son; my Son, my God.

ELIZABETH ODELL

Correspondence

Dear Sirs:

I've just finished reading the last issue of your magazine, and I thought you might appreciate knowing how well-liked it has become in the seminary here. Two copies arrive each month, and within a week they are both dog-eared. Each one passes through about twenty hands. But of course, such a magazine as yours would naturally find an appreciative audience in a seminary, for its aims are those of every priest and priest-to-be. If we could only get the majority of the laity thinking along the lines of *Integrity*, we priests and seminarians could spend more time catching up on St. John of the Cross and St. Teresa instead of preparing sermons on mortal sin, et al.

* * *

Sirs:

... May I also praise your magazine at this time. You'll never know the help it has been to me in a non-Catholic college.

* * *

"Tis good to know that there are people even in America who have studied the Summa of St. Thomas"!

* * *

I have spent five years in a seminary. One cannot do that, and think, and study, and talk with God, and still look pleasantly and smile at Life as it is portrayed in and typified by the magazine of the same name. But on the contrary, one is overjoyed to see another magazine that typifies and portrays that Life as it is extolled in St. Thomas and the Fathers, and is the throbbing activity of the Church, and which the Word of God came to give us.

I received the three issues of *Integrity* which you so kindly sent. I spent hours with them, and now they are making the rounds of the seminary. Yesterday, I received your letter. It was a thrill to read it. I'll tell you why.

When one gets absorbed in an idea or a plan, and dreams about it, waiting for the day to break it loose and share it with others, it is very discouraging to discover with a jolt that it is not the desired thing with the masses: it has been tried before and was rejected: that the adherents to such a plan are considered commonly to be radicals and rather odd — when such a discovery is made, then you get somewhat confused: you were convinced that this was the truth. But you begin to feel a little odd, like a poetic Sir Galahad, like a dreamer. And you tell yourself — "get back to earth, stop dreaming, think like other people . . . "

If you can do what you are doing: . . . and still believe you are right, then the rest of us surely can dream (if it is becoming to classify as a dream, the desire to feed people with the substantial food of dogmatic theology instead of the candy of unsound devotion, to feed them Christ as God instead of a mythical character of uncommon sweetness).

I had better stop — I have gone on like this before about the Liturgy and such things and sometimes sound too big for my shoes.

Anyway, what I hope you'll realize is this — you have given me a lot of new hope, not that I would ever see things otherwise, for who can lose what you called a "passion for first principles" once they have been displayed to a reason gifted with Faith?

You know, sometimes I have questioned myself this way about folks like you — there is the Baroness and Eddie Doherty, Dorothy Day, Ade de Bethune, the Orate Fratres, Tom Barry at the Sower Press, etc., etc. — why don't they get together? (a 20th century question, I know). Do they know each other? Couldn't they be stronger if they organized?

Well, I have answered the question for myself in my mind. But it seems as though, by instinct or something, questions are always answered in your mind before you put them verbally in black and white. I'll be able to express it some day if I keep thinking about it. But, you are right. "Every man to his own little puddle" (your own expression).

Well, this about uses up my time, but I could go on and on. When I find a common bond with someone, other than the Holy Ghost and charity of course, I find it too easy to talk sometimes. Maybe it's because you were converted from bourgeois paganism and the Sacramental life in Christ, and myself from 1940's class of what doting parents nowadays call the "plucky little teenagers and bobby-soxers."

You have found a constant place in my intentions for Mass and Office daily — all of you, however many make up your staff. I hope you'll remember a deacon of Christ, for the next four or five months anyway.

* * *

...And we like your views on modern society. In this automotive center, which local wowsers like to call Dynamic Detroit, we see industrialism in many of its worst aspects. I get a sinking feeling when I pass an auto plant and see the thousands trudging into work at their machines. It is plant life, but literally.

* * *

Comment from the South

I have been reading *Integrity* very carefully... I must thank you for the very great generosity your work evidences and may God bless you and prosper you in all your undertakings for your studies cover a very wide field, thank God.

The urgent motive behind my letter today is to thank you for your discussion of Protestantism... I have often meditated on the wisdom of the Early Church in maintaining the discipline of the secret. So many non-Catholics had familiarized themselves with the doctrinal terms that Catholics hold dear, but which through the years, had been wrested from their true signification, and been debauched by heresy. Your letter from the "Liberal Protestant" in one of the great secular universities bears out what grieves me; Catholics go ahead and state doctrines to those who do not have the gift of Faith — and then take umbrage when their dogmatic teaching is repelled.

Personally I am of the opinion that we shall never be able to attract Protestants to the Church by no matter how clear the enunciation of dogma. Our Lord began to do and to teach. The doing preceded the teaching. If we Catholics could concentrate a little more strictly on the new commandments so that those outside may, like Pliny, remark our mutual love and support of one another, we shall get somewhere. What we need is a good auditor's analysis of our trading with our heritage.

I believe that we will have to drop the use of the Catholic term in presenting truth to those outside the Church and teach them the thing itself first; when this is grasped, crystallize it with the Catholic term or definition. Had you thought of this?

* * *

From an assistant professor at a Protestant seminary

Although the recent issue on Protestantism was obviously a "window shopping" view, it was highly contributory to one's sense of humility; there was genuine judgment here. At times I felt I was under the eye of Our Lord rather than under scrutiny by Edward Willock and Carol Jackson and Co. At other times I felt the writers needed to come into the direct gaze of Him Who is the Light of our world.

The cover picture — magnificent! and done with no real malice. That poor little ewe lamb above the word: PROTESTANTISM. Could be ready for slaughter, too!! — slaughter inside the covers, yet it reminded me of some words of Christ: "Other sheep I have, which are not of this fold . . . " St. John 10:16. (Of course, you'll emphasize the rest of the verse; I the part quoted.) I do have an appreciation of "the fold," the Roman Church; I have also a love (which I trust is more than a sentiment) for the Shepherd who must judge that or any fold.

I do not hold a brief for Bishop Oxnam — many of his "Catholic utterances" give me a pain in the neck. However, it is hardly urbane to dismiss him in a sentence and with a description that scarcely does him justice — "on a hysterical, low intellectual level." Come, come now; have you ever heard Oxnam!

And what happened to Reinhold Niebuhr? On the blurb you presented to the public for your coming out party, you distinctly said you would refer to him in this issue. I find no references. He's not far away; you'd be welcome at that stronghold of liberalism — Union Seminary, up in Corpus Christi parish!! After all, Dr. Neibuhr is a figure to be reckoned with in Protestantism, why waste paper knocking down straw men?

And many will dismiss the excellent article (corking good bibliography) on Protestantism and Economic life with one question: "What about Franco?"

Yet, despite these criticisms, thanks for packing a real wallop in this issue. Enclosed find a check for $2.00 for 8 issues sent to me for circulation among my friends and in class — best ammunition I know to get students to think through their positions. Our Seminary Hymn is Father F.W. Faber's "Faith of Our Fathers" — never more than today do we need his advice:

"We will love both friend and foe
In all our strife."

* * *

Dear Sirs:

A few days ago I received your fifth issue of *Integrity*, subject: Protestantism; I have read it through. I was much impressed by one word in your editorial "Truth." It is mentioned five times on page one. Being a Protestant, I am much interested in your editorial, and interested to know: what is truth?

Your discussion of Protestantism throughout the book seems to be one of negation.

I don't want to go through the torture of getting acquainted with all the error in the world in order to decide that what is left over must be truth. Now if you have some short pamphlet or some article setting forth in the fewest words possible: What is truth, or the Faith of the Roman Catholic Church condensed into the fewest words possible, it will give me something to compare modern Protestantism by: or if you care to publish it in *Integrity* in the near future, that will be perfectly satisfactory to me.

Hoping to hear from you at your earliest convenience,

* * *

On the Mental Disease Issue

Dear Sirs,

In my position as chaplain of a State Hospital the contents of your 4th issue hold special interest. I've heard Freudianism extolled and therefore would like to counteract it with a few copies of this issue. The excuse for using Freud was that there was nothing better. But I told them they were too easily satisfied or too lazy. After showing them this 4th issue they promised to study it but we would rather keep our copy which we get by subscription and distribute a number of extra copies where they will do the most good. Is it possible to obtain 8 extra copies of this issue?

* * *

The January number is an invaluable treatment in the vernacular of mental disorders in a simplified, yet sound and adequate, form which should be useful to any psychology teacher. I am urging my students to get copies.

INTEGRITY, March 1947

* * *

I appreciated very much your last issue, on the subject of mental disease. It is the first clear-cut discussion on the subject from the Catholic point of view I have seen. I appreciate it more because I studied the subject in college, under a man who once told me, in private, that he was an agnostic.

* * *

May I congratulate you on your January issue of *Integrity?* It was a daring project and showed tremendous study over a long period of time. I have read and reread it several times.

* * *

Dear Sirs, P.C.,

I enclose a dollar. Would you be so kind as to send me four copies of the January '47 issue? It is a gem and I hope to put it to good use among my friends in the medical corps. May Christ and Mary bless you and your work!

* * *

I recently received a copy of *Integrity* and found a number of interesting items in it. Certainly, the illustration on the cover of your fourth issue was quite apt for the subject under consideration. Likewise, I can certainly approve of the general task which you have set for yourself in publishing this series.

I am not certain that I can go along with you in your attitude towards psychiatrists. Certainly, there are quite a number of them who have questionable qualifications for the job that they have set out to do. On the other hand, it is my feeling that the essential roots of the problem presented by mental illness lie in our community and social structure, more than in the prevailing philosophy of those trying to improve the lot of individuals suffering from mental disease.

Correspondence

I know that you will agree with me that no church has made a major contribution to the care of those who are mentally ill, and that we do owe a vote of gratitude to those psychiatrists who have tried, even without public support, to bring order out of chaos in our public institutions.

Sincerely yours,
HAROLD BARTON
Executive Secretary,
National Mental Health Foundation

* * *

I have been interested in *Integrity* since its inception, but did not decide to subscribe until your fourth issue came along, "Subject: Mental Disease." I found your presentation of Catholic philosophical psychology, that is your graphic description of basic notions concerning the Intellect, the Will, the Passions, Man's Final End, etc., particularly good and timely. Other portions, however, are not as praiseworthy, such as your glib treatment of Psychoanalysis and the Unconscious. One ought not dismiss such topics in so summary and dogmatic a fashion. It would seem to me that a more critical and evaluating attitude is appropriate when discussing subject-matter that is still controverted. For a more dispassionate analysis, I refer you to the following works: Jastrow, "The House that Freud Built"; or Healy, Bronner, and Bowers, "The Structure and Meaning of Psychoanalysis"; or Sears, "Survey of Objective Studies of Psychoanalytic Concepts."

Outside of these two bits, I am very much pleased with the distinctly Catholic twist you have given to certain drab facts of Abnormal Psychology. A Christian, theological approach to problems of mental abnormality is like a breath of fresh air in a charnel-house.

More power to *Integrity* and its staff.

* * *

"A Christian Abnormal Psychology," January 1947 issue, of itself justifies the launching of *Integrity*. I am enclosing a check for eight additional copies.

* * *

The previous issues of *Integrity* have been passed among my associates in the field of social work by me, but the fourth issue, I feel, must be in the hands of each worker to keep forever. Therefore, will you please send me eight issues of volume four at your earliest convenience. It contains the sort of thing I revolted against in graduate school and am fighting in the field at present. May God bless you in your Herculean task.

* * *

Dear Mr. Willock and Miss Jackson:

I think your fourth issue of *Integrity* on the subject of mental disease is by far the finest and frankest thing of its kind I have ever seen and perhaps the most needed approach in the Christian world today. I wish I had the means of sending a copy to every clergyman of my acquaintance. Enclosed is a check for $2.50 for which I would like to have ten copies at your earliest convenience.

You people are doing an amazing and wonderful kind of missionary work and I am sure that the hand of the Lord is upon you. Be assured that you are in our prayers and that we ask God's blessing upon your every effort.

* * *

To the Editor:

Your attempt to wrestle with modern psychology in terms of Catholic philosophy deserves credit as a worthy intention. There is hardly a greater need today than to coordinate the efforts of modern psychology with the substance of Catholic teaching.

One of the more obvious faults of the psychologist today, however, is that he appears to assume that he is addressing an audience incapable of thinking for itself. I regret to observe that this attitude afflicts your current authority likewise.

Whence, pray, this amazingly archaic differentiation of human types into the medieval "humours"? The informed reader feels disposed to advise the author to resort to bleeding in the hopes that his mind will clear.

And the temperamental differences of the sexes seems to be handled with no more enlightenment. Such antiquated statements hardly seem possible today in the light of evidence. Peter Michaels[1] aligns himself against the Freudians, and yet the Freudians have done better.

Is it possible that you suppose the reading public today is so ignorant of the necessity of substantiating statement that no one will question the credentials of "Peter Michaels" in venturing to deal with such a complex and much investigated subject? If he chose to rest under the screen of anonymity, he should at least have published his sources. Even the undergraduate mind recognizes the necessity of a bibliography.

It is to be regretted that your courage has outdistanced your qualifications in the fourth issue of *Integrity*.

* * *

Gentlemen:

Please send me *Integrity* for one year. Begin with January 1947, which is excellent ... I am chaplain to a government mental hospital, 8,000 patients, 2,000 of them Catholic. Why do so many priests, nuns and brothers suffer from mental disorders? ... what is needed are (a) Catholic doctors who are willing to take up Catholic psychiatry under Catholic teachers — when I say Catholic doctors I mean holy men, too! (b) A greater awareness of the fact that psychiatry as practiced today, for the most part, is the

[1] Carol Robinson's pseudonym. — Ed.

great heresy. (c) Priests in every city parish with a modicum of training in diagnosing the beginnings of mental disorders, with specific hours for consultation and advice on moral living.

* * *

My dear Mr. Willock:

I want to tell you of the pleasure with which I have read your paper on "Mental Disease" in the copy of *Integrity* which came to me through "Letter."

In particular I want to commend Part V, "The Way Out." For a number of years I have been doing psychotherapy at the Boston Dispensary. I have had to talk in most intimate fashion with Jews, Catholics, Protestants, and Nothingists, and as a part of psychotherapeutic approach have included the matter of religion. It has been of greatest interest to find that I could talk with Catholics and Jews on this profoundest of all subjects, I, a Protestant, with absolute frankness, not trying to change their faith but trying to have them put their professed beliefs into practice in the little and great difficulties of daily life. They have been helped, thus, by religion as well as psychology, and talking with them has done me no end of good personally.

It is one God and one humanity, and it is well that we should learn to bring the profound realities of thought into our day by day dealing with hungry and suffering souls — and also those that are not consciously either suffering or hungry.

Lives there a man with soul so dead,
 Who hasn't to himself at least once said:
"These are MY hands and this is MY head,
 To lead my own life, and not be led."

BOOK REVIEWS

Women's Task

EVE AND THE GRYPHON
By Gerald Vann, O.P.
Blackfriars, Oxford, England

> The fate of the family, the fate of all human relations is at stake... every woman has the strict obligation in conscience to go into action so as to hold back those currents which threaten the home, so as to oppose those doctrines which undermine its foundations so as to prepare, organize and achieve its restoration. (Pius XII)

In the light of Our Holy Father's recent address to women (Feast of St. Ursula, 1945; Lady Day, 1946) emphasizing their crucial role in the reconstruction of society, these four essays on the vocation of laywomen are particularly apropos. Father Vann's uncommon penetration never outstrips his compassion. His clarity never surpasses his charity. His brilliance does not glitter; it glows. "Love-knowledge" is not just a happy phrase in his vocabulary. It is the expression of his inner soul. (One can just guess what terrific tensions have been met and resolved by so keenly perceptive a person.) Hyperbole is Hollywood. Suffice to say that all Gerald Vann writes is altogether out of the ordinary. In serious discussions he is never heavy; everything is leavened by his all-pervasive charity, rooted in God, radiating on men.

The chapter headings are indicative: "Seek ye first the kingdom," has St. Catherine of Siena as its model — she who spent 3 years in solitude and prayer and the most rigid asceticism before launching into activity. "Let us salute in her her wisdom: it was a wisdom that she learnt in prayer — not the acquired wisdom of a powerful intellect but the infused wisdom of a humble heart, the intuitive grasp of truth, the love-knowledge, which as we shall see later is the wisdom most proper to women's vocation in the world."

"The Mystical Body and the Vocation of Motherhood" has Our Lady as its supreme exemplar. Speaker of her, he says: "Mary, the Queen of the Seven Swords, knew as no other woman has known the length and breadth and height and depth... She knew the length because she knew, she saw in her son's story, that immediate failure is often ultimate success and apparent success is often ultimately failure: she knew that what is wisdom in men is often folly to God. And those who share in her vocation have to share in her length of view: theirs is the majesty of bringing up souls for God, their eyes fixed not on the immediate and often illusory objectives of money and social advancement but on the ultimate objective of the fullness of eternal life."

"The Vocation of Tears" — lest we forget that the Liturgy prays for the "Gift" — has St. Monica as its central figure, and "The Leadership of Love" Dante's Beatrice. Herein is the clue to the book's enigmatic title.

Particularly pertinent passages include the following:

> To study the life of Our Lady or St. Monica is to gain an impression of an influence silent, secret, self-effacing, patient, working in the background. But we shall miss its meaning if we think of it as something passive, or as limited to the task of supporting and sustaining, comforting and encouraging, expiating. It is active and creative: it not only sustains activity, but calls it forth... The mission of women is not merely a passive, an expiatory one: it is the active mission of the leadership of love... Love is what seeks the good of the one loved; and sometimes that must imply severity.

Woman "must first of all be herself a contemplative: she must learn how to look upon the Sun. Then she must learn the vocation of tears: she must learn how to sympathize, to co-suffer, she must learn how to have pity and how to comfort and sustain. But she must learn also to be strong enough to have, like Beatrice, the kind of compassion in which there is also a taste of severity; resisting temptation to do his will when it is stupid or sinful even though he think her refusal a denial of love. And as her prayer and her pain and her joys and her labours teach her the wisdom which is divine, so that in her eyes there begins to shine the reflection of the eternal light, so she will teach him to turn to her not as to a rival of God or of the work which God would have him do, but as the one who will empower him for this work and help him to do it wisely and humbly in the sight of God; and she will labour, as Monica did in her life with Patricius, not in impatient distress at the difficulties and failures of every day, but with her eyes on the distant horizon, on the end of the journey when at last she will have imparadised his heart."

How much distinction there actually is between the sexes has always been a much mooted question. On this, Father Vann takes an unequivocal stand. "Underneath all the varieties of individual qualities and characteristics there lies the greatest of all natural differentiations: which is that between man and woman."

Some books are arid; others are brilliant but cold; few have the faculty of combining light and heat as this book does.

Addendum: In any discussion of work, it would be unpardonable oversight not to call attention to Father Vann's incomparable meditations on man the maker and man the lover in "The Heart of Man," which, by the way, is an excellent companion piece to the above, elaborating as it does on the masculine as opposed to the feminine virtues. It is the rare writer who can evoke such joy in the contemplation of truth. "The Economics of Personality" and "A Policy of Integration" in "Morals Makyth Man" should also be singled out on this subject. Since sloth and work are opposed, it is good to know the roots of *accidie* (acedia). This is well handled in "On His Fullness" by the same author in a chapter of that title. Sloth is "an aversion in the will from work, arising from a lack of interest and joy in, and desire for the divine good. Not disinclination for virtuous action, but for that divine good, the goodness, and love, and glory, of God in which charity rejoices." As we have not gotten to the roots of the problem of work, so correlatively we have not gotten to the roots of its enemy, sloth.

S. T.

Courteously Presented

WHEREON TO STAND
By John Gilland Brunini
Harper & Brothers

That there are non-Catholics desirous to learn more of the complex anatomy of the Church is something I must accept on hearsay. I never met one. The knowledge that disposes man for the Faith when we consider man philosophically in his perfection as a lesser-god is not quite the same disposing agent when we encounter man as he is today, fallen from grace for the second time. Having been redeemed once made the second fall even more disintegrating. To presuppose even a natural good will toward the Church on the part of those without the gates is to underestimate the totality of the darkness which enshrouds our times. Indeed many men are seeking the light, but the light they require must be shed upon them and their environment. They will ever remain skeptical as long as we merely tell them that it exists hidden within the inner sanctuaries of the Church. We cannot wholly blame them for that, since even the Catholic is rare who has shed scales from pragmatic eyes and dares to look at his Church and see it as the spouse of Christ, and He God of the universe.

Just as it is impossible for a man to admit a God when He is imagined as a benevolent bearded patriarch, it is equally impossible to conceive universal beatitude boxed up within a particular church. The man is right who denies validity to the former or questions the possibility of the latter. Unfortunately, that is the way that God and His Church appear to men today, a fact that we cannot admit without a thrice repeated *mea culpa*. Many people will risk a dollar at the entrance to a theatre to seek a pleasure, the quality of which they can only judge from the ads out front. The same kind of advertising outside the door of the Church will attract fewer customers. The entrance price is too high, and there will be a greater price if you decide to leave before the show is over.

Mr. Bruini has painstakingly and with admirable scholarship compiled a book about the faith. He courteously answers the questions of the curious in matters doctrinal and historical. This is in the nature of an informal text-book, and will probably be read index first, in spite of the logical procession of chapters from Creation to Fall, from Fall to Redemption, and the historical fruition of the Church. It is what it purports to be, "a popular handbook on the Catholic Church." There is no doubt that for many Catholics a frequent consultation of these pages will serve to give them a better understanding of their Faith, and perhaps increase their apostolicity by making them more articulate. I do not think that its value for the non-believer will be so great.

The United States is ripe for conversion, but apologetics will not do it. The battle of the Reformation has been fought, and the Church has emerged victorious. It is victorious in that it has survived. Only a Church divinely sustained could have survived. Those years are behind us. What was once the enemy is now a bleeding, undernourished, bewildered group of displaced persons. It needs only now for Catholics to live out their Faith, to bring light out from under the bushel of private devotion, and all the world will see whence the light emanates. The breakdown of our civilization, although occasioned by man's denial of the Faith, will not be restored by our telling him the cause of his downfall. It will be restored by our bringing Christian practice to bear on every aspect of our life as we live it. The facility with which we accomplish our husbandry under the husbandry of God "in the Holy Ghost, in charity unfeigned, in the words of truth, in the power of God," will make men wonder, and then they too will come and drink from the same spring as we.

ED WILLOCK

The crisis we are experiencing is unique in history. It is a world which must burst out of a crucible in which so many different energies are working. Let us thank God that He makes us live among the present problems... it is no longer permitted to anyone to be mediocre. All men have the imperative duty to remember that they have a mission to fulfill, that of doing the impossible.

Pius XII

: the seventh issue :
April 1947 Vol.1, No. 7

EDITORIAL

OW AT EASTER IS A GOOD TIME to recall that we Christians are the only people in the world who are fighting a battle that has already been won. Our world is wrapped in the dark mantle of Good Friday. Where is the promise of the Resurrection? It lies only in that first Resurrection, repeated in soul after soul, generation after generation, from the first Easter to the end of the world. Christ's merits, won on the Cross, are sufficient to save us all, are intended to save us all. We have but to apply them.

Our present world testifies overwhelmingly to one thing: to the hopelessness of men to save themselves. It is folly to disregard the weapons by which, may we repeat, *the battle has already been won*. As long as we do things our own way the world will get darker and darker. What we need is not an intensification of effort, but a change of strategy.

Why don't we believe it when Our Lady says that the powers of darkness (she specifically mentioned Russia as the place they would be fomented) will be conquered if men again turn to God and lead holy lives? But no, she was obviously wrong. What we need are tanks and parleys and committees and international trade and atomic bombs. It wouldn't be prudent to trust in spiritual weapons now. It wouldn't be prudent because spiritual weapons are irrelevant to our own natural, human methods. So we go on winning wars, only to lose them; seeking peace where there is no peace.

But the victory we seek has already been won. Christ it is who conquers. When we stop trying to do it ourselves and let Christ make a new world through us, then we shall see the dawn of Easter. In the Christian battle, dying we live, falling we rise, and in defeat is our victory. In the world's economy, diamonds turn to glass in our hands and the most splendid civilizations unaccountably corrupt. In God's economy, good is perpetually triumphing over evil; Good Friday is always followed by Easter Sunday.

Where is there that Christ cannot conquer if we will let him? There is no concentration camp so degrading, no life so sinful, no society so materialistic, no international situation so tangled, no heart so heavy that it cannot be transformed by the promises of the Resurrection.

THE EDITORS

Resurrection: 1947

MOST PEOPLE WILL ADMIT THAT CHRISTIANity has been a powerful influence in the history of the world. But many fail to see the fact that this power proceeds from the witness which the Christian Church has always borne to the Resurrection of the Lord, or the further fact that the Resurrection is not only in the past perfect but also in the present tense, a constant, recurrent principle of life for all the generations of men.

Go back to the fountain and headwaters of the Church's beginnings and see what was happening there. No other way can you so convincingly grasp the meaning of the Resurrection and its always contemporary relevance to the changing history of man. In those first Apostolic decades of the Christian era, so amply and reliably recorded in the contemporary documents which now form our New Testament, we find a microcosm, organically perfect, of all that the Church's life will ever mean or convey to men's souls — the Light and life of the Risen Jesus, not alone as a past Fact becoming each year more and more remote, but as a perennial Reality in the Sacraments which Christ left to be its infallible instruments. Faith in the Resurrection, but even more, Life through the Resurrection, elevating men to another dimension, transfiguring and energizing them with Christ, and invigorating them with joy, these are the notes which characterize the Christian communities of the Apostolic Age. To this day these notes have never failed the Church, nor will they ever, although again and again her children have fallen short of their proper measure, and will, in the fickleness of human strivings, continue to do so.

A candid study of the documents of the Apostolic period, both Scriptural and patristic, shows that the Faith was built upon the Fact of the Resurrection. Then as now, there were those who denied the Fact, not for lack of evidence, but for some prejudice on doctrinal grounds. In our days the prejudice is against the possibility of miracles; in those days, it was against the possibility of the body's resurrection. Then the prejudice was formed out of Platonic conceptions concerning an "antagonism" between body and soul; now it is formed out of Liberalist conceptions concerning an "antagonism" between science and religion. Every age has had its Christian apologists to meet its prejudices with suitable demonstration. In our time, to name one who is good for the general reader, we have Mr. Arnold Lunn, whose *The Third Day*[1] prefaces its admirable summary of the arguments with two chapters on miracles. In the Apostolic days, it was St. Paul, who confronted the skeptical prejudice of the Greeks with convincing answers on the resurrection of the body. The Fact of Christ's Resurrection stands solid and incontrovertible before anyone who gives it candid attention. Prejudice must be removed to allow this candid gaze to focus unreservedly on the evidences for the Fact, and so there will always be need of contemporary apologists.

LIFE-BEARERS

It seems quite certain, however, that the people of our age stand in greater need of apostolic witnesses of the Resurrection than they do of apologists. Ours is not only a Truth and a Way: it is a Life. And that Life is Christ's, or more truly, it is Christ — shared with us, possessing us, using us as the instruments of His work. Our best witness to the Resurrection is not with our tongues nor the propriety of our conduct, but with the transfiguration of our lives by the power of Christ, in such a way that the Risen Savior stands clearly in us before the men and women of our generation, choosing "the foolish things of the world that He may confound the wise, and the weak things of the world that He may confound the strong." (Cor. 1:27)

---

[1] The Newman Bookshop: Westminster, Md. (1945)

Resurrection: 1947

St. Athanasius writes, in his great treatise on *The Incarnation of the Word of God, Ch. 30:*

> The Savior is working mightily among men, every day He is invisibly persuading numbers of people all over the world... to accept His faith and be obedient to His teaching. Can anyone, in face of this, still doubt that He has risen and lives, or rather that He is Himself the Life? Does a dead man prick the consciences of men, so that they throw all the traditions of their fathers to the winds and bow down before the teaching of Christ? If He is no longer active in the world, as He must needs be if He is dead, how is it that He makes the living cease from their activities, the adulterer from his adultery, the murderer from murdering, the unjust from avarice while the profane and godless man becomes religious?[2]

These words come from the fourth century, but their ring is timeless. While they testify to the imperishable Truth of the Risen Savior, they stand as an evidence of the force which Christians, permeated by the Life of the Risen Savior, can exercise upon the people with whom they live and work.

CHRIST-CONTEMPORARY

It will be the purpose of this article to show, first of all, how Christ has provided that the power of His Resurrection will always be contemporary, and, secondly, how that power is relevant to the spiritual disorder of our times.

In the divine plan of our Redemption, the Resurrection of Jesus is integral with His Passion and Death. It marks a high stage, though not yet the climax, in the sequence of the redemptive work. When Jesus was preparing His disciples for these final

[2] Translated by a Religious of C.S.M.V.: Macmillan, N.Y. 1946

events, telling them of the dire Passion He was to undergo, He finished His announcement with the words, "And the third day He (the Son of man) shall rise again." And on the night of His Resurrection, He instructed two of the disciples on the road to Emmaus, "Ought not Christ to have suffered these things and so to enter into His glory?" The humbling unto death and the exalting unto glory were phases of one continuous Work, correlative with the casting out of sin and the restoring of the new life.

There is a radiant passage in St. Paul to the Colossians, well worth meditating upon for this thought:

> You, by baptism, have been united with His burial, united, too, with His resurrection, through your faith in that exercise of power by which God raised Him up from the dead. And in giving life to Him, He gave life to you too, when you lay dead in your sins, with nature all uncircumcised in you. He condoned all your sins; cancelled the deed which excluded us, the decree made to our prejudice, swept it out of the way, by nailing it to the cross; and the dominions and powers He robbed of their prey, put them to an open shame, led them away in triumph, through Him.[3]

LIFE-GIVER

We know, of course, that the redemptive work produced the casting out of sin and the restoring of the divine life, and that this was for us. *We consider lovingly how Jesus gave His life for us. We do not consider deeply enough how Jesus gives His life to us.* The answer is given in the passage just cited from St. Paul, and this is only one of several similar references. The answer is Baptism, which Christ has made the sacrament of our renewal, our regeneration, our resurrection. Not only does Baptism incorporate us into Christ, but into the purging and vivifying

---

3 Col. 2: 12–16 (Knox translation: Sheed and Ward)

energy of His Passion, Death and Resurrection. It plants the cross within our nature, conforms our soul into the image of the Crucified, and penetrates us at the same time with the victory-grace of the Resurrection. Through it, in Christ, we die to sin, and live to God.

St. Paul gloried in the Cross of Christ. This, Cardinal Newman reminds us, was not the material cross only, on which the Lord dies, nor yet only the Sacrifice of Him who died:

> but it is that Sacrifice coming in power to him who has faith in it, and converting body and soul into a sacrifice. It is the Cross, realized, present, living in him, sealing him, separating him from the world, sanctifying him, afflicting him. Thus the great Apostle clasped it to his heart, though it pierced it through like a sword; held it fast in his hands, though it cut them; reared it aloft, preached it, exulted in it.[4]

And this glory which comes to Christians from the Cross was bestowed by the victory of the Resurrection. The Cross bestowed the immolation of the Victim: but the Resurrection was God's necessary ratification of the Sacrifice. In and through the Resurrection, the Cross has become glorious, *crux fidelis* . . . . . . the jewelled, resplendent Cross *crux gemmata,* of ancient Christian art.

TRANSFIGURATION

The fact that Baptism is the sacrament which incorporates and transfigures us into the Death and Resurrection of our Savior makes it eminently an Easter sacrament. In the present discipline of the Church this association of Easter and Baptism is not readily evident. But there was a time, a long period in the early Christian centuries, when Baptism was normally administered

---

4 Lectures on Justification, p. 178: Longmans, London: 1924.

only in the Easter time, and then only on the terminal feasts of the season, Easter and Pentecost. Even now the liturgical blessings of the baptismal font is reserved to these two occasions (more strictly, to their vigils). In spite, however of the changes which prudence and necessity have brought about in the time and manner of baptismal administration, it is for him who receives it an Easter sacrament, at no matter what time of the year. At that moment, Christ's Death becomes our death to the "old man of sin" in us, and our spiritual affinity to the ancient Adam is destroyed; and Christ's Resurrection becomes our resurrection into the new life of the "second Adam," Who takes us then into affinity with Himself, giving us rebirth into His life through "water and the Holy Spirit," so that we have full right to appropriate to ourselves the exultant cry of St. Paul, "I live, now not I, but Christ liveth in me."

OCCUPATION

This vital occupation of our nature and its operations by the energy of the Christ-life is a fact of primary importance to a proper understanding of Christianity. Our duty is not solely the imitation of Christ. Even more is it cooperation with Christ. We have been made His dwelling, and our faculties have been appropriated by Him as His organs of Redemption, not merely for ourselves alone, but for all those others as well whom divine Providence has appointed to us. Our being is an occupied country, the old diabolic usurper having been cast out by the Risen Conqueror: and now we, His conquest, become conquerors with Him enjoying the privilege of collaboration in His Redeeming Work.

IN THE SHADOW OF THE CROSS

The conquest, however, is far from complete, even inside ourselves. The effects of original sin abide with us, permitted by God so that, in justice, we may feel in our own flesh and spirit some of the agony of Christ, and thus share in His atonement as in His victory. Though Christ has robbed them of their worst sting, they are still not easy to bear, and offer a constant threat of betrayal. Besides these attacks and vexations from within, our warfare is "with princedoms and powers, with those who have mastery of the world in these dark days, with malign influences in an order higher than ours".[5] In the inward struggle, Christians are given many comforting intimations and assurances of victory. But in the outward warfare, there are periods in history — and ours seems to be one of them — when the fighting is grim and the issue dark, times when the Cross is more bloody than glorious, and hope is the only assurance of a victory we shall not live to see. As Pascal said, "Ours is not to see the victory of Truth but to fight in its behalf."

THE ACTION IS THE PASSION

Whether in the personal arena of our own souls or in the catholic arena of the Mystical Body, world-wide, the struggle is Christ's, and His Passion fulfills itself in countless ways as generations come and go. "As long as you did it to one of these least, you did it to me." (Matthew 25:40). "Saul, Saul, why persecutest thou Me?" (Acts of the Apostles 9:4) You and I, and all of us signed with the Cross and christened, made into Christ, by Baptism, must feel the brunt of the Passion, not only when it drives against us personally, but just as much when it is hurled against our brothers who are one with us in Christ's Body. We need constant discipline and reinforcements, each for our own struggle. But seeking them, we should not forget the others, for the Christ in them calls out to the Christ in us.

This is what gives such urgency to Lent before Easter. It is a time of renewal and reenforcement, a season of retreat in which to rally our strength and training. But not for each of us alone, personally: it is the whole Church, the Mystical Body, purifying

---

[5] Ephesians 6: 12 (Knox trans.)

herself by mortification, and strengthening herself by discipline. And in her and with her, it is Christ extending His Passion so that on Easter the power of His Resurrection may be more manifest than ever in her, and in each of us. In the early days of the Church, Lent was the training time of the catechumens for the Baptism on Easter. So is it today for the Church a training time for our baptismal renewal in Christ's Resurrection. If with all our hearts we pray and fast to do the works of Mercy during the Lenten days, our baptismal life will be increased in us on Easter, and the Church will be renewed and strengthened to extend the victory of Christ to new conquests.

It is reported that the Communists are contemptuous of the strength of American Catholicism. The measure in which they are justified in such an evaluation should be for us the measure of the distance we have departed, both singly and corporately, from the Easter power of our Baptism (and its pentecostal strengthening in our Confirmation). It is good for us to have these sinister judges who make emulation to what we fail to accomplish by inspiration. These gibes at Christians are unintended compliments from the Left to the real power of Christianity.

THE ZEAL OF THEIR HOUSE

Communists are notoriously zealous, tireless in their Cause. Their sacrifices for it are enormous, in time, prosperity, energy, and honor. It is ironic that they can be called the modern parallel to the early Christians, in everything except faith and charity. We brand them as scourges of Christianity: a more caustic estimate would call them God's scourges on His Christians. Let's apply the cautery even though it hurts. We have the Risen Christ for our Cause, but theirs is no risen Lord. Lenin is cold in death, and only his corpse can be seen by pilgrims to Moscow. Yet his apostles are truer to him than many of us to our Lord. Not only is the tomb of our Lord empty, but He has made us His dwelling, full of the light and fire of divine life. But most of us are lazy and listless in His Cause, while they, indwelt by nothing bigger than themselves or what this life can furnish, give themselves little rest, day or night, mentally or physically, wherever and whenever the Cause can be advanced.

The hope of the future is not in Marx and Lenin, but in Christ, and therefore not in the Communists, but in the Christians. It is we to whom the word was said, "You are the light of the world," and that light is not our own but what Christ Himself has given to us from His Easter victory. If we are those to whom the world must look if it is to find Christ, the reflection of Him must be clear in us. Through the gifts of His Holy Spirit, we must learn how to walk in Christ and to work in His power. His apostolate is now ours, or rather it is His in us and through us. The power that once went out from Him to heal and to save must now go out from us, or from Him in us. Our zeal in the spiritual and corporal works of mercy must extend His Resurrection in us to the world around us.

To a world that considers Christianity out of date, we must show its present power in our lives. To a world skeptical about life beyond the grave, we must bear witness by ardent faith in the truth of the Risen Lord within us. To the world's despair and obsession with death and destruction, we must bring Christ's divine compassion; to its appalling burden of sin and suffering, His Calvary imprinted in our own lives; to its gross carnality, His sweet purity radiant in us; to its false philosophies, the clarity of His teaching; to its utopian quests, the evidence of His heaven already present within us.

Does all this seem an excessive interpretation of our Christian responsibility? Each of us, of course, will have to discover his own place in the divine plan, by prayer and cooperation with grace. But each in his place, and in his allotted degree, must be magnanimous, heroic, ready for larger enterprise than merely keeping out of mortal sin. Until a far greater number of us, laymen as well as priests and religious, take far more seriously our responsibility of being active witnesses of the Lord's Resurrection in us, Christianity will not get a grip on the world. Easter of 1947 and the years ahead will seem little more than a nostalgic souvenir instead of a contemporary Resurrection.

RESURGENCE

But the Lord Who is with us "all days even to the end" will not have it so. The signs of contemporary Resurrection are unmistakable. We see them in the widespread fidelity to the Eucharist, in the growing appreciation of the Church's sacramental life and of her character as the Mystical Body of Christ, in the development of the retreat movement for the deepening of the spiritual life, in the manifold efforts to solidify Christian family living, and (perhaps most significantly as a fruit of this all-around intensification) in the appearance and perseverance of numerous apostolic lay groups whose dedication and zeal are not put to shame by the Communist apostles: the Christophers, the Catholic Evidence Guilds, the Jocists and their English-speaking associates, the Young Christian Workers, the Legion of Mary, the Ladies of the Grail, the Catholic Worker group with its Houses of Hospitality, the Friendship Houses — for interracial justice and equity — to name the more conspicuous and influential of them.

DEATH IN LIFE

In all these, and in much else besides, the victory of Christ is conquering and going forth to conquer. They radiate intense faith and confidence, love and joy, and they are blessed with boundless energy. Their joy is saved from frivolity by the Cross they willingly bear with them; and their dedication to the Way of the Cross is saved from gloom by the joy of the Risen Savior Whom also they bear with them, as He carries them forward to the works of His apostolate. They are martyrs in the literal sense of "witnesses" to Christ's Resurrection. Those who know them can testify that their enterprise is keyed up to the spirit of apostleship described by St. Paul to his Corinthian converts:

> We have to show great patience, in times of affliction, of need, of difficulty; under the lash, in prison, in the midst of tumult; when we are tired out, sleepless, and fasting. We have to be pure-minded, enlightened, forgiving and gracious to others; we have to rely on the Holy Spirit, on unaffected love, on the truth of our message, on the power of God. To right and left we must be armed with innocence, now honored, now slighted, now traduced, now flattered. They call us deceivers, and we tell the truth; unknown, and we are fully acknowledged; dying men, and see, we live; punished, yes, but not doomed to die; sad men, that rejoice continually; beggars, that bring riches to many; disinherited, and the world is ours.[6]

REV. BENEDICT EHMANN

EPITAPH OF AN EDUCATOR

Under this stone
  Lies Professor Pfyffe,
He knew everything,
  But the purpose of life.

---

6 2 Cor. 6: 4–10 (Knox trans.)

The Size of It

Dear Editors of Integrity:
I am Mr. Big. I have just finished reading the March issue of *Integrity* on work. It impressed me profoundly. Now I want to make a searching examination of conscience. I want to know what God wants of me here and now. And I am resolved to carry out His Will as perfectly as possible.

I am the president and chairman of the board of directors of a Washing Machine Company. I own 60% of the stock in the company and my share is currently valued at $120,000,000. I am married and have seven children, ranging in age from four to eighteen years. I live with my wife and family in my own home in a near-by suburb. It is a large place set on a plot of ground 60 acres in extent. We employ six servants to maintain the house and grounds. I am also supporting my own wife's parents. We have a place in Florida and have been in the habit of spending January and February there.

I started out to give these personal details with the idea of listing my most obvious obligations so that I might have a basis for deciding what would happen if I sold or gave away my entire holdings in the Washing Machine company and started to do the most perfect things, — striving to do, insofar as I could, fully and completely what God wants of me.

But even at this point, before I have begun to consider what will become of the company if I pull out — its 5000 employees, the holders of the other 40% of the stock, and my associates in managing the concern — I can begin to see that so drastic a step will probably be fraught with disaster for my dependents. What to do?

My plant is in a large city. I am tying several thousand people to this unhealthy, urban life to manufacture and sell my product. Maybe it would be better for the women of America not to have washing machines. Perhaps many of those who buy the machines and use them devote the leisure, which machine as contrasted with hand-washing leaves, to sinful pursuits. My conscience has been thoroughly aroused; and I want to do what is right. Am I obliged to study the habits of those who buy my machines and restrict sales to those who use them properly? And just what is proper use? You can see how I am becoming enmeshed in the problem. I am trying to think this thing through objectively and not to bring in petty or irrelevant details....

* * *

Dear Mr. Big,

The first suggestion that comes to my mind is that you liquidate your company, give the money away (say half to our Holy Father for war relief and half to your workers), and spend the rest of your life going from house to house doing family washings gratuitously. In this way you will satisfy your intense longing (the one you have so often expressed in your advertisements) to ease the pain of housewives' wash-days, while at the same time doing penance for having bollixed up the economic system.

I hear you protest. You are too old and too proud to wash clothes... you fear for the future of your employees... after all, women almost have to have washing machines.

Well, all right, I can see anyhow that you would probably not be a good laundress, so we'll settle on that score. Suppose then you try to use the power and wealth you've got together for some good purpose. Suppose you try to right your wrong within the order of washing machines. (It had to be washing machines you make. Only the most calloused brute would deprive a housewife of her washing machine. And I decline to play the role of calloused brute. Nonetheless, be it noted that I think things may of their own accord come to such a pass that nobody will care about washing machines.) Now I am a pessimist, the sort of pessimist who thinks that if you have, say, been married and divorced seven times you are not going to make your peace with God by some simple expedient, such as taking an eighth and yet more charming wife. No, Mr. Big, if you are a man of conscience, you put your Florida estate in jeopardy merely by asking my advice.

Since you insist, here is the relatively painless way out. It ought to reduce you to something like your normal size in easy stages. It may work. Don't mind my gloom.

You make washing machines, Mr. Big. Not for profit now (remember?) but to ease the toil of American housewives. What housewives need washing machines most? The housewives with lots of children and no maids and little money. These should be your customers. They can't buy your machines on time, either. That would only make it harder on them, wouldn't it?

So, Mr. Big, you have to find a way to make washing machines available at $25.00 each or say $35.00. Don't faint. Remember, you don't have to include your salary in the cost, in case it turns out that you are extraneous.

First, I'd like an analysis of your costs. I think you will find (you are the one who should be figuring these things out, not I) that advertising, selling, transportation, distribution, executive salaries, and red tape account for a large part of your costs. No? Well, think up a scheme that will eliminate these major items of expense. It will mean small, local, independent manufacturing units, won't it? Where do you come in? Maybe you could be one of the small, local makers.

Next, I'd like you to put your investor's brains, and your own, to work to see if you can devise a washing machine that could almost be made by a boy scout out of his manual. After all, I've seen washing machines. Nothing could be simpler as to principle. We can dispense with the glamour. And let's experiment with different materials for the body of the machine. Of course this machine won't have to dry, hang up, iron and wear clothes. All it has to do is swish them back and forth and have a wringer attachment.

The Size of It

When you have the machine design perfected, call in all your workers (if the unions still allow you to talk to them). Confess your economic sins, exhort them to do likewise, explain that you are giving the plant to the city for a greenhouse, and tell them that any who want to become owners of small businesses can have your secrets and your training and enough money to move far from Detroit to set up a modest local concern of their own.

I can't carry the details any further, Mr. Big. You can see already that it wouldn't work. Think how the workers would laugh! The truth of the matter is that they are no more compassionate of housewives than you were. It might work if they got converted too, if somebody started the leavening among them. But you are hardly the person to start it, although you might import some Jocists to do the job.

And think of the housewives. They wouldn't like it either. They want a Bendix. They want glamour. And they aren't having lots of babies, partly because they can't have both babies and Bendixes. Your advertising department had a lot to do with making them that way. Now you want to advertise in reverse? Oh no. It doesn't work that way. Advertising is auxiliary to the commercial exploitation of people, in respect of which it pays dividends of its sort. It is no part of the Christian synthesis.

So it all works out the way it should, doesn't it Mr. Big? It ought not to surprise you that the Christian millennium cannot be brought about without Christians, that no system can succeed without a healthy human ingredient.

And don't let me hear of you buying your workers sweet little cottages (all alike) in the outskirts of Detroit. That isn't the answer, and you know it.

Sincerely yours,
MR. LITTLE

INTEGRITY, April 1947

WALL STREET FOREVER

We pledge as long as we shall live,
 It never will be banned:
The very highly manipulative
 Law of Supply and Demand

Road to Reality

IN 1941, I GRADUATED FROM ST. JOHN'S OF Collegeville, Minnesota, after a not altogether uneventful four years. Without fully appreciating it at the time, it was nonetheless there that I got the historical, philosophical and theological background which helped me eventually to travel the road to reality.

While at St. John's, I became acquainted with the Social Institute, which did much work with farmers. I met there the men interested in the Rural Life Movement: Fathers Dom Virgil Michel and Martin Schriber, both of the Benedictine Order; Monsignor Luigi Ligutti; Professor Emerson Hynes and others. I read there the writings of Eric Gill, Peter Maurin and others who pointed a way from the mess we are now in. From these men I learned that "in a Christian society, there is no kind of physical labor which is either derogatory to human nature or incapable of being sanctified." I learned that "It is good that a man should glory in his own handiwork." From them I learned that labor was the work of slaves before Christianity made itself felt, and that in this new pagan era, labor was again losing its dignity. Unfortunately, I acquired most of this knowledge academically. I stored it in an academic corner of my mind and proceeded to act on quite other principles.

When I left college in 1941, I had the usual idea of those who have a college diploma, from C.C.N.Y. TO U.C.L.A., namely to earn my living in some sort of dignified white collar or professional work. Ed Willock's jingle would apply to many of the country's graduates of that fateful year:

My daddy was a laborer,
And good Lord so were you,
But now that I have my degree
Must I get dirty too?

INTEGRITY, April 1947

In the course of this article we shall see whether I did or not. I had a long road to travel but it was worth the trip for the knowledge it gave me. I started in behind the desk of a fine New York hotel, and inside of less than a year, I was acting night manager. I also doubled my salary in that time but never really felt a great deal of satisfaction in my work, even when I figured out a system of doing four hours work in about an hour and a half.

While working there, I turned to carpentry, but only to fill a temporary need. I built a solid bookcase, designing it, sawing the wood, putting it together, sanding it and painting it myself. I "gloried in my own handiwork" and felt a sense of accomplishment that office work did not give me, and never would give me.

In my groping for work that really satisfied me, I got a personnel job, and as office jobs go, it was excellent. I had the run of the office, and could come and go almost as I pleased. They gave me a temporary feeling of importance by seeing that I had a personal expense account, a private dictaphone, and the privilege of ordering any and all supplies the office needed. Another thing they let me do — the *ne plus ultra* of office work — they let me sign the president of the company's signature on letters that I answered for him even though I had never met the man. Such is the impersonalism of office work all too often, doing work for people you never meet, doing part of a job that you never see completed. My job by contemporary standards was supposed to satisfy, especially when, only on my saying so, ship captains and engineers were signed on for world-wide trips. However, I knew a good office boy could do the job I was doing. Having arranged the office work completely to my superior's satisfaction, and seemingly on the way to a career, all were flabbergasted when I told them I was leaving. But leave I did, and I never did meet the president whose name I signed, nor did I see him.

I tried teaching, but soon found my error in thinking it was for me. In my opinion, I had tried the run of white collar and professional jobs, and had jobs which most people really envy, but I could not work up a sustained enthusiasm over any of them.

Slightly in desperation, I enrolled at Farmingdale Agricultural Institute on Long Island. I entered in the summer when the students do all the work under the supervision of instructors, the work on two farms totaling about one thousand acres.

The work at the Institute is so arranged that each student becomes acquainted with every aspect of farming, no matter which particular field of agriculture he may specialize in. Naturally, those taking a special course get more intensive instruction and work in it, but all get the same fundamentals in all branches of field work and farm practice. The work begins as early as five A.M. depending on one's chore, and ends about five-thirty P.M. Each student is assigned to some barn work — poultry, dairy, hogs, horses etc. And does chores in connection with them both morning and night, with the time between taken up with other farm operations. The instructors, trained in teaching city boys to become farmers, are patient and considerate, and do their utmost to help those who try to do their best.

My first barn work was with pigs, and my first day on the job I had to help a sow deliver a litter of fifteen. I considered this something of a sign. The summer followed with my doing every conceivable type of farm operation — all new to me — but second nature to any farmer's son.

My office hands which had not gotten beyond lifting a typewriter or adding machine now lifted dairy bags to load feed bins. I harnessed horses, horses that towered over me; and I felt like a Roman charioteer driving them. I sweltered while I cleaned out the bottom of a silo, and I got soaked from head to foot while filling it with ensilage. My office pallor changed to a ruddy hue, and my hair got bleached by the sun. I could sing aloud at my work, as was the custom when labor was the work of love, and my voice improved in the fresh air. I developed callouses on my hands, and I was as proud of them as a boy wearing long pants for the first time.

I learned how to milk a cow and developed my hands by milking more of them. The first two weeks of milking I soaked my hands in warm water both morning and night, but I got over the soreness. The great day came when I milked out six heavy producing cows in the time allotted me, thereby passing my milking test, a requisite for graduation.

I loaded corn on wagons till I thought my back would snap, and then loaded more corn on more wagons. I weeded the vegetable garden and picked beans by the basketful.

I worked on the mowing machine, the thrasher and the hay baler.

I worked thinning apple trees, picking peaches, pears, berries.

All this work, since it was close to nature, and varied, was befitting a man. I gloried in my own handiwork. Adam gloried in the same type of work, the first occupation in history.

The variety was something that office work lacked. And there was a sense of accomplishment at seeing a silo filled, a field mowed, a crop harvested or even a barn cleaned or a cow milked.

I found that this type of work appealed to me. It gave me a chance to use my stocky body designed by nature for manual and physical work. In using it for the work for which it was obviously designed, I was happy. I saw the complete work of my hands, the complete cycle of work and life; from taking a cow to be bred to delivering the calf, from planting to harvesting. I knew what I was doing, and why I was doing it, and that it was completely honorable. There was in the work that completeness which makes a whole man, which helps to integrate a man. There was in it that natural quality which is like nature itself, appealing to the natural normal average man. I might add too that I knew everybody with whom I was working, or for whom I was working, without the anonymity of the personnel worker, and they had the humility and helpfulness about them which comes with close contact with the soil, and from a recognition of true values.

There was a certain creativeness in the work, actually a making of new things. It gave me a chance to impress my own person into my work, to put the stamp of my own nature on it. Man, by nature resembling God, is creative and needs to see that extension of his personality which is so abundantly seen in farm and craft work.

At the end of the long summer days, I could sleep the sleep of the just . . . the just exhausted. I had used every muscle in my hands, my arms, my back, my legs. My sleep was sound. My tiredness was not the tiredness of boredom which comes from office work with its repetition of work which because of its limitations is often almost meaningless and disintegrates people. My whole being was used. I was close to nature.

The summer went by and fall registration was at hand. I registered for general farming, but found my true forte in the farm shop course when it came to working with wood, iron, and leather. I found I was first in my class in iron work and second in woodwork and saw this was even more appealing than general farming, so I decided to place more stress on shop work. Actually no matter which of the courses you specialize in, you still wind up with a general knowledge of farming, more than enough to run a subsistence farm, because the work is so planned that all get a general, generous minimum. The planning and detailed work behind this on the part of all the faculty, to achieve such a result, is the work of genius.

After woodwork and leatherwork, we went to blacksmithing, welding, concrete work, and the use of dynamite, again with practical work in all branches covered. Along with this work, all have the usual farm chores, such as milking, and feeding hogs and chickens.

My farm schooling was interrupted to come to my sister's farm, where my background of schooling proved to be invaluable. We raise and butcher our own beef (we had some of it today for supper), our own chickens (we killed one for tomorrow's lunch, by way of variety), our own ducks and a few turkeys (we ate one for Thanksgiving), and can get an occasional deer from our woodlot, during hunting season.

Among the wonderful things about farm life is the outlet it offers for so many of man's talents: carpentry, plumbing, husbandry, and the joy in his own handiwork. Another and very important thing is that on a well-run farm, in the winter a farmer has many days in which he can further develop himself. Almost every evening on the farm, when supper is over and the chores are done, a person can pursue whatever hobby or craft interests him — from wood carving or painting to playing the violin. Or the farmer can use the evening for social, mental or spiritual development. This is not so true of city life with its hectic pace. But farm life is especially leisurely in the winter, and seems to be designed so by nature for the rest and recreation of man after the hard work of the other three seasons.

One of the most wise, most truly wise and cultured men I know, is our neighbor here who spends much of his time after his light winter work is done, reading. This shows in his every word, and is proof enough to anybody who has met him that life in the country can be truly cultured and dignified.

In the winter, the peace and quiet of the farm is exceedingly conducive to study, or anything which will improve man's mind or soul. One has the room in the country to do the things one has in mind, because country life is not so cramped as it ordinarily is in the city.

My one regret about the road I had to travel is this. I know that after the fall of the Roman Empire Europe went into a stage of darkness in which the youthful Catholic religion, then known as Christianity, converted Europe. The Church did it by the "Cross and the Plow." It set up its centers, its monasteries, all over Europe and civilized the barbaric tribes by religion, and the teaching of farming as a way of stable, normal life. Now my regret is this. The marvelous Catholic Church, with its armies of geniuses in every field from theology to biology, from philosophy to animal husbandry, does not seem to be fully aware of its power, and its history. The need now, as in the dark ages, is for monasteries to convert the Street Arabs and to show them the real way out of industrialism, not only by showing the contemporary errors in thought, but by teaching blacksmithing along with theology, animal husbandry along with history, field crops with foreign languages, butchering along with economics, and carpentry along with the history of social thought. All of these subjects would make a great deal of sense in the college course, which would train men for life in the country on the ideal type of farm, a subsistence farm; and give them skill in a craft, which could be followed along with farming. This was the custom years ago when farming was a way of life and the craft presented that natural diversity in labor which all men unconsciously look for. Until that day comes when there is less emphasis on business courses in Catholic colleges, the few who will find their way to freedom will have a hard road to travel.

JAMES P. EGAN
Crestmont Farm
Susquehanna, Pa.

THE BIRTH OF THE BLUES

Envy and Greed were talking one day,
   Said Greed to his spurious neighbor,
"I know a game that we two can play,
   I will be Capital, you can be Labor!"

The Psychology of Anti-Semitism

IF THERE IS ONE FORM OF MENTAL HEALTH that really needs a searching analysis from the Catholic viewpoint, it is this question of anti-semitism.

It isn't an easy subject to analyze.

Some years ago, Milton Meyer of *the Saturday Evening Post* wrote an article on the Jews which raised a hullabaloo. There was even a shakeup in the editorial department over the article.

Yet all that Meyer said was that Jews in many cases were not living up to their own ethical and religious traditions, something which could equally be said of Catholics.

For a Catholic to write on anti-semitism and be honest, it is of no use to say merely nice things, as for instance that we must love Jews because they are our brothers, children of the same God, our Father.

The Jews are accused of being money-mad, seekers after the goods of this world, makers of bad movies, creators of pornographic literature, Freudians, Marxists and upholders of science divorced from religion, and it is quite true that all too many Jews are in different types of evil like these; still it would be unkind and unfair to claim that these are Jewish monopolies.

The Jews have no monopoly on the seven deadly sins.

The task for Christians who have a better ethic is to show them the true way and not berate them for going after false gods.

But it is of that peculiar hatred of Jews and continual blaming them for all and sundry evils that we would like to write. It becomes a sort of obsession with so many Catholics, and leads to all forms of uncharitableness.

It so often happens that the materialistic Catholic is the chief offender in this business.

We have often pondered on this fact and have wondered if the real cause is not that Christians who seek after the same things of this world as the Jews, find themselves outstripped by minds which are better, and a consequent envy is born.

It isn't an easy subject nor can it be over-simplified but there are a few angles concerning this emphasis on materialism which can clarify the subject somewhat, we believe.

THE THREE MODERN HERESIES

The three great heresies of today, Marxism, Freudianism and "Pure Scientism," can be called the three great temptations of Christ in modern form, the temptation of the world, the flesh and the devil.

It is no small point that Jews so often go towards these heresies and fail to see the much greater and deeper truths of Catholicism. Probably the answer is that Catholics do not know their stuff and haven't given enough thought to the implications of their own religion and consequently are unable to enlighten the very acute Jewish mind.

When Christians are intent merely on more money and power and wealth, they certainly fail to enlighten the Jews on the superiority of Christianity. If, however, there was a rebirth of the early Christian spirit of the counsels, Jews might come to say of the Christians "see how they love one another" and might be tempted to join Catholicism.

There is a marvelous unity about everything studied in the light of Catholic theology and the present mental-breakdown epidemic, anti-semitism, and a too eager grasping after the things of this life are all closely associated.

Some years ago in a series of articles on mental health we put forth the suggestion that maybe a great deal of this ill health came from a disregard of the three evangelical counsels, voluntary poverty, chastity and obedience.

We said it was noticeable that men who went after money and power so often committed suicide not only after they lost their fortunes but even when they still had them. In one case, they seemed to think that life had no more in it to make it worth living and in the other case they had exhausted their imaginations in trying to buy happiness, and had failed to grasp the fact that happiness rests alone in seeking God and that we must come to God through Christ, who said that the poor are the blessed ones.

THE WORLD, MARXISM, AND VOLUNTARY POVERTY

We said you could call this temptation of money and power the temptation of the world and that it had a curious relationship to Marxism which offers us the material splendours of the world if we only would bow down and adore its anti-God tenents.

The three words that sum up so much of modern day thinking are "security," "inhibitions" and "frustration." "Security" seems to be the over-emphasis on faith in material things and a very definite falling away in belief in a personal Providence Who watches over the sparrows and the lilies and Who loves man much more than these.

"Inhibition" and 'frustration" are related to the questions of sex and obedience.

St. Thomas speaking of money says that it is not real wealth, for you can want it to infinity and for a finite mind to want a finite thing to infinity is an irrational act. That is smart thinking. A Boston woman, working in the financial district, made a similar observation once to us. She said that money had a mystical quality about it. The more you had of it the more you wanted of it. We have watched miners going into the Arctic from Edmonton, Alberta, cutting themselves off from civilization for a year at a time just to get gold and suffering indescribable hardships in the process. Once a year they would come back to Edmonton and blow their money in a grand drunk. Then back to the north country.

Cobalt Jim McDonald, who discovered the famous cobalt, Ontario gold mine, one of the largest gold producers in the world, once told us that the companies in northern Ontario had to remove the gold bricks from the sight of the workmen in the smelteries because when the gold was left around, the men would stand watching it in a spell all day and would do little or no work. It evidently spelt dreams for them.

"Clean mad for the muck called gold," Robert Service once wrote of the Arctic gold seekers.

THE FLESH, FREUDIANISM AND CHASTITY

The mental breakdowns from an overindulgence in drink and sex are a sure testimony to failure to practice the spirit of chastity.

The peculiar perversity of so much Freudian reasoning is this obsession with sex as being the root cause of people's troubles.

Catholic ascetical theology has a far more intelligent understanding of the question of sex than the Freudians will ever dream of having.

St. Paul says that the union of a man and wife in lawful marriage is a symbol of the union between Christ and his Church. If we ever stop to meditate on that statement, we shall have entered into one of the most magnificent aspects of our theology. We shall learn what is the depth of love and its magnificent meaning. We shall begin to comprehend the sacrifices of Christ on the Cross. We shall begin to understand the pain Christ suffered from love in the Garden of Gethsemane . . . The Canticle of Canticles will open up with wonderful new vistas of thought.

The Freudians talk of the return to the womb as a fundamental drive of human beings and they are fond of the phrase "Oedipus complex," which can better be translated into "Mamma's boy." Catholics shouldn't fear these seemingly horrendous statements for they know that in the womb of Mary, the elect are born in a marvelous spiritual union with Christ who was constituted head of His Mystical Body in that marvelous womb.

And every true Catholic is a "Mamma's boy." Only Mamma is the greatest Mother of all, the Mother of God, Queen of the Angels, our "tainted nature's solitary boast."

THE DEVIL, "PURE SCIENTISM," AND OBEDIENCE

The third word "frustration" today reveals a subtler temptation. Everyone is talking about being frustrated, which boils down to this, that people are not having their own way. Consequently they are unhappy. They forget that God's ways are not their ways and God's thoughts are not their thoughts and that God knows what is best for all and draws us firmly by His grace to do His will when we have good will.

The Holy Father in his encyclical on the Mystical Body speaks of Christ gently bending the wills of His followers to do His will. It is struggling against God's will that really makes us unhappy. And perhaps because the Jews are nearer to God in the sense that they are God's chosen people, this struggle is the keener and more painful with them. A proud people don't like to bend the neck. That is where the Blessed Virgin must come in with her gift of humility or of humiliation to bring them to the light.

"He hath taken the mighty down from their seat and hath exalted the humble," she said in the Magnificat and she is the treasury of God's graces, who gives out the necessary spiritual aids.

The very exceptional mental gifts of the Jews may be their stumbling block in coming to the truths of faith. Their temptation can be the special and third temptation, that of the Devil. St. Thomas says that the purpose of obedience is to offset the devil who is an angelic intellect and can easily delude a merely human intellect.

The idea of a "pure science" divorced from God is a dream of the irreligious scientists today. They boast of their humility even and they accuse the Catholics of being proud because they are dogmatic, claiming to know divine things with certainty. Why, we only claim to know a few things, these scientists say, and we use our scientific method carefully to ascertain these things. This is the final surrender to pride.

From the visible things of the universe, our minds should rise naturally to the invisible as St. Paul says but pride has so disordered the thinking of these scientists that they are actually being fooled by the angel of darkness posing as an angel of light.

St. John of the Cross tells us that we shouldn't go to fortune tellers for fear the devil may use the fortune teller to predict purely natural events, such as happenings dependent merely on natural circumstances. Thus we could easily be deceived into believing in the superior lights of the fortune teller and would be drawn into error by the spirit whose sole aim is that we refuse to do God's will and so fail to get to Heaven.

The fool has said in his heart there is no God and atheism is a form of insanity.

A false mysticism and scrupulosity can also be forms of mental ill health and the only answer here is right mysticism, guided by good spiritual directors and obedience to these directors. Then those marvelous lights if they are real lights move under the power of the keys of Peter and we are protected against the devil who shall never prevail against these keys.

If the Jewish mind is going after the three false ways of life, of Marxism, Freudianism and "pure science", then the Christian answer is not to berate them but to show them the evil of those philosophies and their shortcomings.

RE-DIRECTING ANTI-SEMITISM

If the Christian is really inspired with supernatural charity and has the love of God and the Blessed Virgin in him, he will have the mind of Christ and will be seeking the conversion of the Jews and he will meditate on the problems of anti-semitism and try to turn that hate into an effective love. Hate is but perverted love. This anti-semitic drive can be changed into a tremendous zeal for the conversion of the Jews if rightly understood.

It is the constant tradition of the Catholic Church that many of the Jews will come to the true faith at the end of the world. In this faith, the Jews will find a meaning for Purim that they never dreamed of in their own study of the Old Testament. They will realize the deep meaning of the stories about Abel and Abraham and Melchisedech and Esther and David and Solomon.

They will come to realize that the sixty or more prophecies regarding the Messias have been fulfilled in Christ and that they have but to turn to His life to find the truth.

We Christians are spiritually Semites, as Pope Pius XI once said, and we have Abraham for our father too as have the Jews. When Christ gave up the ghost on the Cross and the veil of the Temple was rent, the Old Law had passed away and the new reign of Christ in His Mystical Body had begun.

The nurturing of anti-semitism by any Catholic is then an evil of the greatest kind, one that might well be called diabolical for if there is one thing the devil wants it is to frustrate the Divine plan which is that all men may be saved. More than this, an anti-semitic Catholic is giving away a very clear insight into his own wrong motives.

Thackeray once wrote an essay about Dean Swift and a very sharp critic said that it didn't tell you much about Swift but it did tell you an awful lot about Thackeray. Similarly, with anti-semitism in a Catholic. It doesn't tell you much about the Jews and their mysterious mission in this life but it does only too well show forth the limitations of the Catholic harboring these feelings.

ARTHUR SHEEHAN
New York City

THE DECEIVED

"This is not love," they said, "that lays down life
Alone on Calvary's hill; that hangs apart
With Arms outstretched, entwined about a Tree of Death,
With broken feet and sorrow-stricken Heart.
This is not love but blindness."

"This is not God," they cried, "Whose power is bound
Within the yoke of wood, the chain of nails,
Whose strength is fastened firm upon a Cross,
Whose kingly might is gone, Whose courage fails.
He is not God but weakness."

"This is not life," they mocked, "that bows Its Head
And yields — the Conquered and the Crucified,
The Christ Who'd claimed the very keys to life
But found this door well locked, for He has died.
This is not life but darkness."

"He is no Friend," they scoffed, "Whose idle boasts
Of triumph and of glory cannot show
His death less real, His shame less true to us
Who stand deceived and shaken, here below.
He is no Friend but coldness."

"Not love nor power nor life nor Friend," they said,
Yet little knew they spoke of Him, the leav'n
Of truth and peace whose death had rent the veil
Of sin and opened forth a living heav'n.
He was their God of fullness.

GERARD SEDLEY

A Retreat to Principle

ANARCHISTS, I FIND, ARE NOT WELL REPRE-sented among my intimate friends. The reader may say now, and even more likely may say it later, that the disadvantage is not to the anarchist, and he may say it quite rightly, for all I know. Still, the deplorable fact remains, and I may consequently be doing the anarchists an injustice when I assert, purely from hearsay, that, at least when they are working hard at their anarchy, they are not likely to be universally friendly or even lovable creatures. However, the one anarchist I know, I like. He is the one we see in the cartoons, with Einstein hair, a beard grown out of all credibility, and with bombs fairly dripping from his shabby pockets. The last time I saw him, he was deep in some underworld burrow, surrounded by thousands of demonstration posters all reading "Down with —!" followed by a long dash, and on one he was hurriedly filling in the name of something or of somebody.

Now I like this anarchist because, whatever be his shortcomings in aught else, he has a nice sense of proportion. After all, what a person is against is a relatively negligible matter, altogether secondary, and may be constantly changing in emphasis. What one is against depends upon the real thing that matters, what he is for. Accordingly as the positive is understood, the negative will develop, and hence there is nothing out of the way in having on hand at all times a certain amount of these posters, ready to be filled in as occasion warrants.

And I wonder if we have always preserved due proportion in the things that we are for and against. Take for instance our battle against communism, or take what we refer to vaguely as "christianizing the social order." The Church's war on communism is an inevitable and holy thing, but far too many of us, without knowing precisely what we are for that communism opposes, and why the Church has filled in a blank with communism's name, have seized a sign ready-marked "Down with communism!" and have rushed out to fight a purely negative war. And "christianizing the social order" may very easily mean nothing at all. Christianity, Michael de la Bedoyere reminds us, does not entail in itself a ready-drawn blueprint to solve the social problem, or any problem, for that matter. It does provide a set of working principles from which Christian men can draw their own blueprint. If "christianizing the social order" is to mean anything at all, it must embrace the definite and specific social deductions from Christianity upon which the Christian social order is to be shaped. The conversion of the world overnight would not of itself bring an end to the world's social and economic and racial injustices. Bishop Sheil said recently, quoting Cardinal Saliege, that it is because we Catholics do not know the Church's social doctrine "that the causes which brought communism into existence have not disappeared, and for this condition, Catholics bear heavy responsibility."

Now, as we are coming more and more to discover, the Church does have certain definite and specific social deductions from Christianity which form the positive basis for her attack on, among others, communism. The Church aims at nothing less than what was known, before secularism put an end to that sort of thing, as Christian civilization. The social encyclicals have stimulated much vigorous thought along these lines, and many of the old labels and slogans formerly accepted uncritically have been re-examined in the light of almost forgotten principles, and it has come to pass that many of them have been found wanting. Today, it seems hardly credible to us that *Rerum Novarum* could have been greeted by sincere Catholic conservatives as merely a confirmation of the existing order. It would be scarcely possible for us to interpret in the same fashion such words as the following of the present Holy Father (Pius XII):

The Church has condemned the various systems of Marxist socialism, and she condemns them still today, for it is her permanent duty and right to save men from currents of thought and from influences which jeopardize their eternal salvation. But the Church cannot fail to know and to perceive that the worker, in his efforts to improve his condition, finds himself confronted by a system which, far from being conformable with nature, is contrary to the order established by God and to the purpose which He has assigned to earthly goods. The methods used may have been and may still be, wrong, dangerous, and deserving of condemnation; but no one, least of all a priest or a Christian, can possibly remain deaf to the cry that rises out of the depths, calling for justice and for a spirit of brotherhood in a world which a just God has made.

Clearly the social pronouncements of the Popes converge to the establishment of a system which will not be unconformable with nature and contrary to the order established by God and to the purpose which He has assigned to earthly goods. That it is for the Church to take the lead in forming such an order is a conclusion from what we shall consider as the first principle which the pope lays down for the Christian civilization. I have arbitrarily expressed the Pope's social doctrine in four principles, without presuming to codify this doctrine, and intending nothing more than to hit upon a convenient way of dealing with the subject. The first principle is this: *that the whole social question is primarily a spiritual affair.* In the same message from which I quoted above (Christmas, 1942), the Pope interprets the Christian obligation for the salvation of mankind in terms of the re-ordering of society:

A Retreat to Principle

Only in one way can we hope for salvation, renewal, and true progress, and that is through the return of numerous and influential sections of mankind to a true conception of society, a return which will require an extraordinary grace of God and firm and self-sacrificing resolution on the part of men of good will and far-sighted vision.

We shall return to this first principle, which is paramount, at the end of this article. If it is recognized from the outset, however, we may be spared the noisy protest of the twentieth-century realist, whose both feet are on the ground, who will invariably give a materialist interpretation to the Pope's words, and who will, therefore, invariably miss the whole point. The twentieth-century realist can see in the papal condemnation of machine civilization run wild, only reaction and Luddism. And he loftily asks if we propose to jettison technical progress and return to outmoded methods of production, or, in the classical phrase, to go back to the Middle Ages.

The answer to the realist is that we do not know the answer. This is a question which deals with men's hearts and minds. A method of economy is not a transcendent item, but is a product of the human mind and will. The technical progress that did or did not exist in the Middle Ages is irrelevant. The only relevance that the Middle Ages themselves have is in the fact, as Pius XI put it, that at that time

> there existed a social order which, though by no means perfect in every respect, corresponded nevertheless in a certain measure to right reason according to the needs and conditions of the times. That this order has long since perished is not due to the fact that it was incapable of development and adaptation

to changing needs and circumstances, but rather to
the wrong-doing of men. (*Quadragesimo Anno*)

If we could restore the atmosphere of the Middle Ages, the
atmosphere of thought and of moral judgment, the methods
of business would take care of themselves. The Pope is not an
economist, and his sole interest in economic technique is to lay
down those certain conditions which we must obtain if we are to
bring back that necessary atmosphere in which a sane order could
thrive (and which we shall consider as principles two, three, and
four). And surely, if to save our souls we need to restore some one
or other simpler habit of life (which means that we would have
to begin to see in technical progress something indifferent, determinable to good or evil, and not necessarily and always good),
then, to save our souls we would, in a sane order, restore it.

Thus, when the existing order is criticized, the immediate
inference should not be an advocacy of surgical operations without anaesthesia or that the plumbing be ripped from our homes,
or even, to a world that is rapidly going out, that it go by horse
and buggy. It is a question of hearts and minds, rather, and the
twentieth-century realist is cousin germane to the racial realist
who resents anyone poking about in the institution of Jim Crow
or suggesting some injustice might be involved in the accompanying murder and pillage, since such business can only lead
to negroes marrying our sisters. The Pope does lay down this
general principle:

> Even technical progress should not prevail over the
> general good, but should rather be directed and subordinated to it.

It would be impossible to say just what might be the fate of
the latest atom-smasher, or even of last year's model, if men began
to subject them to moral judgments instead of accepting them as

the inevitable advance of science. A writer recently in *The Weekly Review* developed very well the principle enunciated above:

> The difference between us and our contemporaries is not a material one, it is essentially a spiritual one... Their advocacy (of a dominating machine economy) is based not on reason, but on mysticism. Their attitude is 'We cannot do without the machine'... We are not prejudiced machine breakers; but neither are we mystic machine worshippers. What we are concerned about is the menace to freedom from the concentration of economic power. We do not believe that the machine was the origin of that concentration. In fact we hold that it might be possible to use the machine for the distribution of economic power. But if any machine cannot be used without concentrating economic power, then we ask what advantages its use will bring us which will outweigh the menace to freedom. If the answer is not satisfactory, then we will keep that particular machine in a museum and endow a few old scientists to take it to pieces and put it together again at intervals. At any rate, we resolutely refuse to say: 'We cannot do without the machine.' That betokens the loss of a free mind.

The second principle for the restoration of the Christian order is *the institution (perhaps it would be better to say re-institution) of private property.* The correlative to this is that at present property is ill distributed. Of the institution of private property is spun the whole fabric of the better society; it is the tone of that society, the atmosphere in which the new order must breathe. The Church's attitude towards private property has been stated best of all by Leo XIII in *Rerum Novarum:*

The law should favor ownership, and its policy should be to induce as many as possible of the people to become owners. Many excellent results will follow from this; first of all, property will certainly become more equitably divided. For the result of civil change and revolution has been to divide society into two widely differing castes. On the one side there is the party which holds power because it holds wealth; which has in its grasp the whole of labor and trade; which manipulates for its own benefit and its own purposes all the sources of supply, and which is even represented in the councils of the State itself. On the other side there is the needy and powerless multitude, sick and sore in spirit and ever ready for disturbance. If working people can be encouraged to look forward to obtaining a share in the land, the consequences will be that the gulf between vast wealth and sheer poverty will be bridged over, and the respective classes will be brought nearer to one another. A further consequence will result in the greater abundance of the fruits of the earth.

The old Christian order of the past, and final destruction of which order Cobbett rightly traced back to the land spoliation of the Reformation, was founded upon the institution of private property. Private property was the guarantee of personal freedom, the ground in which grew personal responsibility. It was that modicum of the world's goods which St. Thomas lays down as necessary if a man is to practise virtue. It was the great leveller, which left no man altogether at the mercy of another, or of a group, or of the state. And it was the destruction of this institution and all that it connoted that depersonalized and mechanized society, and that has thrown us upon the horns of the dilemma of socialism and industrial capitalism.

The fundamental and Christian nature of private property has been developed exhaustively in the writings and the activity of all those who have formed the various communal farms and other land movements, the groups advocating the small shop and small businesses, the private craftsman and the small farm. The whole philosophy of ownership was perhaps never better stated than in Chesterton's *The Outline of Sanity*.

The third principle is a restriction, or rather, an amplification of the second. It is clear that by the concept of private property the Holy Father does not envisage merely, in the case of the worker, the wage contract, however just and equitable. He says, in fact:

> The dignity of the human person normally demands the right to the use of earthly goods as the natural foundation for a livelihood; and to that right corresponds the fundamental obligation to grant private property, as far as possible, to all. The positive laws regulating private property may change and may grant a more or less restricted use of it, but if such legal provisions are to contribute to the peaceful state of the community, they must not prevent the worker, who is or will be the father of a family, from being condemned to an economic dependence or slavery irreconcilable with his rights as a person.
>
> The dignity of labor demands, not only a just wage, adequate to the needs of the worker and his family, but also the maintenance and development of a social order which will render possible and secure a portion of private property, however modest, for all sections of the community.

This is plainly in accord with the view of society taken as the ideal by Mr. Belloc, and thus defined:

a society in which property is well distributed and so large a proportion as to determine the general tone of society.

From this, it is a mere deduction to the fourth principle: *property must be redivided.* In his speech on the anniversary of the outbreak of the war, in 1944, the Pope called for the "setting up of an economic and social order more in keeping with the eternal law of God and with the dignity of man." And this, he said, "appears to every follower of Christ not only as a step forward along the path of earthly progress but also as the fulfilment of a moral obligation."

Return of property to the many is the way out of this system in which there is an

> excessive concentration of economic goods which, often hidden under anonymous titles, are successfully withdrawn from contributing as they should to the social order, and which face the worker with the virtual impossibility of effectively acquiring private property of his own.
>
> The social and economic policy of the future, the controlling power of the State, of local bodies, of professional institutions, cannot permanently secure their ends, perfect a genuine productivity of social life, and normal return on national economy, except by thus fixing and safeguarding the vital functions of private property in its personal and social values... The State may, in the public interest, intervene by regulating its use or, even, if it cannot equitably meet the situation in any other way, by decreeing the expropriation of property, giving a suitable indemnity. For the same purpose, small and medium holdings in agriculture, in the

arts and trades, in commerce and industry, should be guaranteed and promoted, co-operative unions should ensure for them the advantages of big business. Where big business even today shows itself more productive there should be given the possibility of tempering the labor contract with a contract of co-ownership.

In Mr. Belloc's *The Restoration of Property*, these principles are extensively elaborated to show the process by which this redistribution might take place, through prohibitive taxation and subsidy, until such time as the new social order would be able to function.

Legislation such as that advocated by the Holy Father would be necessary in the creation and preservation of the mental change which is necessary for the Christian society. Where that mental change has been effected, there is no validity to the argument frequently urged, that redistributed property would quickly revert to the hands of a few. Where the proper mind exists, where the social implications of property have been grasped, Chesterton advised land speculators to try to make no corners, as for example in a Spanish village. The objection overlooks the fact upon which the Christian social doctrine is premised, that property is natural to man, that the present reversion of property into the hands of a few is the result not of natural development, but an organized conspiracy. Where the proper mind existed, monopolies and trusts would be recognized for what they are, and in the well-ordered society they would be punished as any other collusion against the common good.

It is upon the first principle that the proposed Christian order must stand or fall. The other three are ancillary, to the extent that they are conditions for the enacting of the first, to the extent that they derive from the first their meaning. Such a system as is considered by the Pope will stand, when the minds of men have been weaned from material secularism, when we have discarded what it called in the Gospel our *pleonexia*, the desire for corruptible goods, and have recognized once more the social significance of property. When society has been given a purpose in life, when the past and the future is given a share in our planning, and when men decide to retreat to principle, then the work will be done.

Such a system once functioned, at least to a great extent. Such a system can still function, as Ireland testifies. There are many reasons, however, naturally speaking, for believing that such a system might not again be generally accepted throughout the world. When Belloc first wrote of the servile state, now a generation ago, he expressed the fear that men had lost the appetite for real property and all therein entailed. He asserted then, what would be even truer today, that it would border on futility to offer a life of freedom with responsibility to the wage slave of our society, tied fast to state and to employer, but with an assured income and social security. The meaning of property, the meaning of labor, the aim of living, these are items buried in the past. As Christopher Dawson tells us, it is in the very nature of the impersonal, mechanized order that it should have dehumanized those caught up in its toils. And the Holy Father has spoken of the natural probability against any change, in discussing the predominant trend of today's thought, found in

> an agglomeration of huge populations in cities and in the districts dominated by industry and trade, an agglomeration that is accompanied by the complete uprooting of the masses who have lost their standards of life, home, work, love, and hatred. By this new conception of thought and life, all ideas of social life have been impregnated with a purely mechanical character.

So, we are brought back to what the Holy Father said in the beginning, that this restoration "will require an extraordinary grace of God and firm and self-sacrificing resolution on the part of men of good will and far-sighted vision." It will require a revolution where all revolution must ultimately be waged, in men's minds.

Because there is every reason for saying we cannot succeed, there is a possibility that we may. We wander now in the penumbra of total war and a precarious peace dominated by the total state; and these are the two supreme achievements of our mechanistic age, the age that was to have ushered in Jerusalem. Blake's sword has long since turned to rust, the sword that was not to sleep in his hand till he had built Jerusalem. Let it lie. I rather think we should not care for Blake's Jerusalem, and, at all events, Jerusalem is not to be had: it is not for this world. What is for this world, which has been so long denied this world, shall return to this world, if we hope aright. And that shall come to pass when the Church militant stretches forth its temporal arm in all its vigor to grasp the sword of the Spirit.

Dies venit, dies tua
In qua reflorent omnia.

BRUCE VAWTER, C.M.

AMERICANA

Under a spreading chestnut tree,
  The village smithy stood.
The site was bought by the A&P,
  And proved to be very good.

Man's Providence

A RECENTLY PUBLISHED BOOK ON THE Metropolitan Life Insurance Company[1] provides an excellent opportunity to examine in detail the insurance phenomenon.

As insurance is one of the institutions which industrial capitalism indirectly brought into being it needs viewing in the floodlight of Christian teaching. When men strayed off the Christian center after the Reformation, things didn't work so well. They declined to retrace their steps. Instead they invented new, makeshift arrangements to cover up their errors. Eventually the makeshift arrangements occasioned new disorders. This is the familiar pattern of our unrepentant society. Insurance is one of the makeshift arrangements. Let us examine it. The Metropolitan is a splendid specimen; not because it is a bad company, but because it is such a good company. We are not looking for accidental chicanery, but for structural defects.

In our society Big Business is playing Santa Claus, Psychiatry is playing Priest, but Insurance is playing God.

THE MET

The Metropolitan Life is the largest insurance company in the world. It represents the largest concentration of private money (over 7½ billion dollars) in the world. Hence its omnipotence.

It began business along with other pioneer life insurance companies in the middle of the last century, as a frankly commercial enterprise (which compares well with some other companies which were swindles, and which met an early demise). That life insurance caught on at all was undoubtedly due to the fact that industrial capitalism had so far separated men from small

[1] *The Metropolitan Life, a Study in Business Growth*, by Marquis James, Viking Press

ownership and broken down their sense of community, that they turned with relief to this new offer of security.

What accounted for Metropolitan's rather sensational rise to first place in the insurance business? Even highly imperfect things like unhappy marriages flourish with the practice of virtue. So it was with Metropolitan. An institution in itself unfortunate (as we shall see) rose to its present position of esteem and prosperity not by shrewd business practice so much as by a certain integrity and benevolence it exercised. First of all it issued industrial insurance in tiny policies to the dispossessed multitudes of industrial wage slaves. Although its motives for inaugurating industrial insurance were mixed, at least the company was visiting the poor with a sort of compassion, instead of vying with other companies for the privilege of "protecting" the rich. It prospered. From 1919 to 1929 Metropolitan had as president a man named Haley Fiske, who was a sort of humanitarian saint. He was also a gifted insurance man (in the trade use of the term), but he appears to have acted as often *first* to seek the Kingdom of Heaven and its justice, as he saw it (a compassionate, but not a blinding vision), as from the principles of expediency. Other presidents and high officials, though of lesser stature than Haley Fiske, exhibited the characteristics of men seriously devoted to the welfare of society in preference to their own selfish interests. In several major investigations, the outstanding integrity of the company was brought to light. From the financial point of view (not the Christian now, but according to the best capitalist ethics), the Metropolitan has not only been phenomenally sound and prudent, but also has shown brilliant initiative. Its handling of farm mortgages during and after the depression, and its vast real estate projects of recent years, are notable examples of financial acumen. More about them anon.

What then can be said against a company so obviously admirable? Really nothing derogatory can be said by anyone who accepts the fundamental presuppositions of the society in which this institution grew. Even the TNEC Inquiry of the Franklin

Roosevelt administration (with it socialist tendencies) couldn't make an indictment. They said the Metropolitan was too big (as it is), but as they only had it up their sleeves to make it yet larger, their criticism fell a little flat. They too were materialists, secularists, humanitarians, and so were wasting their time. It is only from the Christian Center, the Catholic Church, that the Metropolitan really shows itself for the curious and abnormal growth that it is.

INSURANCE SUBSTITUTES FOR CHARITY

All insurance is simply this, in its essence: it is a system of getting the fortunate to contribute to the welfare of the unfortunate, but without charity. All insurance calculations are based on statistical averages. Of a given 1000 men 35 years old, 3 or 4 (or however many it is) will die this year. Of 1000 factory workers, 6 or 7 will hurt themselves at work. Let the living undertake the support of the widows of the dead; let the able-bodied pay the doctors' bills of the injured, through the intermediary services of the insurance company. Now as Christians we are bound to help each other anyhow, for the love of God.

There are three major differences between the one and the other method of distributing largesse.

The first is that it costs more to do it the insurance way because you have to pay all the insurance people for the red tape and investigation that is involved.

The second difference is that the insurance plan benefits only those who can pay dividends, whereas the Christian plan benefits especially those who cannot (and therefore need it most).

The third difference is that the Christian scheme of things encourages the flow of the virtue of charity, which is the oil of society, whereas the insurance plan tends to destroy charity. A man buys insurance for selfish reasons (see the advertisements. How far would insurance get by advertising: "A man is run over. It might be *your neighbor*." Oh no. The ads read: "It might be *you*."), or at least for reasons of a love not extending beyond his own family, and this despite the fact that he does participate, by buying it, in a group plan by which his money is distributed to help others. Insurance is a way of effecting the material results of charity without charity, and therefore without merit in the sight of God. This situation was occasionally eased in the case of the Metropolitan, as we said. The system in itself cuts out person-to-person charity but the company itself exercised a certain charity when small policy holders were pressed by showing a leniency to which they were not bound by contract. The company is so set up that this could be done almost entirely at the will of one man at the top, but all of the thousands of agents and clerks participated a little in the merits that flowed from it. We see here very clearly the advantage of capitalism over socialism, as going not quite so far in the same direction. Capitalism allows the free exercise of virtue in one's work to only the top few, but socialism would allow it to no one. A Christian social order would make it generally possible. The Christian should not deplore the exercise of charity by the few who are able (and therefore withhold a genuine admiration for the Metropolitan officials), but rather work to make the practice of charity more generally possible.

There is a story attributed to the Baroness de Hueck. It describes the instinctive reaction of a solidly Christian, Russian (pre-Soviet) woman to life insurance. A young man of a certain village went to the city, where he became a life insurance salesman. Returning to the village he pressed his wares upon one of the native women. The first time he explained the workings of insurance to her she didn't understand what he was talking about. He tried again. This time she understood.

"You mean," she said, "that if I pay you a certain amount of money every month, that if my husband dies you will take care of me and my children?"

"Yes, that's it," he answered.

"But why," she said, "should I deprive my friends and relatives of the privilege?"

INSURANCE IMITATES GOD'S PROVIDENCE

To listen to insurance salesmen you would almost think that insurance would protect you against every eventuality of God's Providence. Death holds no terrors to a man adequately covered, while theft or fire can be positively a boon.

A Christian lives by faith, which means, for one thing, that he frankly faces his utter dependency on God. Of course he is utterly dependent on God whether he faces it or not, but few men can stand naked and dependent as did St. Francis. It used to be clear that God provided through nature and the weather. Industrialism blurred that fact. Man found himself in a precarious position, in which he was especially vulnerable to the solicitations of insurance agents. So it came about that God's Providence was to operate through a man-made, mechanical, system rather than organically through nature, and with that it came about that men shifted their faith in God's Providence to faith in men's providence through the regular payment of premiums.

Some day we shall learn why the Irish fell for this in droves. That they were poor and dispossessed is part of the reason, but hardly all. They developed a positive mania for insurance (and civil service jobs), to the point of indecency for Christians who have been assured that under certain circumstances all things will be added unto them.

THE OMNIPOTENCE OF INSURANCE

The omnipotence of insurance companies is something which, as the investigators pointed out, tends to snowball. It's worse than they thought, however. The key is usury.

Let us go back to the original simplification of insurance. We said that it was a matter of getting a group of people to share a risk which would prove fatal to only several of their number. The reader may have wondered about life insurance, which in the long run proves fatal to all of them. Life insurance represents the same principles as originally stated, with added complications. It still is based on group age statistics, but let us consider another aspect. Any one man making out life insurance, even though he live to be very old indeed, never pays the full amount which his heirs can claim. Where does the difference come from? It comes from the compound interest on the investments of the insurance companies.

A man should risk losing his money in order to deserve getting interest on it. He should at the very least risk getting no returns in the way of dividends. Insurance investments (according to their own concerted efforts, and also to government regulations) are notoriously unrisky. Specifically they go in for bonds, preferred stocks and mortgages, all of which are usurious[2] according to Church teaching and the natural law. They are usurious because they entitle the investor to interest, whether or not business makes a profit. (Common stock, by contrast, pays dividends only when business warrants—in other words, it increases the investor's wealth only when there has actually been an increase in real wealth. At least this is the theory. There are other counts against common stock at the moment, and these might have contributed to Metropolitan's vigorous opposition to a recent proposal to rescind the existing prohibition against insurance companies' investment in common stock.)

This is what happens when people practice usury: bad times inevitably come, when interest is not deserved. Those who pay it have to scrape it up from their general wealth somewhere and eventually, if times are hard enough, all the debtor's wealth gravitates to the usurer. This is what happened to the Metropolitan's farm mortgages. When the farmers fell upon prolonged hard times in the thirties, Metropolitan had vast mortgage holdings. As long as they could they adjusted policies and extended payment dates instead of foreclosing. Strictly from a Christian point

---

2 Usury is here used in the technical, not the popular sense. It does not mean charging exorbitant interest, but charging any interest at all on unproductive loans, and it is rooted in the truth that money does not fructify.

of view they had no right to do either. They were exacting their pound of flesh and the longer they took interest (where there was not money to pay interest) the less kind, not the more kind (as some farmers pointed out) they were.

Well, in the end they did foreclose, and to such an extent that Metropolitan became the largest single owner of farm properties in the country. They then hired an executive with agricultural training, and invested large sums of money to recondition the farms (which had been exhausted partly in an effort to meet their own exactions). Eventually they sold the improved farms, often back to the original farmers whom they had kept on as tenants.

Note the gross injustice of the whole process according to true economics. Metropolitan would argue that it had a sacred trust, etc., but actually Metropolitan's policy holders (it is a mutual company) are not entitled to bleed farmers out of all their possessions on any account. Why are policy holders more sacred than land owners?

There are two interesting side-lights to this affair which serve to show that the best interests of the Metropolitan Life Insurance Company are not always synonymous, or even harmonious, with the common good. The stable kind of farming, the kind that would have saved the farmers, is subsistence farming or the growing of what one needs first, and then selling the surplus. Metropolitan knows this. Yet subsistence farming was not in fact encouraged at a time when the company, through its propaganda and local agents, in addition to its temporary ownership, could have done much to change the commercial nature of American farming. Was this because subsistence farming is no way to keep up mortgage payments?

The other interesting point is that Metropolitan was reluctant to have the mortgages finally paid off and to sell the farms. That a man should be independent and debt free is not a beautiful sight to a usurer.

With city mortgages the story was similar. Metropolitan

almost had to take over the Empire State Building at one time, but eased its interest rate in order not to destroy the goose which was laying its golden eggs.

Of another evil, there is only the faintest hint. Yet who has not observed it? Life insurance has made it possible for almost everyone to have a $500 funeral, and in so doing has been accessory to changing the undertaking business from a reasonable facsimile of a work of mercy, to a racket.

THE FUTURE

Goodness knows what will happen to insurance. It ought progressively to cease to exist, but this is impossible to it (did it wish to, which it doesn't), as the payments which will fall due are to be paid in part out of new policy premiums. Indeed, the Metropolitan must not only stay large, but also (according to its president) continue to grow. When you set out to be Providence, you can't help seeing that it would be easier if you were also Omnipotence.

Were an atomic bomb to fall on New York that would probably finish the Metropolitan. Even if its own structure were to survive, the claims would be ruinous. You can provide for most contingencies, but you can't provide for universal disaster.

A less noisy sort of atomic bomb is inflation. Companies don't like to mention this, but they keep urging the general populace not to buy *things* but to *save* money and pay insurance premiums (while they, along with other shrewd financiers, invest heavily in real estate, which is the only bulwark against inflation). Severe inflation would certainly ruin insurance, and us too. Still it would be poetic justice of a sort—something like "those who live by the sword shall perish by the sword."

The third alternative is that the government take over insurance. This is not imminent at the moment (although they have already done so in part with social security). There is this to be said for the government's controlling insurance: the government would include the less good risks (like the Negroes, whom the Metropolitan has rejected with some vigor), if only because governments are allowed to operate at a deficit whereas insurance companies are not.

There is this to be said against the government: It isn't God either. It might be bigger and more omnipotent, but it is considerably less efficient than private companies. If the Metropolitan can't take care of us all and balance the budget, much less will the government be able to do so.

Can it be that the virtue of charity could have done the job economically? Can it be that the cost of red tape and executive brainpower represents *the precise uneconomic factor?* If so, then one way or another we have to return to the simple practice of personal charity.

CAROL ROBINSON

INTEGRITY, April 1947

GAY ADVERSITY

The boy stood on the burning deck,
   His future was assured.
The clever lad, before he sailed,
   Had had the ship insured.

BOOK REVIEWS

Apostle of the Genteel

AFTER BLACK COFFEE
By Robert I. Gannon, S.J.
McMullen

It is not always true that you can judge a man by the company he keeps. The consternation of the rich and successful of His time, at seeing Christ in the company of thieves and publicans, was hardly justified. It is not more justifiable today to bewail the presence of the reverend President of a Jesuit University among real estate operators or capitalists. We may feel safely assured that with the disciple as with the Master, the end is not to condone but to convert. Thieves and publicans have no right to boast of their hospitality, as though it were to their tables alone that Christ is invited. How unfortunate if the Faith had no one fit to grace the tables of the rich! To be all things to all men needs men who can accept the challenge of a gilt-edged invitation, and answer in kind.

The one subject upon which the most friendly of men fail to agree is the various methods for catching fish. For the harpooner of whales the delicate craftiness of the fly caster seems an ignobling concession to the tastes of the fish. The Isaac with the bamboo pole and his can of worms writhes with contempt at the sight of a Walton with gleaming shaft and roller-bearinged reel. It is the fish, however, and not the fisherman who decide the efficacy of the technique. When the day's catch is counted, it is not alone quantity but quality that counts. One salmon is sometimes a greater victory than a netful of conglomerate plebians of the deep. Captain Ahab was a weak man indeed in shallow waters.

Father Gannon is a fisher of men, and of a clan whose creels are seldom empty. In this collection of after-dinner speeches given at various meetings of Upper Crustians, we see the agile and patient tactics of a skillful fly caster. There is no landing hook or net in his equipment. His gear is as light as the fish that he plays. Within his very shadow the wary salmon pounces upon the juicy speckled fly rated as desert on any menu, and then he is away leaping with delight. And so far is he from the fisherman, before his flight is halted with an angry tug, that he does not relate the fisherman with the hook. For one of Father Gannon's victims, it may be a week later, seated at his club, that he suddenly becomes aware that he is caught. He has gone as far as the line will go, and the hook of his conscience bites deep.

Calling a spade a spade is a mark of integrity, but there are times when it is best not to tell the spade to his face, especially a face that has been recently filled and corked with a cigar. That is why our after-dinner apostle must tell real-estate dealers about the vices of the Communist, or tell members of the Chamber of Commerce about the weakness of the educational system. When you can find nothing nice to say about those present, the next best thing is to find fault with those who are not. Within that palatable bit of gossip is hidden the hook of universal reproach, and there is a good chance that for the crime of Communism, real estate practices today are accessories before tomorrow's fact. The lesson for the Commercial man is more subtle. Here, to land the fish, you hope that he, in a crusade for better education, may discover that the foul odor from the schools is but the fetid breath of business being blown back in its own face. About that, the chambered commercialist could probably do something.

All of this is only a criticism of the first third of the book. Father Gannon's speech to a tolerance group in Boston is a masterpiece. In this you see the more direct Irish approach. The tongue is in a more derisive position than in the cheek. The Jesuit is never at his best among straw men. When Father Gannon concludes, tolerance is recognized as a pimply boy sent out upon the man's errand of Charity. There is also some very nice erudite stuff about culture and education.

As long as there are going to be gentlemen around we will need men like Father Gannon to remind them that there is no more in a dinner jacket for all its glory than what will emerge from it on the last day.

EDWARD WILLOCK

Where Do They Fit?

THE RELIGIOUS AND CATHOLIC ACTION
By Reverend Stephen Anderl and Sister M. Ruth, F.S.P.A.
G.A. Keller Print
La Crosse, Wisconsin

To the growing body of Catholic Action literature, "The Religious and Catholic Action" adds an important emphasis. If the laity are the bridge between the spiritual and temporal orders, surely those who pursue the straight and narrow path to perfection by vow are no hindrance to the spread of the Kingdom! How then do they participate? Catholic Action is lay action. They are religious. "Catholic Action can expect on their part not only incessant prayers but also an active participation even in the case of religious who have not charge of souls" said Pius XI. "This is especially true for all contemplative religious, of religious nurses, of those occupied in the care of orphans, the aged, the poor, the sick – collaboration less apparent than others, perhaps, but most powerful with the Heart of Jesus." But a paramount role is to be played by teaching religious, who, by their intelligent understanding of C. A. through advanced courses of study on the subject, can inform and inspire so many malleable young minds in that direction, minds and wills and hearts eager to espouse a revolutionary cause, a messianic mission. Indeed, forward-looking, dynamic Bishop Ross of the Gaspe Peninsula requested all the teaching institutes of his diocese to form J.E.C. cells in their schools, in a brilliant pastoral letter in which he comments acidly on the vast number of "invertebrates" who shall not restore the world to Christ! "Mediocrity is, perhaps, more fatal to society than the obvious evil that inspires defiance or horror." "The world is full of flabby Christians, Christians without radiation, the best of whom are content with not being dangerous –and how admirably they succeed!"

Part I deals with the relation of religious to C.A. Part II backs this up with papal and episcopal letters on the subject.

Part III includes an outline for the study of C.A., suggestions for the development of the apostolic spirit among children and a good bibliography.

FRANCES O'REILLY

The Right Road

MORALS IN POLITICS AND PROFESSIONS
By F. J. Connel, C.SS.R., S.T.D.
The Newman Bookshop

Most of the chapters of this book have already appeared in *The American Ecclesiastical Review*, and so may be familiar to priests. We rejoice that they are now available to the laity.

This is practical, hard-hitting, moral theology for doctors, lawyers, nurses, public school teachers, social workers, soldiers and sailors, judges legislators and politicians. The book is filled with close reasoning rather than pious vagaries. It sets forth general principles and makes unqualified decisions. It talks not about abstract problems but very concrete, contemporary ones like artificial insemination, the "third degree," the atom bomb, and the distribution of prophylactics to men in the armed service.

On the whole Fr. Connell is of the strict observance. Anyone who thinks *Integrity* exaggerates the difficulty of leading a

Christian life within the present framework of society should read this book. Without pulling any punches Father Connell flatly upholds moral principles wildly at variance with what everyone else is doing. Hear him on morals in politics:

He says legislators must vote according to the common good, and that if they subordinate the common welfare to personal or political motives they not only sin but may also become liable in conscience to make restitution. He says that a politician who appoints an incompetent to a job is bound to make restitution to the public treasury for the damage resulting from the incompetency.

He says quite firmly that expediency is "out" as a basis for the conduct of public office.

This book is not the whole story, but it is an excellent statement of what is right and wrong in specific situations. The author has a very good sense of the actual situation in the professions with which he is dealing, especially in the realm of statesmanship. However, I doubt that he realizes the full extent of the difficulty that is involved in applying the moral law in some of the professions. Take nursing for instance. It is good to hear it firmly said that the dying must be warned they are dying. There are many hospitals where a nurse will immediately lose her job if she does not conspire to keep the patient ignorant of his imminent demise. This is not a situation which can be met simply by applying the moral law. It calls urgently for a Catholic Action type of spiritual revolution of the nursing profession. Nonetheless, you do have to apply the moral law, and begin now. It is no criticism of Fr. Connell that he sticks to his theology. It is the work of *Integrity* and other lay efforts to complement his teaching by an analysis of the temporal problems.

CAROL ROBINSON

INTEGRITY, April 1947

It Might Happen Here

DESIGNS FOR CHRISTIAN LIVING[1]
By Peter Michaels (Carol Robinson)
Sheed and Ward

Given the principles the Church already possesses, and the breath of the Holy Spirit which is already sweeping our land, who knows but what might not happen? Here is one imaginative vision of the possibilities.

Designs for Christian Living not only talks about a Christian social order, but pictures it for us in glowing colors. Peter Michaels takes us upon a tour of a Christian society built of the stuff of 1947 and eternity. We visit a grocery store and a theatre, a library and a hospital, the office of an insurance company and a sanctuary for the insane. We listen to a Christian radio station, and consider the methods of a Christian underground college.

In order for a writer to do this convincingly, three gifts must be his:

1. He must appreciate the position of the Church in relation to the temporal order.
2. He must see that relation of Church to temporal order synthesized and manifested in the daily activity of the Christian layman.
3. He must be able to write so well that the reader can see it also.

As evidence that these gifts are undoubtedly his, the reader puts down Peter Michaels' book with a feeling of nostalgia, as though he had actually experienced a society already restored.

For each reader some one particular chapter of the book will

---

[1] This book will be available from Arouca Press as part of Carol Robinson's "Collected Works".

be most appealing, the nearest approximation of his own experiences. Or, perhaps, as I have done, he will especially treasure an excerpt that rings true on the bell of universal experience.

I liked the chapter on "Women's Wear" that begins like this:

> Charles (Pronounced in the French way and seldom followed by a surname) sat in his chartreuse-and-cobalt studio awaiting the preliminary showing of his 'Peek-a-boo' dress. Charles designed for the $79.95 wholesale dress trade. His influence on women's fashions was strong, bad, and usually anonymous. Charles did not mind the anonymity, since he was well-paid and quite gratifyingly famous, or infamous, in the closed circle of self-conscious and dissolute commercial artists which formed his world. The women who bought his clothes (whether at over $100.00 as originally planned, or in the Union Square pirated versions selling for under $10.00) belonged to a remote world of regular hours, where some effort toward monogamy was still maintained and where conversation still had certain prejudices against lascivious piquancy and merciless calumny.

Later you hear Charles musing about his art:

> When you drop a woman's skirts to her ankle, you lift the woman to a pedestal. You endow her with grace and dignity. Her admirers stop coveting and start worshipping. If women wore long, full skirts all the time, the world would turn into a Sunday school. That's why high fashion has always fought against this influence and tried to counteract it. The best counteracting influence is some version of the decollete neckline, which, in effect, simply belies the purity suggested by

the skirt of a long dress. You see it in today's evening dresses and in court styles throughout the ages.

The knee marks the limit of decency. Shorten skirts to just below the knee and you take away a woman's dignity; raise them any more and you have cut into her decency. Women don't realize this because they don't understand men. Because there is no falling off, in fact there is usually an increase, in made attention, women often fail to perceive the subtle change in the quality of the proffered admiration. The measure of respect is better gauged by the courtesy of subway strangers in the matter of seats than it is by the vapid cooings of predatory males.

Peter Michael's apostles set a standard of daring and courage that makes our lauded commercial initiative look very timid by contrast. He implies that being fools for Christ's sake requires an active intellect and imagination, as well as the fortitude that flows from grace. His librarians stock only good books, and rather than discourage bums that come in out of the rain, they read them excerpts from Tolstoy or the lives of the saints. His librarian is not just wet-nurse to a mess of indifferent books, but a gentle and persistent custodian over the minds of men. His restaurant keeper and grocer feel (of all things!) personally responsible for the increasing health of their patrons, and serve them accordingly, making the good foods attractive and discouraging the purchase of those that are not. A converted movie director produces films presenting life in "the light of eternity," and he discusses with his photographers the technical details of the "spiritual vantage point of the camera."

Two chapters are devoted to the Christian Design for Modern Medical Practice. The question raised by the author is whether we can hope to remedy the physical ills of man without interest or intercession to the God Who sustains him in existence, and whether a recognition of this sustenance does not suggest a clinical technique more Christian and consequently more effective.

For those who have read Peter Michaels, either in *Integrity* or in *The Torch* (where all except one of these articles first appeared) these pages will serve to answer that question provoked by his biting criticism of the existing order of things, "Then what will we do about it?" After you have read *Designs For Christian Living*, the way will be much clearer.

ED WILLOCK

Gotham To Gethsemani

A MAN IN THE DIVIDED SEA
By Thomas Merton
New Directions, Norfolk, Connecticut

From the sophisticated pages of "The New Yorker" to the bare walls of a Trappist cell is a spiritual pilgrimage somehow appropriate to our day. Such a pilgrimage is reflected in this volume, a collection of fine poems written over a period of seven years since young Thomas Merton's conversion to the Catholic Faith.

Some, produced while he was still in the world, were first published in popular periodicals; those of the last four years come to us from beyond the silent walls of the Abbey of Our Lady of Gethsemani, Kentucky. These later ones, quite rightly, possess the rarest beauty and clarity, being products of the distillation of thought and prayer that prove the contemplative life so conducive to perfecting the gift of poetry.

Of this group, perhaps the loveliest and most profound is "The Blessed Virgin Mary Compared to a Window," which begins:

> Because my will is simple as a window
> And knows no pride of original earth,
> It is my life to die, like glass, by light:
> Slain the strong rays of the bridegroom Sun.

Others will find "Clairvaux," "Trappists, Working," and "The Trappist Abbey: Matins" memorable in thought and style. Although, like all good literature, these poems improve with rereading, they do not require intensive interpretation, as does much that passes for poetry today.

A Man in the Divided Sea is the work of a distinguished poet. It is more — the work of a distinguished spirit.

ELIZABETH ODELL

Prayer and Poetry

THE ROMAN RITUAL, VOL. III: THE BLESSINGS
Bruce

In Latin and English with Rubrics and Plainchant Notation Translated and edited with introduction and notes by Rev. Philip T. Weller.

This is the long awaited translation of the Roman Ritual into clear and beautiful English. It includes blessings for Sundays and feastdays, for persons, for places and objects designed for a sacred purpose and for "other irrational creatures." The seven penitential psalms (the most lucid renditions we have yet read), the Litany of the Saints, and an appendix including prayers for travellers and blessings at meals complete this substantial addition to the Liturgical Revival. Blessings range from prayers for the extermination of vermin to the dedication of airplanes, from the blessing of seed to the dedication of seismographs. Like Christ Who prophesied that He would draw all things to Himself, His Bride, the Church, takes all material things in her embrace. Everything from bees to bells, from oats to ale, from lard to lilies, has its appropriate blessing. For a world gone berserk dabbling in a chaotic and meaningless symbolism, here is the material for an intelligible symbolism; here poetry flourishes; here the imagination is quickened and drawn up to heavenly things. If we do not have our share of good poets this is one answer; the Cartesian dichotomy lives on. Exorcisms are frequent (and tremendous in their impact) attesting to the recognition of an earlier Church (much more attuned to preternatural as well as supernatural realities) to the persistent attacks of the devil.

Familiarity of congregations with a volume like this should deepen their sense of the sacramentality of life and penetrate them with an awareness of the Providence of God. Here is the Roman Liturgy in all its humility and its humour, its terseness and restraint, its homeliness and its splendour.

FRANCES O'REILLY

INTEGRITY

DO + THOU + BRING + TO + HAPPY
ISSUE + THAT + UNION + OF + WHICH

THOU + THYSELF + ART. THE + AUTHOR

: the eighth issue :

MAY, 1947   Vol. 1. No 8
     SUBJECT — THE FAMILY

EDITORIAL

THE CURRENT ATTITUDE TOWARDS the family is the same as that of a crowd toward a man who has just been hit by an automobile. No one dares touch him for fear of adding to his injury. Some shrug their shoulders, others murmur a prayer, and all make the resolution to be careful not to suffer a similar misfortune. Unlike the injured individual, the injured family has no hospital to which to be taken. The only Physician Who can help the family has great difficulty in having His prescriptions filled because of the general prejudice against Him. The family is in a bad way.

An apple tree is no better than the apples which grow on its branches. A society is no better than the families of which it is comprised. No one can praise today's tree unless he ignores the diminutive, pale, and wormy fruit. Measured by the standard of familial health, our present social system compares unfavorably with any other except the materialistic totalitarian state toward which it logically proceeds. Refusal to face this fact is to betray the family. A continued demand that the family deform itself to fit the hole assigned to it now is the policy best designed to unleash the wrath of God and of nature on this nation.

A good society is the sum total of its families, containing within it as much as possible of the spiritual and material goods necessary to meet the common needs. Any individual within the society who seeks his own good or his family's profit, *apart from* the common good, is an enemy of that society. Any individual who preaches a philosophy of self-interest *apart from* the common good, is guilty of subversive activity. The first end of a good society is the soul's salvation of its people. Its government adjusts its policies to bring about a state of affairs encouraging to virtue, and discouraging to vice. It does everything possible to facilitate the ministry of the Church in her concern for souls, and protects and aids the family from every adversity. That is society as it should be.

The present state of society is a startling contrast with these norms. Our economic habit of seeking for individual profit *without consideration* for the common good, is fundamentally a subversive doctrine. Each seeking what is his own can bring nothing but economic chaos. (Or have you read the papers lately?) Consequently, the relation between individuals, between classes, and between families is a state of concordat, a state of limited hostility. Each family is considered autonomous, and completely responsible for its own welfare. Aid by organized charities is administered much as a pinboy removes deadwood from a bowling alley so that the competitive game can go on. A sense of community, or the common responsibility for children has been lost. Thus it falls upon the parent to accept the whole burden which, by its nature, should be shared with his neighbors.

The profit-seekers are left free to prey upon the lone family amputated from the community. Advertising is the thin-edge of the wedge being used to split society. In addition to the obnoxious use of semi-nudes to sell their products, at the price of feminine modesty and masculine fidelity, virtues essential to the family, the ads set child against parent and neighbor against neighbor. For instance, parents are encouraged to vie with one another in the outfitting of their children. "Oh mamma," says little four-year old Ann, "Why can't I have a new dress like Mary Stoopnagle has?"

"My daddy owns a Nash!" says the little brat in the advertisement. Popular opinion mirrors the competitive snobbery provoked by the advertisers. A campaign against birth control will continue to be ineffective moralizing, without simultaneously breaking down the urge for the selective breeding of well-dressed delinquents.

Editorial

The truncated family, successful at achieving its own ends, partly because it is truncated, and partly because it has picked a winning number in the economic lottery, sets the standard both nationally and parochially. Families of somewhat more than *normal* size (though considerably more than *average*) that manage to survive with respectable dignity, are accorded the same Sunday-supplement notoriety that attends the less rare birth of triplets. Emulation is hardly more expected in one case than in another. Normality in size could give our average father about five dependents, which, if he were without God's grace, and possessed the vaunted American desire "to have something better," would tempt him to accept the usual suggestions of his fellow workers to "go and see the veterinary!" Four children is the estimated average necessary to continue the human race under present conditions. Birth-controllers, as evidence of God's marvelous way of bringing good from evil, do not perpetuate themselves. Until they die out, however, they will continue to set the standard in many things as well as the high price of diapers.

Without normal families to set the standard, we have already become a nation of selective breeders. Society is now for the elect, and church for good people. The conscientious gardener of another age when asked "How does your garden grow?" did not stamp through a tangle of stunted week-choked blossoms, and proudly point to a lone and magnificent flower. This has, however, become the practice of the individual who refuses to face the fact that there is not wide enough distribution of economic manure or sufficient social cultivation to support any more than a few well-cared for families. Unanimous opinion is that a normal family is impossible in a society which doesn't know what normal is. This opinion is correct — if we overlook God. With Him all things are possible, especially a normal family.

* * *

INTEGRITY, May 1947

When preparing this issue, we realized that dedicating it to the family was somewhat redundant. Every issue of *Integrity* is a family issue. All the ideas pertaining to the reintegration of religion and life directly concern the family, for next to the salvation of souls, there is no other task more important than the holiness of the family. As a blow to our pride we must admit that the sum total of children represented in this issue by their contributing parents, is a paltry fifteen. Inability to meet our deadline scratched the proud parent of five, which might have brought our total to twenty. We let the reader in on this secret to assure him that we are very hopeful of the future of the Christian family. That hope is not increased one iota by anything we read in the daily paper. We have forsaken the providence of big business for the Providence of God.

A wide-eyed pessimism for the way of the world has already led some Christian parents to a happy conclusion. This conclusion is the one that explains God's permitting this fruitless social order to come into being. The sterile habits of a dying era have prompted these parents to look into the bosoms of their families and see there the nucleus of a just and noble society to come. The economy of this new order, they have delightfully discovered, is already in operation, and has been since the time of Adam. It is not a niggardly penny-pitching economy of scarcity, but an economy of abundance. Each new child is a further guarantee of prosperity. Each new child is a citizen of the new community. Each new child is an apostle for Christ. They have turned their backs upon a philosophy of fear, and fastened their eyes upon God, anxious to anticipate His every desire, for in this lies their entire future.

It is the desire of these parents that the old order die with them, and in their children will be the resurrection of the new Christ-life. Thus all of the mores and habits which for generations have militated against the Faith may be sweated out in their efforts to renew society and furnish it with Christian leaders.

Editorial

They do not presume for an instant that so heroic a task can be accomplished by sheer will-power or self-negation, but they seek in the Sacraments the grace to accomplish that which grace has ordained. Their task will be made lighter when others less fortunate in the Faith but wealthier in talents turn their hands also to the common problem.

When disaster comes, it may be these homes that God will spare, and upon their hearth-stones erect the "new heaven and the new earth wherein justice dwelleth." Whatever God's Will may be for the future, these families at present can supply the curious with a living example of that strange phenomenon — a normal family.

THE EDITORS

A Holy Thing

*"Wedding is a holy thing; and it should be
dealt with holily." (Council of Trent)*

MY DEAR FRIENDS,

You stand here together in the sight of God to bring about the fulfillment of your cherished plan. You are still engaged, but this chapter is about to be closed and a new one opened. Yet it is not merely a new chapter you are to begin, but a new life: the life of two-in-one. You are soon to be joined together by your consent: "I will." However brief a word, it is of greatest import. It is a word of vigor and courage, full of readiness and joy, bespeaking fidelity and love. "I will" is a word at once human and divine.

"I will" is the word God spoke in creating heaven and earth. "I will that light be," was His Command, and light was made. In repeating the word the Lord spoke at the beginning, you partake of His creative power. It is yours to perform almost a miracle, to bring new beings into the world, children able to wonder at God's creation, having the unique power to love, and capable of holding God in their hearts. May you often kneel together and recall your dignity as instruments of the Almighty, co-workers of the loving God.

"I will" is also a thoroughly human word. It was spoken in profound humility by the Blessed Virgin when she replied to the message of the Angel: "Behold the handmaid of the Lord. Be it done unto me according to thy word." What other meaning has this most perfect consent than: "I will His will"? Marriage, all marriage, is the answer of two hearts calling to one another. Christian marriage, however, is something more; it is the joint response of two persons of God. After Mary's model, you are to unfold your being before Him. Like her, you will let yourselves be overshadowed by the Holy Spirit. Marriage is the mysterious union in the flesh, but as a sacrament it is even greater — the inexplicable union of grace.

A Holy Thing

You will be one in body, but you ought to be increasingly one in soul, one in grace. What a delight it will be for you to possess earthly goods in common! But in sharing the eternal, you will find joy even deeper. No longer will you live for yourselves, but for one another, and I am sure you will also live for Christ. Indeed, you would fail one another and betray your deepest vocation, you would dim the image God has engraved upon your souls, did you not dedicate yourselves wholly to Him. So potent is this participation in each other's lives that your pains will be mitigated and your happiness exalted, the joys you share will be doubled and your sorrows divided.

Your consent opens the gate to conjugal love, a divine gift to you for time and eternity. Our hardships here below are many, but they are more easily endured together. Marriage is intended to ease some of our burdens, but also to heighten our responsibilities. By discovering to each other the beauties of nature, by enjoying in union music, literature and art, by giving your minds to the pursuit of truth, and above all, to contemplation of the splendor of the eternal mysteries, your love will open up a vast store of treasure. Sanctifying each day the Lord gives you by uniting in prayer and joining with Christ in His Holy Sacrifice, you will find the riches of His Kingdom. You are given each to each to grow together in wisdom and age and grace before God and man. You are given each to each to grow together by mutual help and understanding. You are no less than companions on the way to God.

Already to the Israel of old, marriage was something sacred, almost a sacrament. It was thought to carry with it the forgiveness of sins to those who entered it with a godly spirit. The devout used to fast, therefore, and confess their trespasses, before assuming its bond. Marriage was regarded as a reflection of the loving union of God with His people. And when the first man and woman became one, says a Jewish legend, angels were the witnesses, the heavenly spirits sang the nuptial hymn, and the Lord Himself pronounced the benediction.

These thoughts of Israel are, having attained perfection, the teaching of Holy Church. Conjugal love, your love, is a reminder, and a reminder of paradise. Marriage is the image of the lasting union of Christ with the Church, His Bride. And your home should be a realm in which God's Kingdom is never disputed. It ought to be a little Church, a mirror of the Church in pilgrimage.

In a little while, you will give your consent; you will say: "I will." Once pronounced, it determines your life forever. Still, to conform to the perfect pattern, you will have to say this word each day anew. Love does not grow of itself to the highest peak. It is for you to say "Yes" to God and to each other every morning, assenting to His word and will, to His wishes and commandments, and to His blessings, be they favors or afflictions. In a moment, you will with great affection declare your "Yes." To keep it strong, to render it impregnable, you must repeat it, especially at any threat of disharmony. For human beings are bound to disappoint one another at times, but to you this should be only an opportunity to show the overwhelming power of love.

In a few moments, each will give and each will wear a ring, an unbroken circle gleaming in the light, blessed on the altar of sacrifice, the symbol of your sacramental union. Often together recall this solemn moment; join your hands and repeat your bridal vow. Disarm whatever might menace your union by saying: "I want thee and accept thee as God gave thee to me." This will keep your love young, and prepare your souls for the boons of God's goodness.

My dear friends, may your marriage be blessed beyond measure! This is my desire for you, and it is the wish of your Mother the Church, in whose name I speak.

JOHN M. OESTERREICHER

Note: This sermon was given by Father John Oesterreicher at the wedding of Jounet Kahn and Margaret Stern at the Church of the Epiphany in New York City. The bride and groom, Father Oesterreicher, and many of those who comprise the wedding party, are converts from Judaism.

Among So Many

*"Husbands, love your wives, as
Christ loved the Church."*

THE SMELL OF WHISKEY ON THE COUPLE behind you turned your stomach, but you kept on reading because you were tired of waiting, you hadn't known you line up for a marriage license like a ticket to a ball game, the only thing you had with you was a missal.

"... *that it should be holy and without blemish* ... "

A muggy August morning. Outside, the sun was shining; it was trying to be a nice day. Here, in this fetid hallway in the municipal building, there were only the insolent officiousness of bored clerks, pale lights, the soiled, dark surfaces of old walls.

The couple three ahead of you were quarreling. The woman was loud and loose, and obviously older than the boy. Her outrageous hat was exceeded by her corsage. The boy was thin and nervous. He shook his head at her and seemed about to walk off and leave her. But the couple behind them had been telling jokes, the girl swept the quarrelling two into the homestretch of her story and finished on peals of laughter in which the neighboring couples joined, and it was all right, the boy didn't walk away, he wasn't mad any more.

Over them all, the sin of Adam ... On all faces, mean, stupid, brooding, gay ... the scarlet sneer, the snicker, an obscure sense of surrender to the goat ... And there was no one to absolve, to sanctify.

The line snaked forward slowly. You edged past a door marked "Marriages Performed." The door was open, and for a few minutes the ritual of civil matrimony was displayed to you. The girl wore the corsage, the man smirked as he put the ring on her finger. The official, despite the wrinkled suit, wore the owlish air of inscrutable corruption.

INTEGRITY, May 1947

"This is a great sacrament — but I speak in Christ..."

The music of the words, the music of your heart, was fading. You tried to strengthen it, to relate it to what you saw, to imagine that somehow, despite corruption, the Word could become flesh. But there was only horror, the retching shame of a vast obscenity.

The line moved forward into the large room with the little barred windows like a post office, and there was a guard to tell you to go to this window or that, and at last you and your betrothed, separate from the mass, stood alone before the high priest of the mysteries, an oily, little bureaucrat. A few quick questions, the filling in of blanks, the money over the counter, the stamping of dates and the seal of the city upon this union, that all might be fulfilled according to law, and then you were free to pass out of the room, out of the building, out into the warm morning and the promise of a great sacrament.

On the way home, you were both silent. Shame would not leave you. You could not separate yourself from the other, from the feeling that they had been betrayed, and that their betrayal was yours. Betrayed not only by that one wretched experience and their own weakness, but by the sum of all the thousand scenes, laws, schools, jobs, that made them what they were, by the whole impact of the mindless, teeming city powdering them to dust and you among them. Marriage thus affronted at the start, how would it go with them afterwards? How would it go with you? For in time to come, as then, you would all bear the cross of an indifferent brutal age, and you knew it and were afraid...

For the moment, of course, you could forget. "Look at my gown, darling. Do you like my gown? Shall I have a train?" She was more appealing than ever as she twirled for you to see and yes, of course, she must have a train by all means. So there was a train and a nuptial Mass, a sung Mass, too, with the priest telling you to smile after his blessing. Then you realized how scared you looked and you smiled as you left the altar with the organ playing and your mother crying and your friends taking movies from the back of the church. So you were smiling in the pictures afterwards and you told yourself always to remember to smile and not be scared.

You did smile, too. The vision was so strongly in you: *"That it should be holy and without blemish..."* It would always be warm and bright and sweet. You would have difficulties, that was natural. But there would be Christ and His Sacraments — and this great sacrament. You would overcome the world.

How could you know what lay ahead? The fatuousness of your zeal, the cloying after-taste of too much ardor? Your adversary the Devil went about, seeking whom he might devour — but not like a lion. Like a banal conversation. Boredom. A nagging irritation. The "world" you had thought to overcome was a penny-catechism world, peopled with dragons of birth control, heresy and the seven deadly sins. The dragons you really battled were diapers, bills, a baby's wait, the blaring radio next door. Armored in faith, you thought you stood your ground. Triviality outflanked you and the slow retreat began.

You were not prepared for it when it came: "... cutting down on the department ... fine worker ... so sorry ... have to let you go ... " Let go! It couldn't be. But the words kept raining on you, it had all been agreed, he was only doing what he was told by the other fellow who had been told ... and it was so. (Pagan Industrialism. Collapse of Capitalism. Not my fault, I tell you.)

Quietly the years passed. Funny, boring, often lonely. Better jobs, a bigger apartment, a house. But no matter where you lived, the world was everywhere and you were you.

The room was full of interesting people and warm highballs, you were heading for the kitchen for air. There she was, your old girl. You wondered why people always wound up in the kitchen, the one place you hadn't groomed. Her manner was familiar as you lit her cigarette. Same perfume, you observed. A child of her own, but still playing Hubba Hubba.

"... think you've done wonders," she enthused.

"It's coming along," you agreed.
"And you're really happy?"
"Oh yes." Not too defiantly.
She appraised your defense.
"But who would have thought that *you* . . . I mean, all this . . . "
" — no, no, not at all like O'Neill! Passion, yes, but *not* homosexuality." Winters and McCutcheon had drifted in with one of their Interesting Discussions. God bless all phonies.

"But don't you agree that sexual depravity is psychic — an effect rather than a cause?"

The fault, dear Brutus, lies not in ourselves...

As the pressure increased, the vision slowly faded. Where was it now? — the Christian home, the bringing up of children in piety and love? Paled by the present need: "I got to make more money." Dulled by the mediocrity of a hundred films, the Philharmonic on Sunday afternoon, the new issue of "Life." Poisoned with loneliness: where was the hand to help, what shall I do, where are my friends?

They dropped in with new clothes and criticism in their eyes. Oh how cute, they said. But their gaze flickered. That makes three boys and two girls, doesn't it? Their mouths made the words, but their eyes had no modesty, they must inspect the empty womb and wonder . . . Their eyes had no sympathy, they must wander over the room, noting the dusty curtain, the disarray, the worn heel.

The well-wishers wearied you more than the hostile. You could argue or be silent with those who spoke solemnly of being Sensible about These Things, who judged you imbecile or careless. But how resent the legend of the happy peasant, his children run about him like unto the olive tree? How react to those who glibly said Yes, I Believe in the Apostolate of the Family, you're doing a fine job, your children are so well-behaved? You longed to tell these hopefuls of the toughness it took to achieve the legend, that there was more to it than quoting Gill. If they could not cure a fever or plane a door, let them be silent. But they were not silent, and you could not silence them, for the knowledge you wanted to give them could not be communicated, only experienced.

And when the visitors had left, the papers been put away, the radio turned off, when all the myriad manifestations of the Paganity of Our Day had been shut away, there yet remained the greatest of these: yourself. The training you had never had, the education you should not have had, all the neurotic complex of your own personality, full of the shame and pride of a twentieth-century ego. Like the drunk and the consumptive, you were always cured, only to awake again from other nightmares of ambition, nerves and lust. Nude Girl Found Dead in Motor Car, story on page three, you were only reading the paper, everyone does that. Lights flashed on the screen, the camera panned across the boxcars of emaciated dead in a concentration camp, you felt the thrill of the macabre as you watched, but kept on looking. The theatre emptied, you walked home purged of violence till another day.

As the vision paled, you came to feel that it was not real, had never been. Idealism of youth. You were over that, now. It had been sweet, part of the honeymoon, like, but you had grown, you realized now that the dream could never have been achieved. Too many responsibilities. The times weren't right. The image of that August morning in the municipal building came back to you, and you knew you had been right. It was too much — too much...

What then? Content yourself with Sunday church, choir on Tuesday, bowling on Thursday, the meeting, you must make that meeting, a famous European Catholic editor is speaking on The Future of the Church? You tired, grew dissatisfied with stimulating talks, mental fornication. As the years evaporated and the dream dissolved, you yearned for a sign, a Word, the way out. What then? Where? How?

Think. Time out to think. Where were you? What had you done? What had you been trying to do? What was this Christian way all about, anyhow? What did you want?

You had wanted to raise a good family, and you had started. You had wanted to oppose by word and example the pagan drift of social forces in your life, but this you had not done. "Why not?" What had happened?

You saw that, despite your ideals, you had never really said no, never really broken, ruthlessly and completely, with the forces you decried. Though you shut the door on Anti-Christ, he was with you daily, in your thoughts, your ill-will, self-pity, bad habits, petty compromise. No matter where you fled or what you did, the world was with you for in your heart you were still with the world.

You looked around and saw that you were not alone in this. Your friends ... Collins ... Gardella ... Had they not all followed the same pattern? You had started out together, in the group, the movement, the study club — scorning the world, dedicated to high purpose. Now you were scattered, reeds shaken by the wind, hurt, whining, ashamed of youthful enthusiasms, afraid of questions. How could a brutal age be overcome by this mystical body of the timid?

Timid, that was it. This Brutal Age, this Pagan Environment were abstractions, excuses for failure. There were no Godless Societies, no Modern Values — as such. Only people. You, multiplied. Living out patterns, everywhere, all over the earth. The children were asleep, the room was quiet, the lamp threw a warm pool in the gloom where you sat smoking and thinking. The Australian shut off his alarm, the ambassador in China yawned and fished for his slippers, and as they scratched their pajamas and shambled off to shave, the Future of the Church and Civilization lay with them. And you. You were all one: fathers, husbands, heads of families, linked in defeat, blaming the forces you could not oppose, creating forces for tomorrow. Fella's gotta make a living. You can't change things overnight.

Perhaps not. But perhaps you could change you. And because you and your neighbors were "things," perhaps you could change "things" too. True, those like you were not the whole. But you and you and you could act, could leaven the lump, could say yes, I will, I will make the break, and saying yes together, might win. For good is ultimately stronger than evil, stronger than the pushing city, the proud nation, the great army... stronger than life.

You could begin simply, at the breakfast table, on the bus. You could become a real Christian father. If a Christian home could not be fathered in the city, you could leave the city. Advertising could not sway you if you did not read it. The pretty girl could not hurt you if you did not look. Bob Hope you could turn off.

But what is there left, O my soul? Can't a fella have a little fun? I do my work, I do the right thing, what's wrong with a little fun?

There is wrong in the littlest funs that adds the smallest grain to the mass of evil already in the world.

This is a tough saying, O my soul. There's so much against you. It isn't going to change. What can *you* do?

"There is a boy here that has five barely loaves and two fishes. But what are these among so many?

You thought of the family at supper. Your wife was trying to slap a mischievous hand without losing the baby off her lap. One child was telling for the fourth time some tiresome tale about what happened in school. You couldn't understand what he said because another had just kicked a third under the table.

"Daddy, daddy, daddy," chanted Brian. "I coasted down on the road today and I didn't even get killed."

Five barely loaves. Two fishes.

You yawned, stretched. Eleven. Must fix the furnace. Wake up the kids, prob'ly. Shouldn't of stayed up. Droopy to-morrow at the office.

You rose, moved slowly toward the cellar.

What were these among so many?

Everything...!

NEIL MACCARTHY
Washington, Conn.

INTEGRITY, May 1947

EQUITY

The Williams and the Fullers,
  Were out for real-estate.
The Williams got eight rooms for two,
  The Fullers two for eight.

Towards a New Generation

So obviously are the forces of evil at work against marriage that even our secular press and magazines deplore the condition of the American family. A recent issue of *The New York Times*, discussing the problem, concludes that if the present rate of divorce continues, the number of marriages between persons marrying for the first time will be exceeded by the number of divorces in the not too distant future. And this month's issue of the ultra ultra *Glamour* featuring "Our Marriage Problem" states that "the failure of American marriage is not a threat but an actuality... and that divorce represents... our first social problem."

Long before the newspapers and slippery covered magazines evidenced concern for the failure of our marriages (for which failure they were in large part responsible as we will see later on) Pius XI exhorted his Brethren:

> to give yourself wholly to this that through yourselves and through the priests subject to you, and moreover through the laity welded together through Catholic Action you may by every fitting means oppose error by truth, vice by the excellent dignity of chastity, the slavery of covetousness by the liberty of the sons of God, that disastrous ease of obtaining divorce by an enduring love in the bond of marriage, and by the inviolate pledge of fidelity given even unto death. (Encyclical, *Casti Connubi*)

Is it not to be expected then, that one of the first problems attacked by the organized apostolate of Catholic Action in the attempt to repair the ravages of secularism is the re-Christianization of the family?

LET'S FACE THE PROBLEMS

The numerous forces at work against Christian marriage might be brought under two broad classifications; firstly, those created by anti-Christian institutions and secondly, those given rise to through ignorance.

From what institutions, for example, do we draw our standards for a successful marriage (the word successful itself is so much in keeping with our times). Pagan Hollywood creates the notion that the conjugal union is a whirl of romance, and our radio scripts, newspapers and magazines carry out this fantasy. So it is that the mind of the individual is formed believing that the all-important element of one's marital life is the physical union granted free rein under the bonds of matrimony.

Similarly accented by those bonds who mold mass mentality is a materialistic attitude toward marriage. The superficiality of *Glamour's* concern over the condition of the family is evident when contrasted with the rest of its contents. "Luxuries are necessities" is the keynote and Susie Jones has just got to have money for her so-called "needs." Of course, it is assumed that Susie will work after marriage, so *Glamour* offers the career bride's trousseau with accent on the office. It is often at this point that Susie decides she won't have children for the first couple of years with the excuse that she's young and has plenty of time before being tied down with a family (and, by the way, youth is lasting longer and longer these days).

Eventually, Susie may tire of marriage but more and more frequently she leaves a back door open — divorce. Each day many Susies challenge the Church's stand on the indissolubility of marriage as is evidenced by the mounting divorce rate. In 1946 alone, one magazine writer tells us that one out of two and a half marriages ended in the law courts.

It is unfair to give our magazines credit for so much of the problem without looking to our scandal sheets. Take *The Daily*

News, with the largest circulation in America, and what do you find — sex slayings, immodest pictures, lewd stories, immoral advertising. But they too are alarmed about the increased divorce rate and the breakdown of the family. One cannot help but ask "Can these mortals be such fools?"

Closely linked with the necessity for re-Christianization of institutions is the need for re-education. Failure to educate our people to accept wholeheartedly the teachings of the Gospel has made them easy prey for the fallacious ideas of the world about us. Instruction, if any, is largely concerned with the physiology of the sexes. The importance of the supernatural and spiritual elements in conjugal life is disregarded in the overemphasis of sexual love. The result of this failure to integrate properly the various aspects of marriage is obvious in the faulty way in which the marriage contract is interpreted. There are those of Jansenist tendencies who draw the conclusion that the separation of the spiritual from the physical confirms the belief that the body is evil in itself. Then with gradations from the Jansenist attitude we arrive at the other extreme held by those who say "So sex pleasure is immoral but let's enjoy it anyway."

Finally there is ignorance in regard to the true role of man and woman in marriage. In their pseudo-emancipation, women have slavishly imitated men, failing to realize that it is the very differences in the sexes which draws them together. And it is impossible to achieve marital happiness in a home where the husband and wife fail to recognize that certain duties rest with each of them by reason of their very nature.

These are the conditions as they exist today, lacking all guarantee of true happiness here and probably preparing many for eternal damnation hereafter. Certainly they do not create a very hopeful picture for the future but we as Christians cannot stand by and watch the slow degeneration of a new generation.

THE REMEDIES

It would be time wasted to attempt to restore marriage to godly principles by re-education alone, for if lasting results are to obtain, complete change must eventually be effected in our anti-Christian institutions. It is to this end that Pius XI cries out for an organized movement of lay people who will bring about this change; people who will live by Christian principles and who in the strength of their numbers will apply them to all phases of society.

Till now the work of the organized apostolate in this country has been limited so far as institutional change is concerned. Yet if one is to consider a Christian institution as a great force for good (Father William Ferree defines our anti-Christian institutions as great forces for evil) there are many large-scale educational changes which might come under this category. Marriage preparation courses, pre-Cana and Cana Conferences are already nationwide. Perhaps the latter needs some explanation. One can easily see the appropriateness of the name for a series of discussions by married couples on Christian family life. The entire conference is dominated by a spirit of prayer, with the problems of married life and their solutions forming a large part of the discussions. At the moment almost one hundred priests are engaged in this work throughout nineteen states.

Undoubtedly at the present time the best work that is being done to rebuild the family is in the field of re-education. At the request of Pius XI for a more thorough preparation for marriage, the Canadian Y.C.W. took up the Pope's directive and in 1938 after studying the papal encyclical on marriage laid plans to communicate their ideas to the working class. Meanwhile they conducted a survey to find the influence of religion on the ideals of marriage, only to discover the ignorance of the masses concerning the Christian ideal of married life and how greatly they were being affected by the pagan, materialistic standards about them. The outcome of a year of study was the Marriage Preparation

Service, organized in 25 dioceses to fit as nearly as could be determined the needs of all the people. Not only were oral courses planned but also courses by correspondence, intended to reach those for whom the others were not available. Since its organization, the Marriage Preparation Service has been a source of instruction for countless numbers of grateful youth.

Patterned somewhat after the Canadian courses are the marriage services of the Y.C.W. in this country. Groups of young men and women study the moral, psychological, physiological and social aspects of marriage in the light of Christian principles.

THE NEW YORK COURSE

For over two years the Y.C.W. in New York has been trying to meet the needs of New York working girls with a continuous series of marriage courses, abbreviating the Canadian course. It is more or less typical of the other courses in the United States.

One of the most gratifying things about this apostolic effort is the ease with which engaged or nearly-engaged girls can be persuaded to attend. This is one service which attracts all sorts and by no means merely the pious. They come hoping for some concrete and helpful information, and they get it. A brief summary of the content of the course would not be amiss here.

Our course consists in a series of five discussions, given weekly. Two are by a priest, two by a nurse and the final one by a Catholic married woman. That these are people convinced of the supernatural vocation of marriage does much toward inspiring the girls to the lofty ideals of Christian marriage. In general, the priest handles the spiritual and psychological, the nurse the physiological and the married woman the practical aspects of marriage, but no lecture is cut and dried and absolutely limited to its field.

A clear understanding of the marriage contract and the grace added to the contract by the sacrament of marriage is given by the priest. Marriage as a union of bodies, of mind and of souls is emphasized, for if the individual puts it on any one level or even three levels it eventually leads to unhappiness. Each of these unions and their inter-relationship is discussed with frankness so that there will be no misunderstanding as to the importance of all of them. The psychological differences between the sexes are then brought out, for it is very often here that misunderstanding arises from failure of the partners to understand one another's temperamental differences. If these temperamental differences are properly understood and accepted they will help them rather than hinder them.

It is only when each adopts the role intended by God for the other that trouble begins. Finally, it is stressed that for those who choose marriage as their vocation sanctity will be achieved only in and through it. With God as the center of marriage, there will follow the beautiful and sublime dignity of the married state and the adventure of continuing the human race through natural and supernatural life.

The talks by the nurse endeavor to clear up misapprehensions in regard to sex. The alarming failure of parents properly to instruct their children is only too evident and so from confused sources come confused ideas which must be corrected. A clear understanding of the physical union and again its relation to the spiritual union is given. The physiology of reproduction is discussed and the importance of good health for child-bearing is stressed.

A question period follows each lecture. Inevitably the priest is asked about rhythm. When giving the Church's stand, it is always emphasized that like any good thing it can be made bad with a bad purpose. The priest also stresses the responsibility these girls have toward the proper training and instruction of their own future children.

The lecture by the Catholic married woman gives an ideal that should be worked toward for a full Christian life. One cannot help but know that marriage is a vocation and not just another job after realizing that salvation depends on the way in which the duties of married life are carried out. Problems of food, clothing and housing are examined in the light of Christian principles and the advice suggested is to "work as if all depends on you and pray as if it all depends on God." Even such small beginnings are a step toward the re-Christianization of the institution of marriage. And these courses do have an effect. Many a girl spontaneously has expressed her gratitude for the frank and accurate information she has received. Her gratitude for a wholesome, integrated view of marriage is also noticeable. Most gratifying, however, are the cases where the girl's whole idea of marriage has been noticeably changed from 100% Hollywood to at least the beginning of some conception of the Christian ideal.

When courses like this have spread throughout the country as they are already quickly doing, it will mean we have attained a foothold for the re-Christianization of American youth.

MARY MANNIX
New York City

OFF TO THE MARKET

"Can we afford a child," they mused,
  Deciding that they wouldn't.
When they had made their pile, anon,
  They wanted one but couldn't.

Life with Mother

THE EXPERIENCE OF HAVING A CHILD should be for every woman, one which brings to her physical, emotional and spiritual maturity. She has been chosen by God as His instrument for presenting another soul to the world for His greater honor and glory. Pregnancy and childbirth are attended by many physical trials and difficulties but these may be amply compensated for by the spiritual rewards of increased mutual love between husband and wife and the joy of participating in the miracle of creation.

A novel that I have recently read, *Walk With A Separate Pride* by Sheila Alexander, aims at describing with a vivid reality the intimate feelings of a woman during her last months of pregnancy and in the pains of childbirth. The heroine, Nessa McKenna, whose husband is drafted in the seventh month of her pregnancy, is left alone to face the unknown terrors of having her first child. Her mother had died in childbirth and she struggles with a morbid fear of the same fate. She goes looking for comfort to her childhood home, arriving in time to be present at the deathbed of a beloved uncle. On her return to the city she faces an empty apartment and the cold soulless efficiency of a City Hospital clinic and delivery ward. Added to her fear for herself and her baby are those for her absent husband.

The whole situation is one that should turn a soul, bereft of human support, in search of Someone higher than herself. It is a time when she might grow tremendously in spiritual strength and in trust in God. Prayer should be her bulwark against loneliness and fear. It has all the potentialities of a great story.

Yet what has the author done with this material? A large part of the tale is told by allowing us to read Nessa's thoughts, or rather, I should say feelings, for there is little real thought there. Nessa McKenna is a creature completely lacking in spiritual perception of any kind, or even the most primitive gropings toward it. She fulfills the definition of a rational animal with emphasis on the word animal. Her emotions toward the creature growing within her are no higher than those of a favored mare, had she the power of expression. The description of the pains of childbirth is dramatic and quite exact biologically. It is too bad that Nessa, or Miss Alexander, did not know that the most excruciating pains may be joyously accepted when offered up to Christ in union with His; in reparation for sin, either our own sins or those of others.

Christ endured His bitter agony and death that He might bring forth Life to all men, that He might give birth to His Church. So too, the Christian mother endures lovingly the racking pains of giving birth, comforted by the thought that she is bringing forth new life even at the risk of her own.

When Nessa does experience joy and delight in her child it is quite animal-like. It is compounded of biological wonder and pleasure at this fruit of sexual love. She is not encouraged to feel otherwise by her experiences at the clinic, which queues up and handles the women as so many cows, valuable ones to be sure, but nevertheless cows.

Miss Alexander captures quite accurately the atmosphere of a modern pre-natal clinic. These clinics are marvels of medical science and aim at providing physically sound babies for the underprivileged who persist in having so many. The poor are given the finest medical advice and care at little or no expense. The result has been healthier babies and a tremendous decline in the infant mortality rate. However the harm they do cannot be compensated for by the good they accomplish.

A couple of years ago, in a burst of apostolic zeal, I broached the subject of a Catholic maternity guild to a parish priest, a good, zealous priest. His answer took me by surprise. He was willing to consider it but really saw no need for one in a large city supplied with several outstanding clinics for those in both poor and moderate circumstances. (They differ primarily in that one has a slightly higher social standing than the other.)

How I would like to take him on a typical day's visit to a typical clinic of the better sort; not as a visitor seeing the wonderful equipment and being filled with impressive statistics but as a patient following the regular routine.

Many of the women like Nessa McKenna are having their first child. Many more are there for the second, third or sixth. Those making many visits, frequently are given a bit of friendly or perhaps reproving advice on birth control, or, as most of the social workers prefer to express it, on planned parenthood.

Let us presume that our typical patient is having her fourth child. She arrives at the clinic between nine and ten o'clock after an early morning rush to feed and dress the other children and to leave things in order for the kind neighbor or friend who has offered to stay with them. Some mothers are not fortunate enough to have such a friend and must bring with them restless two or four year olds who have to be kept within reasonable bounds during the long dull wait. If she is able to arrive quite early the process is not too long. If she comes any time after nine there are already at least forty or fifty before her.

She goes to her desk, presents her identification, waits while her record is checked, receives a number and is sent to the next room for tests. This first detail is handled by an impersonal, efficient person, who, after long years at the task, often acquires the attitude that "that kind of people has to be kept in their place." A person so unfortunate as to arrive a minute or two late, or to have missed an appointment for whatever reason, is publicly rebuked and threatened with being dropped from the list.

In the room where tests are made our patient stands in line to be weighed, to have her blood pressure taken and a urinalysis done. The results are marked on her slip of paper and she returns to the waiting room to wait until her number is called!

She goes and sits on a long hard, overcrowded bench. The

women in such places usually speak with an intimacy and frankness shocking to the newcomer. Conversation is easily picked up and the topics center around morning sickness, labor pains, interesting complications, the swapping of birth control information, (strange in such surroundings) and intimate details of sexual life. If someone shows herself above these discussions she overhears someone wondering "who she thinks she is?" She learns to sit quietly, attempt to read a book, smile pleasantly and say as little as possible.

After a wait that frequently extends into an hour or two, she is interviewed by a doctor. He has her record and the results of her tests. He asks routine questions; any dizzy spells, vomiting, bleeding and have you any difficulties, mother? This is done rapidly with the sense of no time to waste if we are ever to get through that long line outside. At the conclusion of the interview she is allowed to go home, or if it is her day to be examined, she is passed along to the next waiting line.

The patients to be examined are told to disrobe. In clinics of the better sort robes are provided. In many the women keep on their slips. The "better sort" also provide curtained cubicles for undressing. The waiting line here is not so long but the examinations last longer than the interviews so that one may spend up to an hour here also.

In the examining room the patient climbs on a table and is prepared for the doctor. The doctor bustles in, usually attended by bored interns or students. The examination is thorough, the position of the baby is ascertained. Then the others are invited to probe and push the patient's stomach, to listen to the fetal heart and to express an opinion. No one bothers to ask the woman whether or not she minds being so probed and pushed. The young doctors have to learn, don't they? They all bustle out and into the next examining room. The patient goes back to the cubicles (this is a clinic of the better sort, remember) dresses and goes wearily home — unless the doctor has decided that she must have an x-ray or other treatment in which case she goes along to the next department.

In our novel, Nessa McKenna instinctively shrank from the cold, mass production methods of the clinic. She did not realize that these clinics are the outgrowth of attitudes such as her own towards birth and the human person. She is wallowing in the mystery of life making life. She is absorbed in the process of biological regeneration separated from any conception of a Creator as its Beginning or as its End.

The Christian mother cannot think of the formation of her child as a purely biological process. If she fears for his death, she fears lest he die without the Sacrament of Baptism. For her, his birth is climaxed by his re-birth in the waters of Baptism into the Mystical Body of Christ. Until methods for providing care and hospitalization for the Christian mother are in keeping with her dignity as a co-creator, only heroic faith and humility will aid her to remember it herself.

DOROTHY WILLOCK

PROGRESS

There was a Crooked Man
And he lived a crooked life,
Amasses a crooked fortune
And espoused a crooked wife;
He begot a crooked daughter
And a super-crooked son;
And the Crooked Spirit got him
When his crooked course was run.

PAUL A. LEWIS

Sins of Flesh and Commerce

SOCIOLOGY IS THE WOULD-BE-SCIENCE OF expediency, and fittingly honored in an age which has abandoned morality for expediency. We no longer act according to objective moral principles, doing things because they are *good*; rather do we do things because they seem to be *expedient,* even if that involves transgression of the moral law. Sociology purports to explain to college students what will be expedient. When expediency is carried into practice on a wide-spread, premeditated scale, it is called planning.

The irony of the situation is that the moral law indicates precisely what will be expedient, on the authority of One Person Who really knows, God. It is exactly insofar as we observe the moral law that things will turn out right. We can never calculate this exactly in advance because it depends largely on the grace of God and the free-will of men, and these are not humanly predictable factors. Sociology has to deny, in effect, that these factors exist, and then make its predictions in accordance with purely materialistic considerations. So sociology decides that education will improve with an appropriation of five billion dollars, and that criminals will soften up if the jails have better facilities, and that we shall have no more wars if we only practice birth control. The more we follow the principles of expediency, the worse mess we get into, materially and morally. Were it not that men's blindness increases in proportion to their folly, this would long since have become evident. To those who still have eyes to see, the true expediency of morality becomes increasingly evident. Even to the myopic it must be evident that the past performance of expediency leaves something to be desired. Another thing that becomes increasingly evident to the observant Christian is the unity of morality, the absolute impossibility of observing anything short of the totality of the moral law. Particularly obvious it is that the sins of the flesh cannot be separated from the sins of commerce. It is irrational to condemn Margaret Sanger and defer to the advertising profession.

One of the preoccupations of sociology is the matter of population. It is also a preoccupation of morality. The fruit of sociological probings are the expedient laws for the regulation of population, chiefly the law of the necessity of practicing contraception, and the law (gradually gaining acceptance) of the advisability of imposing euthanasia.

The moral law has lately been struggling along (firmly, but losing ground in practice) on one wheel. It has affirmed in a loud voice that we shall not practice contraception. It has been relatively silent in regard to the commercial sins which have been accessory to the crime of race suicide. It will be useful to show the profound relationship that exists between the sins of the flesh and the sins of commerce.

THE LAWS OF FERTILITY

Fertility is the measure of fecundity. It varies according to laws which are not wholly fathomable, at least at this point. Many a birth-controller is discovering that it is not really in our power mechanically to regulate the quantity of human beings who walk this earth, much less their quality. There are not a few unhappy modernists who have found that years of conscientious contraception have evidently been quite unnecessary, for they are sterile. Here are some of the real laws of fertility:

I. Under conditions of hardship nature will preserve the species at the expense of the individual.

This law is readily observable in plant life. It also applies to the human species. If you are growing carrots and there is a drought, the carrots will absorb the last moisture in the soil, using it *not* to become bigger and better carrots, but to go to seed, i.e. to preserve the species carrot.

So it is with human beings. One obvious example is furnished by the pregnant woman and her child. If there is not enough calcium for the two of them, the fetus will get its full quota of calcium, and never mind the mother's teeth.

However, the law works much more generally than that. If undue hardship is put upon a people, they will have more children than they would otherwise have had. The classic example of this is the case of the Israelites whom the Egyptians hoped to exterminate by oppression. The worse the Egyptians treated them, the more they increased in numbers, as the Egyptians themselves observed and lamented. See the first chapter of Exodus for details. Incidentally, the sociologists and other modern law-givers might learn quite a few things from the Bible. For instance, the whole theory of "rhythm" is contained in the Book of Leviticus, whereas modern "scientists" had it completely backwards until recently. Needless to say, the concern of the Old Law was in the interests of fertility, rather than vice versa. The fact that the Jews observed this law, together with the recurring persecutions they have suffered, probably furnishes the natural explanation of the survival of that race.

But one need not go back to Egypt to observe the workings of the law that a hard-pressed people will have more children than usual. It was the commonly observed phenomenon of the industrial system that the poor were always having too many babies.

And from the law certain simple deductions are obvious. The first is that you don't have to press contraception on the poor; if you just give them more to eat (that is to say, if you just practice a little justice and charity) they will oblige by having fewer children anyhow. The next is that we and God are not of one mind in the matter of species versus individual. After all, God it is Who made the laws of nature, Who arranged that the species should be preferred to the individual. Whenever we get

a chance, we decree just the opposite. Most all family limitation schemes are based on solicitude for the well-being and comfort of those already here. Abortion, of course, is a gross imposition of our preference, even at the expense of committing murder. So also is the custom of choosing whether the mother or the child shall live in a case of difficult childbirth. No human being has the right to make the choice. Non-Catholic doctors do make it though, and customarily in favor of the mother. Were the choice put to a truly Christian mother, she would certainly decide otherwise.

11. The birth rate fluctuates with the death rate.

Increasingly enough, (and characteristically) the sociologists have this law backwards. They are always trying to show that if you fix up the birth rate (by contraception) the death rate will go down. This is the old story about it being better to have *one* healthy child than *five* unhealthy children who will die young. But children do not die of having too many brothers and sisters, they die of tuberculosis or diphtheria or something, which may come partly from being poor. The causal relationship is between poverty and death, not between large families and death, and the obvious thing to do is to treat the poverty.

However, the law does work the other way around. Changes in the death rate tend to be reflected in the birth rate. Taking the matter in the large, it appears that throughout nature the birth rates of species have adjusted to their chances of survival. That is why some species have abundant fertility (the conger eel lays fifteen million eggs a year) while others, whose chance of death are slight, reproduce slowly (the fulmar petrel lays one egg a year). It is because of this tendency to adjust that a balance in nature is obtained and the world is not over-run by two or three conquering species of animal or insect. It is devotedly to be hoped that the advent of D.D.T. and its possible irresponsible use will not, by too sudden changes, upset the balance nature has established.

Within limits, the birth rate can adjust itself to changes in the death rate. When salmon are preyed upon heavily one year they return the next year fairly bursting with eggs. When human beings make wars, the carnage thereof seems to be followed by an increase in the birth rate which cannot be entirely attributed to the more loving nature of veterans.

Note that this law works in both directions. If there is an increase in the death rate, there is liable to be a corresponding increase in the birthrate (as shown, for instance, in the tremendous increase in the population of Ireland during the famine years. It is useful to note here how God uses our sins for His own purposes. This tremendous increase in population among the Irish forced them to migrate, and served to carry the Faith to many places).

On the other hand, if you bring the death rate down, the birth rate lowers of itself. There was a striking example of this in the Suez Canal area during the early years of this century. Owing to malarial conditions in the region surrounding the Canal there was a very high death rate. Officials hesitated to improve living conditions by a drainage project for fear that then the population, which also had a very high birth rate, would outstrip its food supply and end up in yet more suffering. Nevertheless, they did drain the area. The death rate dropped as anticipated, but to their surprise, the birth rate fell correspondingly *of its own accord*.

The moral of this law is that nothing but good will come of our pursuing a virtuous course in reducing death rates, as notably through modern medical advances, but that we should stop interfering artificially in the matter of births.

III. Fertility decreases with luxurious living.

It is because of the operation of this law that the rich tend to have fewer children than they would normally, and this even apart from contraception, which greatly aggravates the situation.

There seem to be two main causes. This first is purely physical. Luxury means soft living, food in excess, and food which makes for fat rather than sinew. Besides there is the important factor of a lessening of exercise on the part of the rich, which further adds to the softness and detracts from the fertility of the body.

The second factor is psychological. Life which is too easy is a breeding ground for neuroses, which mitigate against fertility quite often.

To take a calloused view of the situation, it appears that extravagance and riches ill become the human race, and so nature goes through cycles of sloughing off those who have become parasitical drains on society. Indeed, it is a well-observed fact that the "best families" are prone to decadence much more than the laboring classes who really don't have time. We are in a period now in which both the quantity and quality of our erstwhile leading families is suffering diminution, and we are still awaiting new leaders with sufficient vitality to lead and save us. Society does not suffer too much from the recurrent renewal of its vitality from below. But see what has happened in our own day. There seems to be no real reservoir of vitality left in America. Why? Because from the physical point of view (the important point of view is not physical but spiritual; however spiritual debility parallels the physical pretty well in this case) we are all "enjoying" luxurious living, and our vitality and fertility is correspondingly drained. For this we can thank the industrial-capitalist system which, as its admirers love to reiterate, has raised the general standard of living in industrial countries to a level unknown in history. We are now all privileged to live in crowded cities, sit hours in the movies, and days in office chairs, eat white bread, drink pasteurized milk and get jelly doughnuts from the bakery. We can all have neuroses too. Only a malcontent would remind us that there is not beauty anywhere, that we have no space and no fresh air, that our jobs are meaningless and dull, and that maybe there would have been more joy in a baby than in a radio. We know better. We have equality. Sterility is no longer the prerogative of the rich.

IV. Populations tend to stabilize within enclosed areas.

All the old birth-controllers' arguments were based on the theory that if you just went on having children the race would increase geometrically by leaps and bounds until very shortly there wouldn't be room for us all, much less food for us all. As a matter of fact, under relatively good conditions, and in a closed economy, the population tends to stabilize itself. This may have something to do with the fact that people living in closed economies do not eat exotic food, I don't know.

The outstanding example of this law is Japan, where the population remained just about stationary between the years 1723 and 1846. This was the period during which Japan shut her doors to all outside interference, especially from western civilization. There was no overcrowding during this time, and a good standard of living (not the American way of life, of course; we speak now of essentials, not luxuries) prevailed. There was an agrarian-craft economy. No birth-control was practiced. There were no major wars, no grievous natural catastrophes, no plagues. At the end of the period, as at the beginning, the population was about 27 million. After this period Japan rapidly became a "civilized" and then an industrial power. With industrialization the mass of people became poorer, and then the population soared. By 1934, it was, with her dependencies, 84 million. One has only to reflect that the underlying natural cause of the late war in the Far East was the over-population of Japan, to have another example of the marvelous benefits which flow from industrial capitalism.

V. God provides a natural spacing between babies in the period of lactation.

All the modern talk about baby spacing (it was up to four-year intervals a while ago, but appears to be coming down) neglects to consider the fact that nature normally provides an interval between children, and that that interval is the period of lactation (which with the period of pregnancy would usually make the children two years or so apart). This fact has been part of the folk wisdom of the race up until now. It has been variously used. Women who wished to avoid pregnancy have nursed their children scandalously long. Chinese women who have sometimes wished to speed up propagation have given their newborn out to wet nurses so that they themselves might become pregnant soon again.

The late Alexis Carrel set down this law categorically in the *Readers Digest* some years ago in an article about the advisability of nursing babies. However, there are probably many doctors who would deny that there is such a natural law, on the grounds that it no longer can be counted on to operate in regard to modern American women. As a matter of fact, deft inquiry among nurses, mothers and grandmothers usually results in a flat denial of the law by young nurses, assent among grandmothers, and a qualified statement from mothers of grown children to the effect that, "Oh yes, that used to work, but it doesn't any more."

Someone ought to make a study as to why it doesn't work any more. Such a study would be complicated by the fact that many women are physically unable to nurse their babies anyhow.

THE CONCATENATION OF SINS

As every liar knows, one lie leads to an ever-increasing number of other lies to cover up the first one. So it is with social expediency. You break the moral law once, and then you have to do it again and again and again and again. There is no end short of a return to the moral law. It is wise to keep this in mind, because the current evils of birth control and euthanasia and abortion are really the latest manifestations of a chain of sins in the service of expediency. It is not so much that anyone desires them of themselves, as that they are more or less inevitable, given the circumstances which occasion them. Let us examine the chain. It will take us back to England, where the industrial revolution began.

Sins of Flesh and Commerce

Be it noted, first of all, that the population of England and Wales remained almost stationary during the 14th to the 16th centuries, at a little less than 2½ million people. As far as we can determine, there was never an increase during that period of more than 3% per ten-year period. This was the Merrie England which we so love to represent on our Christmas cards and assiduously avoid imitating in our daily life (if it were still possible, which of course it isn't — the face of the earth has changed from a Sherwood Forest to the wasteland of industrialism.)

The chain of circumstances which started with the Reformation and culminated in the industrial revolution profoundly changed England. There is no need to go into the well-known details here. First there was the confiscation of the monastic lands, which was followed in time by the enclosure laws and wholesale evictions. Meanwhile the widespread pauperization occasioned by the dissolution of the monasteries (it broke the whole framework of charity, and in addition set the religious in vagabondage) was dealt with first by inhuman laws against beggary and then by Poor Laws which were not any good either. Meanwhile small farms (through evictions) were consolidated into large farms, two or three families sufficing where formerly there had been several hundred, and arable land became pasture. County people were forced into the city, where they lived wretchedly and where they became grist for the mills of industrialism, which was just then unfortunately beginning. One can scarcely read the account of the industrial beginnings in England (which have finally culminated in the evils which beset that unfortunate country today, not to mention the ills and ugliness which have spread to the far corners of the earth from it) without weeping. Still, it is the purpose of this paper not to lament but to note the effects on population. *The most notable effect of the industrial revolution was a tremendous increase in population.* There are some people so misled that they would like to make out that this shows how good the industrial revolution was.

Note these increases:
Prior to 1751 — never more than 3% increase in population in any ten-year period.

1751–1761	6% increase
1761–1771	6% increase
1771–1781	6% increase
1781–1791	9% increase
1791–1801	11% increase
1801–1811	14% increase
1811–1821	18% increase

During the years between 1800 and 1820 there were famine conditions in England. After 1821 a vast emigration set in, so that 18% represents the peak increase percentage.

During the early period of industrialism children were welcomed because they were useful in the factories when they were as young as four years old. It is better to pass over this period swiftly.

In time industrialism began to regret the high birth rate. Technical improvements in machinery made child-labor unnecessary, as also a lot of adult labor. Periods of unemployment were setting in. Over-production was at first compensated for by exploiting all the unindustrialized countries of the world, but as other countries became industrialized themselves, the consequences of over-production caused more and more misery on the home front.

It was at this period that a few advanced and far-seeing souls started to see the advantage of contraception. Basically the advocates of contraception have always argued in the same way: Here we have a situation which is inevitable and cannot be changed (why not?), and therefore we have to go on to show mercy (or protect our own financial interests) through birth control. It is one of the mysteries of iniquity that industrial capitalism has always been considered immutable. Legion are the immoralities which have been perpetuated to the chant of "industrial capitalism is here to stay."

The next stage of industrialism, which is the one we are still in, is the stage in which it was realized by the capitalists that the worker is also the consumer, and that he must buy the luxuries he makes, even if he has to go without the necessities to do so. Here is where advertising comes in, which now surrounds all of us, inciting our concupiscence in every direction. Now the worker is willing to practice birth control, because he has to cut down somewhere and the advertisements will not let him cut down on clothes, extravagant food, amusements or labor-saving devices. Besides, his wife is usually working to help keep up the new standard of life.

But if a man does not practice birth control, he is still in a rather bad way as regards propagating the race. First of all, there is the danger of sterility from luxurious living and neuroses. But besides that there is the fact that his wife will have children with increasing difficulty.

It has been shown that soft, luxurious, depleted modern foods make childbirth increasingly difficult, through nutritional deficiencies which narrow the pelvic girdle. The increased difficulty leads in turn to increased need for hospitalization, more expense and elaborate anesthesia, etc.

All the way along the line, from the dissolution of the monasteries (which marked the destruction of the Catholic Church in England and its moral authority), all the way along from the banishing of the priests to the turning out of the cottagers, to the crowding in the cities, to the poverty, the materialism, the introduction of contraception, all the way down to the Raleigh cigarette ads of our own glorious day, an increased sexual license has accompanied the process. The birth control people may not be in favor of high school delinquency, but they are certainly fostering it. So and so, who has a 40-million dollar factory, may not personally like adultery, but he is certainly providing a breeding ground for it, if only because of the dullness and uncreativity of the jobs in his plant. Do advertisers regret that they have to break down our will power in order to make their pretentious livings? One has not heard it.

THE FUTURE

It is evident now that we are in the crescendo part of the development herein outlined. In the cities, there is a rapid intensification of all the evils: overcrowding, adulteration, pretension, pornography, despair, luxury. There is no sign of repentance, no sign of a reversal of direction. Take, for instance, the persistent efforts of city people to prevent decentralization. Consider the curious circumstance under which the United Nations' Headquarters came to choose a site in the heart of New York City. It looked for a while as though the United Nations was going to settle in Philadelphia, but the Rockefellers stopped that at a cost to themselves of, as I remember, some eight million dollars. Now obviously peace can be deliberated as well in the City of Brotherly Love as in New York. Why is it worth eight million dollars to the Rockefellers to keep the United Nations in an already hopelessly congested area? Can it be to protect their real estate interests?

In the country, the situation is comparable. Large holdings and commercial farming are the rule. This tends to depopulate the country and so lessen the yield per acre (although it increases, temporarily, the yield per farmer).

The birth rate has been falling in England since 1900, and is in a bad way here (although temporarily buoyed up by a post-war boom in babies). With a falling birth rate you get a preponderancy of old people, who must be supported by a decreasing number of young people. Hence our preoccupation with social security. It would normally be quite a burden for the young to care for preponderantly large numbers of old. Who dares say that this does not present a temptation to the practice of euthanasia?

Even the Planned Parenthood Association is now concerned about the lack of fertility in its clients. It is expediency again, and not a return to morality. It will presently be expedient, especially if we get a dictator and are going to have another war, for the state to pay double for illegitimate children. By then we shall have committed just about all the sins it is possible for us to commit from having departed from the laws of objective morality.

THE REMEDY

The only remedy, of course, is to start immediate, strict observance of the *entire* moral law. Let those who marry have children as God sends them. It will comfort them to remember that God is not bound by the laws of a bad economic system, and that He will provide, somehow, extra (extra rooms and extra food) for the children He sends. It will take an heroic faith to act upon this principle, and a willingness to sacrifice a materialistic way of life. It is characteristic of our day that nothing less than an heroic faith will suffice. But there is no alternative, the mediocre will go under.

There will have to accompany this heroic trust in God's Providence, a general spiritual revolution against the materialism of our time. Let us preach the *un*importance of being well-dressed. Let it be bruited about that it is a sin to incite concupiscence, whether it be a lust for an all-electric kitchen, incited through the courtesy of the *Saturday Evening Post* and the advertising agencies; or whether it be smart pornography in fashionable night clubs. Let us somehow or other leave the cities, somehow or other get wholesome food again.

Let us forget about the American Way of Life, and start the Godly Way of Life, which will bring down graces upon us to rectify all the messes we have made of things.

CAROL ROBINSON

INTEGRITY, May 1947

TOO LITTLE AND TOO LATE

Planning parents can hardly hope,
   With two or three but seldom more,
To match a Catherine of Sien'
   The last but one of twenty-four.

Our Child is Mentally Defective

THE PRESENCE OF EVIL IN THE UNIVERSE OF an All-Good, All-Powerful Creator is the springboard from which philosophers and theologians have taken to the waters of turbulent discussions. Lo, these many years.

The problem constitutes more than an academic challenge when it confronts you, the Man in the Street, in one of its protean, material forms. A solution becomes then an urgent, personal necessity. You cry, with Saint Augustine:

"Whence is this evil?"

When the doctor told us that our baby was mentally defective, our reaction was one of incredulity. Surely he — only a country practitioner, after all — had made a mistake. It wasn't possible that we were the victims of this Thing that happens, the doctor said, only once in ten thousand times.

Whistling in the dark, we left his office to begin the long pursuit of the will o' the wisp of hope. It beckoned us into the office of an ear specialist — perhaps the child was deaf only. "Just deaf" would be infinitely better than the other. It led us into the modernistic salon of a Park Avenue biochemist. He told us nothing at ten dollars a minute for five minutes. Perhaps we ought to see a brain man, we thought next. Thus hope teased us along a path of cruel self-delusion for many months. Like tenderfoots lost in the forest, we came back to where we'd started — and we were still lost.

My husband began to avoid the company of the child. He never went into the nursery and he made it plain that any conversations on the subject were painful. I began to dramatize myself as a valiant figure, fighting this battle in noble aloneness. I am ashamed to admit that I even did my husband the injustice of considering him callous and unfeeling. I had forgotten that fathers want to be proud of their sons, that they normally take them fishing and watch them play football, that a father's loving folly prompts him to buy an electric train long before the little fellow is old enough to know the difference between a transformer and a caboose. My husband's grief was inarticulate. His only armor was to act the role of tough guy. From the perspective that time has since afforded, I see now that I was far from alone in this desolate period.

One son was two years old when Mary was born. She came into the world, charming and alert from the moment she filled her lungs with the alien Connecticut air and started squalling with the same virtuosity she has exhibited in everything else she has done since then. Every day thenceforward the difference between the two children became more marked as Mary followed the normal pattern of development. She outstripped her brother in only a few weeks.

The time had come. We could ignore no longer the fact that emerged from the fog of wishful thinking in which we had obscured it in our unwillingness to face the truth of the situation. With nothing left to explore or exploit, we now acknowledged that no human agency however skilled could restore wholeness to the congenitally defective son whom we had brought into the world with expectation and joy. We had to go on from there.

Our prayers bombarded Heaven. We had Masses said and the Sisters made innumerable novenas for our importunate intention. God works miracles all the time, we reassured ourselves, not yet really reconciled. I remember spending hour after hour trying to teach our son whom we had brought into the world with expectation and joy. To him, just once more, whispering, "Little Flower, make him do it, make him do it, this simple, little gesture!"

But he never learned to do it.

Time mitigated the shock of acknowledgment but it aggravated the heaviness of heart that comes with living with sorrow intimately, month after interminable, unrelieved month. Our emotions were spent. Psychologically this was, as I look back on it, the most crucial phase of our readjustment. For it was then that we were tempted to search the Will of God. Perhaps we were no more than His pawns in the pastime of Eternity. Omar's philosophy was beguiling, if specious. Why had the hand of the Potter shaken as he scooped up the primeval clay, imprisoning an immortal soul in the imperfect vase of our child's body? Was He a sadistic god, using power in the manner of an Infinite Bully because its exercise filled him with brutal exuberance? These thoughts came to me many times as I watched the little boy with the aureole of golden hair. They came, unbidden, during the night when his constant wailing filled me with that sense of indescribable desolation that Matthew Arnold called "the eternal note of human sadness." I thought beyond this present and personal grief and saw it as only a microcosm in the tide of war, disease, corruption and sin that engulfs all mortal things. That I had company in my sorrow did not alleviate the misery. It served rather to enhance it. I was aware that it had universal implications — Weltschmerz pervaded my thinking.

I discussed these thoughts with my confessor. He told me that God would send me the grace I needed, that even Our Lord had cried, "My God, My God, why hast Thou forsaken Me?"

Our child was very ill during the first days following her birth. This incident precipitated a decision to which we had been reluctant to address ourselves. We placed our son in the care of a woman whose name you would not recognize but whose work on behalf of a small group of other defective children has been heroic. She was a trained nurse. She had foresworn an easier phase of her profession because of her concern over the lack of facilities for the care of these children and had opened a twenty-bed hospital. When I took our son to place him there, she took me into the ward. As I looked at the monstrous infants in the little, white beds, I said to her,

"How sad this all is — they would be so lovely if they were normal!"

Her answer was vehement. Stroking the head of a tiny, hydrocephalic baby, she replied passionately,

"They are lovely — otherwise God would not have made them."

Her face was ridiculously low and she never asked parents to pay for extra items such as oxygen or special medications and doctors' consultations. Our association with her was an important factor in the rehabilitation of the emotional and spiritual damage we had undergone. She had opened a door!

Our child has never come home again. We believe that the care he is getting now is far better than that which we could provide and that his presence would prejudice the psychological welfare of the three little daughters who are entitled to the environment of a normal home. We seldom talk about our son and we visit him only when an emergency makes it advisable. This arrangement originally required a degree of self-discipline on our part. It appears, for us, the wiser course. Conforming to it has become automatic. Only once in a while do I remember, as it is written in "Kristin Lavransdatter,"[1] that a mother's heart is never delivered of its burden as the womb is.

After fifteen years of trial-and-error groping for the answer to Saint Augustine's "Whence is this evil?", we have found the answer.

The answer, found, surprised us. It was the realization that what we thought to be evil was in reality a manifestation of God's goodness. Our prayers have been answered — and far more generously than we had dared hope for in the days we prayed for a miracle.

This experience has brought us from shallowness and doubt, to the deeper, unsounded waters of spiritual understanding and human sympathy. It has not made saints of us — we are too blamed ornery for that — but we hope that it has purified our lives of much that was superficial and worldly. God has given us

---

1 Trilogy of historical novels written by the Norwegian Nobel laureate Sigrid Undset from 1920 to 1922. — Ed.

a precious commodity, the gift of interior peace that comes when one has finally achieved an unconcern for the ephemeral and the temporal. He has honored us with a privilege unwarranted by our worldliness for we have been the vessel in which has been raised to Him a soul utterly uninfected by the contagions of sin. Our son's life has been a constant act of reparation for the irreligion and materialism of the world in which he will never move.

Supplementing these spiritual blessings, God has even provided temporal blessings with splendid largesse. He has sensitized us to His Face in the stars and the seas and the panorama of the Seasons. He has increased our capacity for joy in the three little daughters who get A's on their report cards, have perennially rosy cheeks and are sometimes derelict in washing behind their ears. This life looks good to us.

I believe that our mentally defective child has justified his existence in time as well as in eternity. The investment of mortal tears will return immortal dividends.

Saint Paul wrote:

"Our own tribulation which is at present momentary and light worketh for us above measure exceedingly an eternal weight of glory." (2 Cor. 4: 17)

What more can we ask?

ANONYMOUS

INTEGRITY, May 1947

MATRIARCH

A tower of strength, beyond reproach,
   Is Mrs. John McBarry.
She loves her girls so very much,
   She will not let them marry.

The Family Has Lost Its Head

THE RHYME ABOUT MR. AND MRS. JACK SPRAT and their divergent tastes in meat is a refreshing relic from some earlier day when it was considered more important that mates should be complementary than that they should be similar. The fact that Jack could eat no fat, and the Mrs. eat no lean is as apt and typical a condition of material dissimilarity as one could find. My wife abhors sugar in her tea, whereas I dislike cream. My friend's wife loves brilliantly colored furnishings, while he prefers neutral shades. This divergence in tastes rather than making married life difficult, is the factor most contributive to its preservation as an institution. Diversity makes for beauty.

In this factor, we see but one in a legion of reasons why the idea of the family and the true relation of its parts is almost incomprehensible to the modern mind. In the modern scheme of things, the concept of unity is not that which one finds in an organism such as a flower or vine, but rather that kind of unity found in a heap of ashes. Instead of dissimilar things brought to a common fruition by a sharing of functions, the modern unity is achieved by the reduction of all things to their elemental form. The relations of persons is no longer a meeting of minds, but a wedding of valences, or, in marriage, the reconciliation of metabolisms. Consequently, the solution to divorce is not the marriage of likes, but marriage based upon a concept of life that finds order and beauty in diversity. The sole requirement for pairing off under such a concept, would be that the man be manly, the woman womanly, and both more or less willing to accept the fact that the children would be childish. All that *needs* to be common to a man and wife, is a common Faith, common sense, a common bed and board, and common children. Beyond this, all other common interests can only cement the marital bond, if they are interests normally common to either sex.

To the peril of the institution of the family, men are seeking to build the common bond upon those habits of the man and woman, which by their nature should remain autonomous. Rarely sharing a common faith, the marital expert insists that the mates read the same books or smoke the same brand of cigarettes. Commonly lacking common sense, the man and wife are counseled to share the same intellectual prejudices. Frequently lacking a normal quota of common children, the couples are advised to baby each other, and play the same games. Now if the basis of marriage harmony is playing the same games, you may be sure that it will be a losing game, and one in which it will be more and more the custom for one child to pick up the marbles and look for another playmate. To say that marriage is companionship is the same kind of lie as saying that Christ was a good man. If that is all that He is, or all that it is, then the human race has been victim of a malicious fraud. If marriage is a question of a man leaving a number of male companions to cling to one female companion, the marriage is a mad institution. It is just a mad kind of card game in which the dummy has the children; it is a kind of tennis match in which the children are the balls, and love is a way of keeping score. It is a race in which the human race is bound to lose.

Marriage is a wonderful thing that only God could have invented. The Church compares it with the union between Christ and His Church, for there is no other comparison on earth to do it justice. This should serve as warning to us that we should approach a study of marriage with great humility, realizing at the outset that this institution has only the faintest resemblance to the modern substitute falsely classified under the same title, and listed in the same book at City Hall.

Saint Paul has something to say about marriage which is of more than passing interest. The Church in her wisdom has incorporated it into the nuptial Mass. The good saint says, "Let women be subject to their husbands as to the Lord: for the husband is the head of the wife, as Christ is the Head of the Church. He is the Savior of His body. Therefore, as the Church is subject to Christ, so let the wives be to their husbands in all things." On the basis of this testimony, with that nasty dogmatism so characteristic of Catholics, I present the statement without debate that "the man is head of the family." This is a conclusion hardly substantiated by statistics. Generally speaking, the American male is not the head of the family. This difference between the counsel of St. Paul and the evidences of our senses in the matter of masculine headship is of prime importance, if we are intent upon reforming the family. The restoration of all things in Christ must include, well up on the agenda, the restoring of the man to his proper position within the family economy.

THE DIFFERENCES BETWEEN THE SEXES

The most obvious fact and consequently the one most overlooked except by simple-minded Christians, is that marriage is a happy relationship because of the difference between the sexes, and not because they are similar. The proper end of marriage is the propagation of children and depends, it has been whispered, on functions peculiar to each sex. This evokes a problem very upsetting to the equalitarian. Difference of function implies difference in status. You cannot say that a woman is the equal of a man, any more than you can say that an apple is the equal of a peach, unless you have a different definition of equality from the rest of mankind. This difference between the sexes is not only physical but psychological, and it is because of these natural differences and not because of any ecclesiastical decree that man is the normal head of the family.

Man's physical qualifications for the job of headship are seldom questioned. His superior physical strength makes him the logical breadwinner, and for obvious reasons the breadwinner should be the head of the family. Women, during long periods of pregnancy, and while nursing, are dependent. This dependency indicates the function of the man. The head of the family must be independent. Adequate as these reasons may be for the establishment of headship, it is more the psychological peculiarities of the man which indicate his proper function as husband and father.

The outstanding male tendency is to be objective. The man can more readily stand off and consider a thing apart from its relation to himself. In a woman this quality, though possible, is rarely developed. She, on the contrary, is personal and tends to measure all things with her heart. For that reason, she is more readily sympathetic and willing to serve. It is this tendency, when brought to virtue, which makes a woman the warm, pulsating heart of the family. When she is free to do so, a woman gravitates to certain interests and occupations different from those which capture the fancy of man. Seldom is she interested in those sciences which demand the utmost in objectivity. The fields of theology, philosophy, mathematics, and academic law have been and always will be the fields of the man. Anything which requires human sympathy and selfless friendship will be most attractive to women. Women succeed as novelists, on the whole, because of their easily stimulated sympathies, and wherever the male novelist is superior it is usually because of philosophic content. Since man's objectivity makes him more interested in universals than particulars, the composition of music, and the making of art objects in their purest form, will always be predominantly male occupations. It is neither by accident nor conspiracy that women have always been homemakers, nor is it male arrogance to say that that is their proper place. The female temperament is most happy surrounded by particular and familiar creatures on which she may be free to exercise her tremendous capacity for loving devotion.

To tell a man that he is illogical is as much an insult as to deny a woman's intuitive abilities. Wives will always say, "John Jones, you make me mad. You're always so coldly analytical!"

The husband will eternally retort, "But you are always jumping to conclusions!" This is the method proper to each for attaining a deeper understanding of truth. The combination of the logical genius of man and the intuitive genius of woman is one of God's most beautiful syntheses, and it is the natural gift upon which the parents' authority to teach their children is based.

Man's other tendencies are a consequence of his objectivity, and his physical prowess. He is by nature aggressive and direct. It is his to initiate and to envision. The woman is by nature more retiring, satisfied to find strength in her husband's protection. She is circumspect, using devious methods to gain her ends, resorting to tact or diplomacy as expedient instruments. All of these innate characteristics help us to determine man's proper place in society and in the home.

DIFFICULT TO PROVE

What I have said here is not all that can be said about the relation of the man and wife in marriage, and you can't prove any of it by the isolated case of John Dee or Mary Daa. It would be even difficult to prove the aptness of categorizing male and female temperaments in this way, by taking a poll among your friends. That is the sad part of it! There is a condition in modern times which, for a lack of a better word, I will call feminization. It is a condition both in the family and in the community which is the result of a preponderance of feminine virtue being exercised under circumstances that demand the masculine approach. The blame, if there were any advantage to placing it anywhere, is upon the men. The women are not usurping the places of the men, nor would denying them that questionable privilege solve anything. Wives and mothers are being forced to take over the throne from which the husband and father has abdicated. The man has become inoperative.

Where it is the function of the woman to be heart and center of the family, it is the function of the man to relate his family to the rest of society for the mutual benefit of all. This *relating of the family to the community* is the root foundation of the married man's vocation. This is his field, his domain. If the man does not control this field then the woman must, and the result will be a disregard for the common good and an over-emphatic concern for the well-being of the individual family. Since the well-being of the individual family should proceed from the common good and not merely be a sum total of all the individual goods, an over-concern for the individual family's welfare will bring about a state of affairs spelling chaos for the whole society. There is a normal tension between the man and wife in regard to the question of the common good. It is the kind of tension that makes for balance. The woman will usually place the good of her family first. For her to do so is normal. The man, if he is truly head of the family, realizes that his family's well-being depends upon the common good and thus will make the common good the first end of his work. With him that sense called social consciousness will not be merely a part-time hobby, but the motivating force in everything he does. When called upon to do so, he will even jeopardize his family's welfare in order to serve the common good. Men have always done this in time of war. It may sometimes be asked of them in time of peace. Today, faced as we are with the need for reorganizing the social order, this responsibility to serve the common good cannot be shirked if we are to avoid complete disaster.

As it was of St. Joseph, the greatest praise for a man is that he be a "just man." The masculine temperament, being objective, logical, and direct, is a fitting occasion for the virtue of justice. This is the virtue most lacking in persons and their affairs today. We have evidence of charity, goodwill, emotional sympathy on the part of many people, all of which fail to compensate for the lack of justice. It is typically feminine to be sympathetic for the lot of the impoverished. It is typically masculine to crusade against the injustices which are the root cause of the deprivation.

MATRIARCHY

The average American family is approaching a matriarchy. Sons are adopting the virtues of their mothers for lack of a substantial display of masculine virtue by the fathers. The movies, radio scripts, and comic strips have all adopted this theme of masculine inferiority in the home, and it rings appallingly true to life. Among the faithful in the Church it is as evident as elsewhere. The expression of the Faith today is primarily private devotion and not public apostolicity, and it is the former that appeals most to women, and the latter which appeals most to men. Even the parochial men's groups have taken on a feminine flavor hardly relieved by an occasional "Sport Nite." Not the least misfortune that results from this feminization is that these male parochial groups act as buffers between the clergy and other men who, though possibly less pious, possess an aggressive masculinity ripe for conversion to the apostolate.

The consent and endless regard of today's good husband for the well-being of his family, so that he saves from the time of their birth for the education of his children while his neighbor's children starve, or while his local political system grows corrupt, or his Faith goes unchampioned, or his brother is exploited, is a sign of the times. It is goodness measured by the standard of the wife, and thus she is the actual head of the family. This is not good headship measured by any objective standard. Such a father may leave an inheritance of wealth to his sons, whereas what they need most is masculine virtue lived out for their emulation. The son in such a matriarchy of predominantly feminine concerns becomes one of those lads whose lack of masculine virtue has been called "momism." Under stress, he becomes inoperative for lack of the soothing hand of a tender woman on his brow. He is of little use to the army and is poor material for Catholic Action. Unless he mend his ways, the son of such a father will prove to be a greater handicap to his future wife than was his dad. He will be just another child for his wife to care for. Until men go back to the masculine pursuits of devotion to the common good, relating the talents of their children to that end, they will fail to fulfill amply the office of head of the family.

THE CAUSES

The cause of a lapsed fatherhood is not difficult to find. I think there are two root causes. The first is immodesty on the part of women and incontinence on the part of men. The second is intellectual irresponsibility bred by modern methods of work.

Modesty and continence go hand in hand. Without either or both virtues men become the slaves of women. The natural tendencies to sexual promiscuity and feminine coquettishness as consequence of original sin have been aided and intensified by the popular use of contraceptives. Previous to their wide-spread distribution, male continence was encouraged by women if not by the moral law, for fear of the social tragedy of bearing illegitimate children. Nature permitted to take its course rendered a punishment that few women would dare risk incurring. Thus for reasons of respectability as well as morality certain social precautions were taken to save men from themselves. The most effective of these was modesty in dress. Another was the custom of chaperons, both good Christian customs. The manufacture of contraceptives (made possible by mass-production methods) changed all this. There was nothing to fear now but God, (which is ironic, because if God were generally feared neither contraceptives nor mass-production would ever have come into existence!). Women set out to be attractive, and men gave up trying to be continent. The whole social attitude toward woman changed so that today a pious virgin can dress to the point of being indistinguishable from a harlot without evoking any comment more adverse than a whistle.

Thus change in the character of womanhood drastically revised the common attitude toward marriage. Having children became arbitrary. The female instrument of contraception placed the decision for having children on the shoulders of the mother. It became her prerogative to say how few children she should have. When you add this fact to the obsolescence of the male virtue of continence it is no wonder that the modern male has become subservient. We would be astonished to discover how many kept women decide the policies of our nation, due to the judicious use of their wiles and the extreme vulnerability of incontinent men.

Wherever the Catholic family continues to maintain the Christian principles of morality in relation to the marriage act, it has to be done unaided by social customs and habits of the same order. Although a wife may be of good will, she may still subscribe to the current social views of female decorum wherever they do not obviously clash with morality. She may still feel that children are arbitrary and encourage the practice of Catholic (?) birth control indiscriminately and for motives hardly sufficient to warrant so dangerous a practice. The man may consider his wife an exception while continuing to hold the current views toward womanhood. This will not only try his fidelity but also make him unfit to guide his growing sons and daughters. Private virtue in regard to chastity will always be seriously threatened until it is accompanied by public customs of morality.

The second cause of the loss of male leadership may very well be a remote consequence of the first. It is otherwise difficult to explain why men have for so long tolerated a social system so detrimental to the fulfillment of their vocations. The concentration of productive property in the hands of a few has left the average husband no alternative but to let himself out for hire. He no longer possesses either the skills, the property, or the tools to set his own motives or standards of work. Returning home from an office where all his conquests have been of doubtful merit to the community at large, or from a factory where his efficiency is measured by mechanical standards, he can maintain dominion over his family only by reversing the habits which have characterized his day. What virtues he does possess can only be revealed to his children under home circumstances much more favorable to his wife. He finds himself helping her in tasks of her own invention, doing work which she initiates. In the eyes of the children and his wife, he soon assumes a subordinate role. It is a small wonder that the suburban husband in more cases than one seems somewhat less formidably masculine than his wife!

TO REASSURE THE LADIES

A casual glance at the foregoing arguments might lead my lady readers to arm themselves against a turbulent and bloody revolution espoused by the menfolk. Housewives might run to the drygoods store for scarlet draping material to match the color of the blood soon to be shed in their living rooms. Dear old dad, they may suspect, will go about like some Charles Laughtonesque lion seeking whom he may devour. Becoming once again the head of the family might go to father's head. By contrast with the new regime of Barretts of Wimpole Street will be considered a family with a hen-pecked father. For that reason, before jumping to such conclusions (or, if you will, arriving at intuitive perceptions), I hope that the ladies' glances will be more than casual. Whatever a male headship may add to a household will be something more satisfying than bruises or broken heads. It might be that peace of mind so vainly sought by neurotic matrons in the book of that same name. At any rate it will be a state of affairs which a more sane people than we considered normal.

Whatever the specific remedy may be, the general prescription is this. Men must return to the concept of manhood in which each man is considered to have a mission to fulfill. This mission is related to: first, the honor and glory of God; second, the common good, and third, to his specific contribution to each. In the work of fulfilling this mission some men take a helpmate, so that in one flesh, and one mind, and one heart, they may more effectively accomplish this mission. As a result of this holy union, children are born. These children in turn are educated by word and deed to a physical, intellectual, and spiritual maturity so that they too may take up the mission to which God has called them. As you can also see that it calls for a kind of apostolicity, and more than that, a conversion. Without this Christian concept, the family has only half a meaning, and that is the women's half. When only this half-meaning is known, the children are all dressed up with no place to go. They are prepared but no one knows for what. Everyone is getting ready for a great occasion which never happens. The meaning that the man gives to the family is purpose, direction, motive and end.

When groups of families get together to discuss these things, Christ will be there in the midst of them, and so too, Mary and Joseph. The job of the men will be to discover what their specific missions are. The job of the women will be to discover how they can best assist their husbands in the accomplishment of their missions. As time goes on with corporate discussion and personal meditation the men will see, as their Holy Father has, that their vocations must be part of the Church's crusade to restore the affairs of men to Christ. This will become the end which gives meaning to their every act. What was first an evening spent in companionable and neighborly discussion will become for them a new way of life. As they look back on their lives they will see as its milestones, not their first pair of long pants, or their school graduation, or the first dollar they earned, or the first time they met their wives, but rather, they will see those magnificent steps to maturity in Christ, Baptism, Penance, the Eucharist, and Matrimony.

The work which fills the days of these men will fall under greater scrutiny. They will reform it to coincide with the laws of charity and justice courageously without fear of consequence, knowing how ridiculous and imprudent it is to seek security elsewhere than in the furtherance of God's Will. They may conclude that the work they are now doing is without merit and directed solely toward the profit of the owners at the expense of the common good. Then they will consider ways and means to abstract themselves from that job, so that they may better use the talents that God has given them for His purpose.

These are the things that men can do to regain the headship of the family. You may wonder that I have said little about religious practices or the cultivation of virtue. Can it be that I am putting too much emphasis on the social problem and not enough on the problems of the spirit? That is not my intention. Once men have become aware of the magnificent mission to which they have been called, they will hunger for the Eucharist as they have never hungered before. Their virtue will not be cultivated merely by quiet spiritual exercises but rather come as the consequence of Christ acting through them in their daily apostolate. With a new purposefulness, the new Christian man will lift his fellows from the quiet desperation of their lives, and in acting Christ-like, he will be setting for his children an example which is the crowning glory of fatherhood.

ED WILLOCK

BOOK REVIEWS

New Vision Through Revision

THE PSALMS—A NEW TRANSLATION
By Ronald Knox.
Sheed and Ward

Msgr. Knox has done an admirable piece of work in this fresh translation of Our Lord's Prayerbook. Written in rhythmic prose and set up in paragraph (not verse) form, it is terse, accurate, vigorous Anglo-Saxon throughout, not a high-flown attempt at the King's English. Psalm 18 and 22, for example, are delightfully done, and add considerable clarity. Instead of: "Who can understand sins? From my secret ones cleanse me, O Lord" we have "And yet, who knows his own frailties? If I have sinned unwittingly, do thou absolve me." And for "The Lord ruleth me: and I shall want nothing" the more spontaneous and child-like "The Lord is my shepherd; how can I lack anything?" "He hath converted my soul" suddenly comes to life when you read "He revives my drooping spirit." The poetic but mysterious "Day unto day uttereth speech: and night to night sheweth knowledge" of Psalm 18 emerges "Each day echoes its secret to the next, each night passes on to the next its revelation of knowledge."

But whether it's old age or obstinacy, I still prefer "I will rejoice at thy words, as one that hath found great spoils" to "Victors rejoice not more over rich spoils, than I in thy promises" (Psalm 118) and "Restore unto me the joy of thy salvation: and strengthen me with a perfect spirit" to the more prosaic, and perhaps more accurate, "Give me back the comfort of thy saving power, and strengthen me in generous resolve." (Psalm 50) And the old Douai "Thou hast commanded thy commandments to be kept most diligently" still seems smoother and stronger than "Above all else it binds us, the charge thou hast given us to keep."

For rich and beautiful variations, it is rewarding to compare "The heavens shew forth the glory of God: and the firmament declareth the work of his hands" with "See how the skies proclaim God's glory, how the vault of heaven betrays his craftmanship!" and "he hath rejoiced as a giant to run the way" with "he exults like some great runner who sees the track before him."

For a nice balance of intellectual independence and scholarly accuracy, Msgr. Knox deserves high praise.

FRANCES CLARE O'REILLY

Glimpses of the Great

THE FACE OF THE SAINTS
By Wilhelm Schamoni.
Translated by Anne Freemantle
(120 authentic likenesses of Saints in full-page illustrations, each portrait accompanied by a short biography.)
Pantheon Press.

This is a book which ought to meet with immense popularity. For anyone beyond the brute stage, be he worldly or wiser, should react like a lyre to the impact of these towering personalities as they face us from these pages. What's more, the writing as well as the photography is superior, even though the biographies are nothing more than thumbnail sketches. Especially notable is the introduction itself which gives as clear a description of the development of the Church's policy in regard to canonization as I've ever read. It may come as a shock to some to learn that Francis de Sales was the first Saint solemnly beatified. And that Thomas More and John Fisher were canonized by Pius XI despite the fact that there were no miracles after their beatification. Others will stop short at Dr. Carrel's account of seeing "a huge cancerous growth ... shrink into a scar." And most of us would hardly be able to define "equipollent canonization" right off the cuff.

But it is the book proper, the Saints themselves in life or death who exert their ineluctable fascination — from sharp-faced, ascetic, distinguished-looking John Chrysostom to soft, luminous-eyed Mother Francis Cabrini. No wonder Teresa of Avila laughed at her portrait; a vainer woman would have winced. The resemblance between St. Antoninus and the late Father Baker, between Francis Borgia and Pius XII and, at least facially, between Jennifer Jones and the real Bernadette, is striking. Among the more awesome but less familiar figures are Mary Frances of the Five Wounds, Veronica Giustiani and Clara of Montefalco. Casimir of Poland, Thérèse of Lisieux and Benedict Joseph Labre stand out for beauty. No one could pass over Catherine of Genoa with her piercing gaze or fail to be struck by the utter peace and happiness mirrored even in the death mask of John Joseph of the Holy Cross.

Of the brief biographies, Conrad Birndorder's stands out. He must have been one of the most lovable men in the 19th century as Philip Neri undoubtedly was in the 16th.

For non-Catholics, this book should serve as an overwhelming introduction to the Saints.

FRANCIS CLARE O'REILLY

Lamb Among Wolves

THINKING IT OVER
By Thomas F. Woodlock.
Declan X. McMullen Co.

The late Mr. Woodlock was for many years an editor and the daily columnist for the *Wall Street Journal*. This is said to be a representative collection of his columns, arranged according to subject rather than date.

What interests me especially in this book is to try to reconcile Wall Street with Mr. Woodlock, or vice versa. First let us consider Mr. Woodlock, who was nearly eighty at the time of his recent and lamented death. His life was without financial blemish and he was personally honored and respected on all counts. He took his Catholicity seriously, even writing a book, *The Catholic Pattern*, in witness of his faith. Just to see him, as I did on nearly his last Ash Wednesday, early approaching the altar at St. Patrick's Cathedral, was to realize that he was a man living very close to God.

What then, of Mr. Woodlock's Wall Street? As revealed in these essays it is the same old Wall Street at its best: Capitalist, conservative, bent on investment rather than speculation, terrified of Communism, scornful and fearful of government control, fighting mad at the packing of the Supreme Court, early alert to the menace of Hitler, and derisive of liberalism.

My disagreement with Mr. Woodlock's economic doctrine is not entire (but nearly so) and profound. That does not so much matter now. What literally astounds me is that there is hardly a single statement in these essays which differs from the "party-line" of a myriad of the more intelligent Republican Capitalists who were, and are, as regards their spiritual lives, poles apart from Mr. Woodlock. It is as plain as anything why Mr. Woodlock was popular with the men of Wall Street. What is not plain, at least to me, is why there was no apparent effort made to bridge the spiritual gap.

Let us put it this way. Mr. Woodlock was a man of prayer, writing for an audience composed largely of the spiritual underprivileged, yet not speaking to them of God. To be sure, he reduced all his arguments (via the Constitution and the Declaration of Independence) to the dignity of the human person, which he then predicated on a supreme moral law or some such (which meant to him the fullness of the Faith, but which, I am certain, conjured up precisely nothing to his largely non-Catholic audience). Aside from that, God is practically not mentioned. Christ is never named in the book that I could find, not even at Christmas. Goodness is advocated under the guise of the natural law rather than the Redemption. But is the Redemption irrelevant to Wall Street? Or even to the preservation of the natural law?

Similarly, there is that common habit of exposing the sins of absent brethren. It is perfectly safe to damn Communists on Wall Street. But what about the sins of avarice and luxury? Where is the prophet who will damn them on Wall Street?

It will be said that Mr. Woodlock was a columnist on a financial paper, not a preacher. He was not hired to save men's souls, but to clarify issues within the Capitalistic system. That is what Mr. Woodlock undoubtedly thought himself, for he was very apostolic, generous, and devout in his private life, and no one could suggest that he was any less than totally dedicated to work for the Church and the preservation of society.

Nevertheless, because I am most familiar with the state of the receiving end of his columns, I wish he *had* preached, and I cannot help but feel that he ought to have done so. Maybe he would have lost his job. Maybe on the other hand, he would have broken down the financiers' morbid embarrassment about discussing the things that really matter. The elder J. P. Morgan used to let himself into an empty church on weekdays because he liked to sing hymns. It is a pathetic little gesture, showing that a man may gain the whole world and not know what to do with his own soul. In the midst of such, where is one's duty? Mr. Woodlock sometimes gives the impression of a man tied in mental knots from trying to reduce the Apostle's Creed to the size of the Declaration of Independence.

It is easy, now that the Faith is on the *offensive* (and no one is any longer really awed at Wall Street) to say these things. It may have been impossible and imprudent to have said them in the era, so recent and yet so finished now, to which Mr. Woodlock belonged. In any case, my remarks are intended more as pricks to our own contemporary consciences than as condemnation of a man who was far better than I am. R. I. P.

CAROL JACKSON

THE THREE AGES OF THE INTERIOR LIFE, VOL. 1
By Reginald Garrigou-Lagrange, O.P.
Trans. By Sr. M. Timothea Doyle, O.P.
Herder

This is the first one translated of a two-volume work on the spiritual life by the most eminent French Thomist. The entire work represents a summary of a course on ascetical and mystical theology which has been given in the Angelicum in Rome for the past twenty years, this volume ending after a consideration of the way of beginners. According to the author himself, this work treats in a higher and simpler manner the same subjects as covered in *Christian Perfection and Contemplation*, and *L'amour du Dieu et la croix de Jesus* and indeed it is much less controversial, and therefore easier, than the former work.

For those who are not familiar with Garrigou-Lagrange, we should say that he is a brilliant defender of St. Thomas' doctrine of grace and that he consequently holds (and keeps reiterating) that the path of the saints through the purgative, illuminative and unitive stages is the normal and inevitable path for all of us; and that most of us are bogged down somewhere on the outskirts of the spiritual life for lack of understanding of the path of holiness and because of resultant general ineptitude in our spiritual lives. So he undertakes to explain the why, wherefore and how. Most of this volume is given over to a general treatment of the life of grace and the spiritual organism. Only toward the end does it come to a specific consideration of the way of beginners.

Let learned men give the author the praise and appreciation owing from theologians. We are not competent to do so. All we can say is that we are abundantly grateful to and for Garrigou-Lagrange. He is *Integrity's* favorite theologian. He is simple enough for us. He is abundantly lucid. Reading this book you are alternately exclaiming, "Oh, *that's why* . . . " and finding yourself carried away by the greatness of the ideal sanctity.

The translation is excellent, as also is the typography.

CAROL JACKSON

The truly mediocre man admires everything a little and nothing with warmth . . . He considers every affirmation insolent, because every affirmation excludes the contradictory proposition. But if you are slightly friendly and slightly hostile to all things, he will consider you wise and reserved. The mediocre man says there is good and evil in all things, and that we must not be absolute in our judgements. If you strongly affirm the truth, the mediocre man will say that you have too much confidence in yourself. The mediocre man regrets that the Christian religion has dogmas. He would like it to teach only ethics, and if you tell him that its code of morals comes from its dogmas as the consequence comes from the principle, he will answer that you exaggerate . . . If the word "exaggeration" did not exist, the mediocre man would invent it.

The mediocre man appears habitually modest. He cannot be humble, or he would cease to be mediocre. The humble man scorns all lies, even were they glorified by the whole earth, and he bows the knee before every truth . . . If the naturally mediocre man becomes seriously Christian, he ceases absolutely to be mediocre . . . *The man who loves is never mediocre.*

From Ernest Hello, L'homme, Bk. 1, chap. 8 (*The Three Ages of the Interior Life*, Reginald Garrigou-Langrange, footnote on page 201).

INTEGRITY

:the ninth issue:
JUNE, 1947   Vol. 1., No. 9
SUBJECT — EDUCATION

EDITORIAL

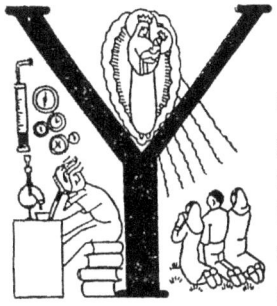

YOU WILL FIND OUR LEADing article (*Our Lady of Wisdom*) hard going the first time you read it through. It's written simply enough, but it's the deep, deep view of a situation we tend to regard superficially. It shows the connection between religion and education ultimately to rest on whether or not we accept the light God wants to give to our minds. If we don't accept it, and modern man has not accepted it, we eventually come out with a curriculum diametrically opposed to the truth. We are in that stage today, when learning which has long since ceased to be for Christ is ever more blatantly against Him. But the evil is not corrected by substituting good information for bad information. The situation has to be corrected radically, which means that we have to overcome our spiritual blindness. When, through Mary, we obtain the humility by which we shall regain the light God has withdrawn from our intellects, then we shall know the truth.

Compared to spiritual blindness, all our other educational ills are minor, even though manifold. Little effort has been made to treat them comprehensively.

We had to point out, because nobody else has (curious fact!) that higher salaries are irrelevant to the teacher-shortage, or rather that money acts as a palliative to a more profound discontent. *Life in an Education Factory* shows why, from personal experience.

Personal experience serves also to press home the case against secular education. Wellesley, our bad example, is not essentially different from other private colleges, except that it has had for years a religion course similar to that which is planned for similar schools. This teaching of religion will, so they say, turn the tide of irreligion. How little they know!

Lastly, we have a lay review of the problem of theology for the laity.

In deference to the full expression of our writers in this issue we have, for this once, reduced the size of our type. We shall revert to the old size next month.

THE EDITORS

Our Lady of Wisdom[1]

YOU MAY HAVE NOTICED THIS STRANGE coincidence, how modern writers at the one extreme, and St. John the Evangelist at the other, are both very much concerned with beginnings? The Evangelist solved the problem quite simply with the help of revelation, writing: "In the beginning was the Word," this right at the beginning of his gospel. In my class, I solve it by a prayer before and after each class, a prayer to Our Blessed Mother.

To an outsider this might seem like an empty formality, something one does in a Catholic university. But, as I understand it, it is the most important part of our class. And that is why I am trying, here, to start in something like the same way. This is the way I understand praying before passing on to formal instruction in the classroom or in the lecture hall; there are three elements in every teaching situation, the doctrine taught, the one teaching, and the one being taught. If what is taught is true, it comes from God, it is a participation in the Being of Him Who is Subsistent Truth. If I am to teach what is true, I must first be moved by that Truth Which is God. If you are to learn that Truth, you must be disposed by God to receive it. In the words of St. Paul, *When one of you says, I am for Paul, and another, I am for Apollo, are not these human thoughts? Why, what is Apollo, what is Paul? Only the ministers of the God in whom your faith rests, who have brought that faith to each of you in the measure God granted. It was for me to plant the seed, for Apollo to water it, but it was God who gave the increase. And if so, the man who plants, the man who waters, counts for nothing; God is everything, since it is He Who gives the increase.*

You and I, then, by the teaching of our holy Faith, and even by the natural testimony of God (Who may be known by natural

---

[1] This lecture was given to the Newman Club of Brown University, Jan. 10, 1947.

reason, to those, that is, who seek to know Him), you and I cannot hope to learn anything which is true, particularly as it is a living truth, except we learn it as we are the instruments of God, united in the holiness of Truth, and seeing one another in the likeness of Jesus Christ, Who is Subsistent Truth. Adapting the words of St. Paul to what is happening here, I say the words, you listen to them, but it is God Who will give the increase. And He will give it in the measure of that love by which I would communicate His truth, and your love by which you receive it.

That, as I conceive, is the meaning of prayer as it is the fitting introduction to learning. And therefore I must beg you to pray that, as we are united in Christ here, in the bond of His Charity, we may together learn something of His Truth.

And now, dwelling on this relation of love as it is found in Christian teaching, pondering the Master's exhortation, "Whenever two or three, or more are gathered together in my name, there am I in the midst of them," I see, in a way that I have already spoken the very substance of all I would say to you.

HE WHO IS NOT WITH ME

For what I had intended to say was this, that Christian learning is holy, because it has its beginning and its end, Alpha and Omega, in God through Jesus Christ. (That, incidentally, is why we pray at the end of class as well as at the beginning.) Whereas any learning that is not Christian is not holy. Neither is it indifferent — here I am afraid I must say something which will shock some of you. But Our Lord, Who is God, has said it: "He who is not with me, is against me." If, then, our learning and our teaching are not in Christ, they are against Him, and, by that fact, they are against God. Teaching which is not in Christ and with Him, and for Him, is the teaching of the devil, because all teaching which is against Him comes from that father of lies, whose end is to seduce souls as it is Our Lord's end to save them.

That is how souls are lost, too, through false doctrine. For men are not mere lumps of matter, or unreasoning brutes. Men are free agents, and they are free just in this, that their appetites must be moved by their reason: that, in fact, is what we mean by being free, free to act for the good *which we understand to be our good.* (The consummation of our free choice, for that reason too, is in making the right choice, binding ourselves to the One Infinite Good, not in being free to make the choice because we always postpone it — as current talk about freedom might lead one to believe. But that is another story, and for another time.) Because men are free, then, they can be brought to God, or kept from Him, only by doctrine, that is, by teaching, rational persuasion.

All doctrine, therefore, is either for Christ, or against Him, all doctrine is ordered either to save souls, or to destroy them. Nothing, not a single proposition is indifferent to our supernatural end. This truth, which is as old as our Faith, I should like to characterize by a new name, this is CATHOLIC PRAGMATISM. And if, as I am convinced — and I think you will agree with me — Catholic thought today does not have the vitality it should have, if it is scandalously true that those whose convictions are contrary to our Faith are more fruitful, shamefully more fruitful than ourselves, it is because they, in their error, have shown an integral purposefulness, where we (like the Jews in a similar situation) have grown content to eat out of the flesh-pots of their culture, serving the enemies of God with our minds as we try to serve the same God with our hearts. This is a terrible wound, not a bleeding gash, so easily seen, which heals as quickly as it is treated, but a slow and furtive, life-consuming cancer which, when it is recognized, has virtually finished its horrible work.

And so I speak to you as men dying of this vicious disease, hoping you will listen even though you have not yet, perhaps, felt the fatal symptoms — even more — just because you have not felt them, because by that time it will be too late: the disease will have destroyed you. You can see now how important my preliminary exhortation was. For here, at the very crucial point of our communication, I must beg you to judge what I am saying, not by the light of your own senses, but by the testimony of the Holy Spirit, even in defiance of your own understanding, as faith animated by love sometimes makes necessary. I exhort you to turn to that Spirit within yourselves, and ask: Is it true, then, that all that I have learned which was not for Christ, is against Him? Is it true that, by my very "education," I am today a house divided, one of whom the Spirit of God wrote: "I know of thy doings, and find thee neither hot nor cold, cold nor hot, I would thou wert one or the other. Being what thou are, lukewarm, neither cold nor hot, thou wilt make me vomit thee out of my mouth"?

Notice, the Holy Spirit says that we *make* God vomit us out by our lukewarmness. Why do you think that is? Why should God tell us that He would prefer us to be cold rather than lukewarm? Certainly He does not want us to sin. The answer is to be found in the words of Jesus, when He told the Pharisees: "I came to save sinners." Did He mean He had not come to save all men, even the Pharisees? Certainly the Mercy of God is for all. But observe the occasion of this utterance. He says this to the Pharisees when they are scandalized because He associates with sinners.

Why were they scandalized? Because they regarded themselves just men. But if they were made by God, why could not that same God make other sinners just? Therefore they looked upon themselves as just, not as sinners made just by God, but as men who had justified themselves without God. And those were the men He could not save, those whose hearts were so hardened by hypocrisy that they could not even so much as think that they needed to be redeemed. But Christ could save sinners like Magdalen, like Matthew, like Peter, — because, through their sin, they knew that they needed to be saved, that they could do nothing without God. And God saves all who ask to be saved, those ask who are not smug in their own virtue.

The lukewarm, who are neither cold nor hot, then, are those who are abandoned neither to God nor to sin. Instead, they keep up just enough of external observance to prevent themselves from being disturbed by their sins, enough to destroy the knowledge of their poverty — by which God calls them to Himself.

The world today is made up pretty much of those who are lukewarm, who are, as they think, neither very much for Christ, nor very much against Him. Particularly among the educated, so-called, the leaders of society. And He is ready to vomit them out of His mouth. These are the men who cry "peace, peace, and there is no peace." Why is there no peace? They ask. They are truly puzzled. Are we not men of good will, all seeking peace? Why then is there no peace? What more could we do to bring about this peace? Listen very carefully to the answer of God, as He speaks in the hatred and war that surrounds us: *If you say that you are men of good will, seeking peace, yet you find no peace, what does that make me? Do you not say, in these very words, that I am a monster who, when his son asks for bread, hand him a stone, hypocrites that you are, why do you not look into your own hearts, to accuse yourselves, before you accuse your God? But, rather than accuse yourselves you will deny my very mercy, the most precious of all my attributes, to show you which I suffered every conceivable suffering. At least, then, confess to yourselves and to me that you do not seek peace. Then ask me, in the knowledge of your own poverty, and I will give you peace — because I will give you myself.*

Yes, it is a fact, as all of us who have tried just a little to love God must know it is a fact that we cannot love Him of ourselves. This is the knowledge, the reward He gives us, when we begin to try to love Him, the knowledge of our abysmal pride and hypocrisy, by which we would not hesitate to use anything to glorify ourselves. What, then, is this strange convention which overwhelms us, by which we assume that we can be men of good will without God, without Christ? Why are we so afraid of our own weakness, we who are the children of a God Who brought us back from the dead? For surely we are afraid to admit our culpability for fear of the punishment.

WHAT IS A NEUROTIC?

Our age, we are told, is "neurotic." There is much talk about the devastating tempo of our lives, and our common language is filled with the terms of psychiatry. But what is the trouble, in the simplest terms? The psychiatrists know very well. They call it by different names, inferiority complex, guilt complex, Oedipus complex, always a complex. But the thing they name is one and the same. Do you know what it is?

Why is it, whatever else is may be called, always a complex? Because it is complicated, not simple; a complex, not a simplex. St. Paul had a "complex" once too. That was what God told him when He said: "Saul, Saul, why dost thou persecute me? . . . I am Jesus, whom Saul persecutes. This is a thankless task of thine, kicking against the goad." Having a complex is kicking against the goad, seeking peace by violating our consciences. Yes, having a "complex," in the language of earlier times, when men used to call things by their right names, is being a liar. But being a liar is a very different thing from telling a lie. For when we tell a lie, merely, we know that we are lying with perfect objectivity. But when we become habitual liars, we not only lie about this or that, we lie about ourselves: we tell ourselves we are not liars. That is the genesis of the *complex*, and we all have complexes because we are all liars about ourselves: we tell ourselves, and we assume with one another, that we are truthful men. Yet we know, at the bottom of our hearts, unless those hearts are utterly hardened, that we are not truthful. And, because we make ourselves out honest and truthful, we make God Himself a liar. That is the hypocrisy that God Himself cannot convert to Himself — because it denies God, because it denies His mercy.

And so the psychiatrists tell us about our complexes, but they do not tell us that we are liars. That would be crude, and they could hardly expect persons to pay for being told that. And the truth is (in defense of the psychiatrists) that, if they did tell them, their patients would not believe it. Because they really are complicated. Being complicated, they don't know, very clearly, that is, that they are liars. And so it wouldn't do very much good to tell them. It might do a lot of harm in fact.

The reason is that lying is more an effect that a cause. No one wants to be a liar, really. No one wants anything bad as such. For example, take a more shocking kind of sin, say murder. No one murders simply for the sake of destroying human life. Why in the world would anyone want to destroy life for its own sake? (That is a terrible habit moderns have fallen into, to conceive sin as though it were desirable for its own sake.) But the truth is that, when we sin, it is always because we want some good. The man who murders does not will death for itself; he wants the money of the man he is going to kill, or the satisfaction to his wounded pride, or something else, but he wants something positive: death is simply a way of getting it — chosen, probably, because the murderer is too stupid to get what he wants in a less drastic way, or to change what he wants. And so with lying. You lie when you tell men, or yourself, something contrary to what you know to be the truth. But you don't deprive your neighbor, or yourself, of the truth for its own sake. That would be like wanting death just because it was nothing. But when we are tempted to want to die, it is to avoid the suffering which, we are persuaded, life is going to entail. We just can't want nothing. We have to want something, and lying is a kind of nothing, the lack of something, the lack of truth.

WHY DO WE LIE?

Why, then, do we lie — to ourselves, to one another and to God, about ourselves, saying that we keep the commandments of God, which are written in the heart of every man of good will, by ourselves? For it is a fact that we are unable of ourselves to keep those commandments. Here is what St. Paul tells us about the matter: "No human creature can become acceptable in God's sight by observing the law; what the law does is to give us the full consciousness of sin." And a little later he adds: "The effect of the law is only to bring God's displeasure upon us; it is only where there is a law that transgression becomes possible." That is why we are all suffering from complexes: we tell ourselves and one another that we *can* keep the law, that we *are* in fact keeping it, *of ourselves*, not by the Faith God gave us and sustains, not by His grace, but by ourselves. And all the time we know it isn't really true. We are in fact quite afraid to look and see what hideous monsters we are without this grace of God. And so, like a sort of family skeleton (only this is one we carry around with us) we assume that it does not exist, locked in the closet of a social convention.

The reason we tell lies, then, is because we are afraid, afraid of the truth, the truth of what we are in ourselves. But why should we be afraid of that truth, even if it is true that we are sinners? Certainly truth in itself is a good, and we would not turn from it as from a good thing. We turn from the truth of our own evil, therefore, only because we are persuaded, somehow, that a greater evil will attack us if we face and acknowledge the present one. We are afraid of despair — because despair is really the worst thing there is. We don't want to go about overwhelmed by our own hopelessness, and the hopelessness of everyone else. And neither does God want us to. That is what poor Judas was doing just before he hung himself. Because he saw the terrible thing he had done. Only there was something terribly wrong in the way he saw it. He saw the evil in himself, but he wasn't prepared to see it. He couldn't take it, *because he had not seen the Mercy of God*, that God's Mercy, great as the sin was, was infinitely greater than that sin. And so he damned himself by trying to pay back his debt to God with his own life, that is, alas! By taking something else away from God, his own life now, in addition to God's life.

That is why we all have complexes, then, because we are afraid to face the truth of our own weakness and malice, and we are afraid to face these because we think we shall be despondent if we see ourselves as we really are. And the point I want to make is that we are entirely right — except for one thing, the Mercy of God, a Mercy, be it remembered too, Which will not permit us to see more than we can bear. For that too would be pride, to want to know our evil more that God would wish us to know it.

Because God is omnipotent, everything whatsoever is under His dominion, including our own acts. Why, then, does He permit sin? He tells us Himself, when Simon, the Pharisee, doubts Him because He had accepted the solicitude of Mary Magdalen: *I came into thy house, and thou gave me not water for my feet, she has washed my feet with her tears, and wiped them with her hair. Thou gavest me no kiss of greeting, she has never ceased to kiss my feet since I entered, though didst not pour oil on my head, she has anointed my feet, and with ointment. And so, I tell thee, if great sins have been forgiven her, she has also greatly loved. He loves little, who has little forgiven him.*

"He loves little, who has little forgiven him." That is the answer of Jesus Christ, to those who ask why He permits sin. He permits it, having paid for it with His Own Precious Blood, in order to forgive it, because He knows the secrets of the human heart, how forgiveness moves it to love, and the more the forgiveness, the greater the love.

MARY AND THE MERCY OF GOD

But we have not yet come to the end of our query. This is where we stand, now: we have all sorts of complexes because we are liars about ourselves: we are liars because we are afraid to face the truth about ourselves, we are afraid to face the truth the fact of our malice, because we do not understand the Mercy of God, how He came to save sinners, not to despise them and to cast them out, how He permits sin as the instrument of His loving Mercy, whereby He teaches us to love Him more, loving Him from the abyss of our own ugliness.

And now we ask: But why do we not understand this Mercy of God? The Spirit of God answers us: Because "wisdom will not enter a malicious heart, nor dwell in a body subject to sin." For this is wisdom, to know peace in the knowledge that God has forgiven us much and therefore we love much. Wisdom is to hope in this Mercy, as foolishness is to hope in ourselves, knowing our own weakness. Therefore, we do not understand the Mercy of God because we are conceived in sin, brought forth in iniquities by a mother herself conceived in sin.

We cannot understand the Mercy of God because it is a gift, utterly for nothing. The prophet calls to us: "All ye who are without money, come and buy." What God gives cannot be purchased by our goods, by our good acts, our good thoughts, it can be had only for nothing, it is only for the beggars, for the poor, the poor in spirit, for those who know their nothingness — and who know that this too is a gift, the knowledge that they have nothing to give. "All ye who are without money, come and buy." "Blessed are the poor in spirit, the kingdom of heaven is theirs."

But why can we not understand this wonderful gift of God, His Mercy? We have said, because we were conceived in sin. Being conceived in sin, our conceptions are warped. We cannot conceive of a Being Who is Infinitely Powerful giving so great a gift to creatures on whom He depends not at all, from whom He has nothing, absolutely nothing, to gain. And the reason we cannot conceive this Mercy, is that we should never, of ourselves, give a great gift to one who could give us nothing in return. For as we are, so do we judge: being ourselves without mercy, we cannot conceive a God Who is all Mercy. If we know ourselves only a very little bit, we know how, day and night, we plot schemes to gain for ourselves, to glorify ourselves, to devour those weaker than ourselves, often hiding our own hardness from ourselves by hypocritical disguises of charity and benevolence. How can we hope, then? How can we hope in the Mercy of God, without which we are lost, unless we can believe in it, hard and unmerciful as we are?

This is what Jesus told Nicodemus, when he came to praise His teachings as coming from God: "Believe me when I tell thee this; a man cannot see the kingdom of God without being born anew." This seems a strange thing for Christ to be telling a person who acknowledges that His teaching is from God, that He is from God. But Nicodemus had been persuaded through miracles, and Jesus wanted him to know that flesh and blood had not revealed this thing to him. For, if he had been persuaded through miracles that Jesus was from God, why would he not be persuaded by his defeat and death on the Cross, that He was not from God, and that He was not God? Nicodemus was puzzled. "How is it possible," he asked, "that a man should be born when he is already old? Can he enter a second time into his mother's womb, and so come to birth?" It was then that Jesus spoke words establishing the Sacrament of Baptism: "Believe me, no man can enter the kingdom of God unless birth comes to him from water and the Holy Spirit."

Many, many centuries later, when the Blessed Virgin had appeared to a little girl in the south of France, the local priest, acting within his rights, indeed by his duty, told the little girl, Bernadette Soubirous, to ask "The Lady" what her name was. Because She was a true Lady, Our Blessed Mother was not offended. It was then, as many of you know, that She announced Her Name "I am the Immaculate Conception."

MARY HELPS US TO BE SIMPLE

Here, then, is the answer to our question, and the end of our quest. We are born again, really and truly born again, in a spiritual generation, of was and the Holy Spirit. This is our vocation, to be other Christs, parts of that first Christ, together with Him constituting that "divine generation" which Isaias had prophesied: "Behold a virgin shall conceive and bear a son." Mary is not only the Mother of Jesus, then, She is the Mother of that whole generation which is one with Jesus. We are born again, by the Sacrament of Baptism, of water and of the Holy Spirit. But, as we learn from the lips of our dying Savior, we are the children of His Mother, we are born again of Mary and the Holy Spirit, as the First Christ was born of Her and of the Holy Spirit. We are "a nation brought forth at once, because Sion (Our Blessed Mother) hath been in labor," in labor at the foot of the Cross where She brought forth all the Elect. We are, therefore, gods, born of God, and of the Mother of God.

Mary, then, is that Immaculate Conception in Whom alone we can see the Mercy of God, in Whom we can become wise, being, mystically, in a body not subject to sin. In Mary, the Mother of Mercy, we can know God's Mercy, as we become one with Her First-born. In Mary we are not afraid of our sins because we know, without guile, that the death of sin has been effected by Our Lord's death, that death no longer has its sting, that death has died. In Mary we are not afraid to hope, because our hope is in Her and not in ourselves; we are not afraid to look at our sins, because, hideous as those sins are, our hope is not in our own virtue. Indeed we rejoice in our weakness, because, through it, we become more attached to Our Lord in His Blessed Mother. In Mary we have confidence that we can overcome all things, because the simplicity of the child wins the kingdom of heaven, and Mary's love, Her strength, makes us children again, burdened down as we may be by our transgressions. Therefore we "run after Her," imitating Her virtues, seeing the blackness of our vices as the background which God has permitted to show forth the wonderful Purity of Our Lady. In Her, therefore, we hate our sins as we strive valiantly to overcome them; but neither do we permit them to overcome us, to take away that joyful hope which God gives in its fullness to Mary's children. If we see ourselves as worse than we had thought, we strive to love Mary more than we had before, we hate ourselves that much more, but not with a bitter hatred, the hatred which is born of a secret fear of evil, and undue fear, but with the hatred which is one with the love of Our Mother.

Therefore, in this new Mother, God has removed the whole principle of our prideful duplicity. For we no longer are afraid to see ourselves as we are, for fear, that is, of despair. We rejoice, even, to see them in order to have the greater motive to love Her, and Her Son in Her. And thus, little by little, Mary makes us uncomplicated, makes us simple as She is simple, makes us mistrustful of ourselves as we become more and more trustful of Her, and of God. Thus we learn, as we learn to love Her more, to love more and more too the Darkness which is the Light of God, dark to us only because it shines in the darkness. Thus too we realize that our intellectual vocation is to be one with God, through love, in this life, as we shall be one with Him forever in the next, not only with that same love which never passes away, but with a light of glory by which we shall know God as He knows us. Then Wisdom will laugh at the devils and the human enemies of God, laughing them to scorn, showing them how all their machinations only helped God to form His Saints.

And already we can hear, as from far off, the voice of that laughter. For did not the prince of this world try to seduce us from the arms of God, telling us that this was the true re-birth, the "renaissance," that we should be born again, liberated from the darkness of our Faith, and brought into the light of human wisdom, of that true infinite perfection, which is progress without end. Did he not seduce our forefathers as he seduced our first parents, with the promise that we should be as gods, this as the reward of disobedience to God? For Lucifer, the light-bearer, can seduce us only through our pride, as Mary saves us through humility. And now, have we not learned, and shall we not learn more and more how much God loves us, through the very instrument of this diabolical trickery? For, having seen, by it, the horrible depths of our uncleanness, we are prepared now to love Our Mother, the Immaculate Conception, knowing how unspeakably wide the gulf is which separates us from Her, so that only the arm of Her Mercy can stretch across it, as She softly calls to us, again and again: "Come over to me all ye that desire me," "Come over to me all ye that desire me, and be filled with my fruits."

CONTEMPORARY EDUCATION IN THE LIGHT OF MARY'S WISDOM

Thus Mary, Our Holy Mother, is the Principle of our life and of our culture. She is God's answer to the malice of the devil which would steal away Her children. In Her we shall see more and more clearly the vicious sophisms of contemporary learning, as we become more and more perfectly united with Her Son. In Her, too, we shall learn to despise all learning which is not ordered to God — not merely, as the prince of darkness loves to insinuate by giving up the truths of the natural order, the very contrary, for, as that terrible liar shall have to hear for all eternity, only we who are the children of Mary, and the children, therefore, of God the Father, are truly solicitous to keep intact the truths of natural reason. Because we know, as that father of all lies knows that only we have a real concern for those truths, because the things of heaven are made manifest by the things of nature, by the things which we see in the light of natural reason. Whereas he, the irreconcilable enemy of God, must distort those truths as long as he is able, to hide from poor sinners the things of God which are manifested in them.

And so this new age on which we are entering, the age of Mary, should be a time of great rejoicing for the taking of new hope by Mary's children — for all the devastation which surrounds us. It has been promised to us, and already we see the beginning of its fulfillment, how the monster of pernicious doctrine will necessarily fall, by the hand of Our Mother, by Her

Who "alone has overcome all heresies." But as the archer needs arrows to kill his quarry, so Our Lady and Her Son need us, to dedicate ourselves to Her Purity, that we may become "as arrows in the hands of the mighty." Everything is poised, now. The whole universe is hushed as it was in that wonderful time when the Angel Gabriel came to Mary with his sublime message. The fate of the whole world was in the balance — until those pure lips uttered their heavenly "Fiat," "Behold the handmaid of the Lord; be it done to me according to thy word." And now once again, the Angel of the Lord comes, to each one of us, asking for our assent, that the Son of God may be born in us, that we may be born again, of Mary and the Holy Spirit. For Mary is God's answer to the problem of Catholic education; Mary is the Educator by Whom we are conformed to Jesus Christ so that we may judge all things as He judges them. What do you say? O, that your answer might be, "Behold the servant of the Lord; be it done unto me according to thy word!"

HERBERT THOMAS SCHWARTZ, T.O.P.
Institute of Christian Philosophy
Georgetown University
Washington, D.C.

Catholic universities,
   Have a few perversities
Like Accreditation
   Of Catholic education.

Commencement Address for a Catholic College

Now close your books of yesterday
And set sweet childhood by.
Tomorrow will be no more dreams.
The storm rides down the sky.

We shall not speak of life's bright dawn
But rather how the night
Comes on too soon with fearful breath
Whispering there is no light.

Yes, though we lit you wisdom's lamp
And spoke of learned things,
Now you shall walk like foolish men
And rule as outcast kings.

Oh you must walk like stupid men
Babbling an outworn creed.
We pray now that you seek to fail
Who taught you to succeed.

Beware when men shall praise your works
And bid you to their feast.
The world loves whom the world does love
But who loves God is least.

Commencement Address for a Catholic College

For every man must sometime find
Within his bitter youth
Our single tragic triumph is
To live, not learn, the truth.

So take the fair words from our lips
And break them in earth's strife.
See if there be the strength in you
To bear a broken life.

And wisdom that we could not give
Shall come to you through tears
In fear and pain and loneliness
Years upon fruitless years.

Then fare you forth from our safe walls,
Your splendor be your loss!
Your hands that tremble touching joy
Be iron upon the Cross!

ELIZABETH ODELL

Life in an Education Factory

IT WAS 1934. THE GRADUATES OF THE CLASSES that had entered college in the depression years of 1929 and 1930 were busy getting jobs as secretaries, switchboard operators, Macy salesmen and saleswomen, and entering fields of work that were not even securely "white-collar." The A.B. that the graduate had won, often at great personal sacrifice and because of the forbearance and help of struggling families, did not even serve the primary purpose for which it had been achieved — it did not lift its owner into a higher social and economic class. Even if the A.B. owner's family had already achieved the stability of belonging to the social and economic stratum where the possession of a college degree was customary and correct, the graduate often had to slip down a cog or two, both in the wage and society scale.

In New York, large numbers of the young women who became A.B.'s in those glum classes of '33 or '34, were only drawn into the economic system by virtue of the fact that so many others were in misery — they became part of the mechanism for the mass production of the works of mercy through serving as investigators for the City Department of Public Welfare.

The goal of most of these young women seemed to be something higher, finer, more rewarding, more secure (think of the promise of *life tenure* in the uncertain and lean days of 1933), more intellectual, more socially acceptable — the goal of Teaching in the Great High School System of the City of New York. The pay was about $2,200 yearly for a beginner, with a long summer vacation and a six-hour and twenty-minute day within the school walls. Though there were thousands upon thousands of candidates for these splendid positions, there were few places. It was a lucky girl who could manage to get one of these places even after a grueling and exacting series of tests.

Even after passing the tests, it was often necessary to wait for years for an "appointment" to a position, since there were for most subjects, long lists of candidates who were appointed in order of grades received in the teacher's examination.

I was one of the searchers after security in those days of 1934. I was one of the few who, having passed the required examination, received an immediate appointment as a high school teacher. My friends told me, many a little sadly because they were still chained to Macy's, how really fortunate I was. I began to think so myself. I had not long returned from a short visit to Europe, and I had seen the terrible, hopeless plight of miners, and industrial workers in urban centers, who had been out of work, or existing on part-time work, for several years. The drabness of their lives, and the corrosive effects of long idleness on the character of the men, had shaken me so that I had taken refuge in writing socially conscious and drab poetry.

THE ASSEMBLY LINE

When my official appointment was announced, I had already served for a full year as a teacher-in-training, and therefore knew more or less what awaited me. My training period was served in a New York high school boasting a student body of upwards of five thousand. As a beginner, I taught no more than three classes a day. During the second term, the remaining periods were filled with the following activities: standing guard in the lunch room; standing guard in the study hall; standing guard in the crowded school hallways; sitting guard in the home room; handing out and counting all the textbooks used in all classes of the English Department. In addition, a dramatic club was given over to my care, and there were various duties in connection with school assemblies and theatricals.

The day began and ended with punching the time clock, and lack of punctuality was no light matter. During the second term of my teacher-in-training year, I finished every day in a more or less exhausted state, but, despite this, I enjoyed the actual teaching hours, and really established a rapport between myself and the students. I was very earnest about becoming a good teacher, and prepared and delivered the lessons with a high degree of enthusiasm. However, my most persistent memories of the period come from the other work that fell to my share. For close to one hour daily, I stood up in a steaming lunch room where about four hundred students milled about, buying and consuming their lunches and chatting and laughing. The roar was deafening. It was broken every now and then by the shattering of a glass or plate. When this happened, there was a moment of silence. One of the few traditions of the school was that the breaking of chinaware in the cafeteria was always the signal for a special kind of howl. One of the duties of the faculty members on guard was to shorten or at least tone down this howl. Often during the lunch room period, students would want to come up to talk about their problems, or ask for advice, or merely to chat with the faculty member. This was hardly possible because there were several infractions of school rules that had to be guarded against.

The study hall was actually the assembly hall of the school — a large auditorium seating a thousand people. Only about five hundred came for study at one time. They had to be watched with great care, because they were not supposed to talk, and the principal visited the auditorium very often. When a pupil was caught whispering to his neighbor, the only way of getting his attention and calling him to order, was by the use of a police whistle supplied to every teacher who had this assignment. There was little opportunity for reposeful study.

Every forty-five minutes a bell clanged over the whole school, announcing the changing of classes. Immediately doors burst open and the thousands of students streamed into the halls to go to the next classroom, to the gymnasium, in the lunch room, to the study hall, or to dash out of the building and home. Student monitors helped keep the lines of students in order. This was no mean task, since the halls were narrow, and it was difficult to hold back the forward rush of students trying to make the next class before the bell rang again. At certain strategic points a teacher was stationed. After a period in the jampacked lunch room, a period in the study hall with five hundred students, even a few minutes in the midst of thousands of students pushing in two opposite directions was enough to make a young teacher wonder if Macy's was not a haven of peace after all.

PERSONALITY PRODUCTION

The atmosphere of high tension and breathless speed was heightened by the attitude of the head of the department in which I happened to be placed. She was a woman in her early forties, ambitious, prepossessing, and full of what is known as "drive." She wanted everyone in her department to be stamped in her image — and kept insisting that all of "her" teachers must have personality. To have personality, I soon discovered, meant to exhibit drive, to dramatize the work, to keep all classes alive and on their toes at every moment. The possession of a quiet, persuasive manner would hardly qualify. I had several pleasant talks with my head of department. She was a good and tolerant woman, interested in the religious faith of those who worked in her department. For herself, she explained, she was an agnostic, and could find no system of belief worthy of her credence. Her main tenets seemed to be the necessity of personality in the teacher, and the duty of such teachers to nurture personality in the students. It was her private revolt against years spent in a large and impersonal public high school. But her idea of personality was on the whole an external one — confined to having the students speak in clear voices, and not restrain themselves if they wanted to comment on some piece of literature or subject under discussion.

As I spent only a year in the department, I never got around to asking her what was the purpose of having a teacher or student develop personality, or what was the final end of our work as teachers. Now that I think back on it, I am very sorry that I did not. But I suppose I was so busy watching out for the development of my own personality (along the prescribed lines, of course) that I would not have had the time to begin such a discussion.

After taking a written examination, an oral test for accepted speech, and an actual practical teaching test in front of an auditor from the board of education, my name was placed on an eligible list and I was given a regular appointment to the city school system of New York. I was constantly reminded by those still waiting for such an honor, of my life tenure, of automatic raises in salary, of the possibility of getting married and even having a baby without losing hold of my teaching job. In point of fact, I really felt that aside from the necessity of earning some money, teaching was really something spiritual, a chance to give meaning to my own life, and to help impress into good patterns the lives of the young. The repetitious emphasis on life tenure seemed to me rather macabre and tended to repel me.

MECHANIZATION AND MORALS

I started my regular teaching career in another school, not quite in the center of New York City life. It was a smaller school than the one I had formerly served in, counting on its rolls only four thousand pupils. I was immediately given five classes of one grade, and handed at the same time a syllabus of what the classes had to know by the end of the term. There was no break between the classes — one followed right after the other. I had to teach the same subject to five classes for five months, and I also had to repeat myself five times a day. After tiring of my role as parrot, I arranged to switch the lessons so that I would teach the same items not more than two or three times a day. Even this was not too simple, because there were exams to be passed, and the same literature had to be taught within a certain period for mid-term and final exams. Nevertheless, the stimulus of young minds and the challenge of a new situation joined to make my first term an enjoyable experience.

Life in an Education Factory

During the second term I was given a little wider latitude and was allowed to teach two different terms of the same subject. During the third term my scope was extended to three different terms — still of the same subject. It was a rather rare occasion if a teacher of one subject, say English, was asked to teach Latin, French or History. Each teacher was licensed for one subject, or one branch of subjects; for example, mathematics. No teacher that I ever met took the liberty of submitting to a series of examinations in more than one subject. The main reason, I believe, was that the examinations were so long-drawn-out, and so extremely detailed and tedious.

In many respects the school was a model public high school. It was run with extreme efficiency — an efficiency that was not obtrusive and that made the wheels of a large institution turn quietly and gently. My fellow teachers were pleasant people, and I made many friends among them. Before long there was abundant proof, had I wanted any, that I was a success as a teacher. The principal gave me significant assignments in the conduct of the school and I found him a sympathetic, forward-looking and idealistic man. He broached the subject of my taking the examination for head of the department, confident of the fact that he had in me a reasonably ambitious, satisfied, high school teacher. By that time I knew I would never take any further examination in the public school system. A blight had fallen over my work as I analyzed it from day to day. Life tenure now took on the guise of a life sentence.

During the course of the day I came in contact with about two hundred and fifty students. They came to my class to study my subject, to pass an exam in it and to pass on to the next course. I think they enjoyed it because on the whole it was a pleasant subject, full of relationship to life and living. I often gave short quizzes to check on their continued application to the subject. Naturally, to their minds, the important thing was to pass the quiz — even if it meant getting some surreptitious aid from a neighbor. I shall never forget the reaction one day when I called off a quiz at the sight of cheating. I tried to impress my students with the relative unimportance of knowing an isolated fact in order to pass an examination, as against soiling one's character by cheating and lying.

"I will call off the test for today," I told the class. "Nothing I can teach you is as important as the true moral base of your characters. If you use my classroom to practice lying, even in a test, it would be better not to come at all." I digressed in such a way in all my classes, and felt that I made some headway. In general, the students made a point of stating that they were unprepared if they had not performed assignments, and after a while I began to have faith in the reasons they offered for such unpreparedness. When it came time to explain why it was necessary to maintain truthfulness, honor and other virtues, I was stumped. A teacher was not allowed to mention God in the classroom. The only time the school ever came near to a mention of the Creator of our world was when a section of the Bible (usually, if not always, the Old Testament) was read aloud in the student assemblies, and when Christmas carols were sung in season.

A COG TAKES COGNIZANCE

I began to have a heavy heart when I thought of the students. They were good material — often full of idealism and of a search for meaning in their lives. Outside of the regular class time, they would often come to me and share their problems and their dreams. I taught them, in general, when they were in the fourth and fifth terms of high school. I never taught the seniors, but I did direct the older students in extracurricular activities. It was heart-breaking to see what happened to boys and girls between the fourth and the eighth terms. At fifteen and sixteen, it was still possible to stress ideals and to have some sympathetic response from unsophisticated minds. They were still in many ways children, and had the unpremeditated response of children. Most of them in the fourth and fifth terms still were under some parental supervision and were not too frequent movie-goers or dance addicts. By the seventh term most of them were "in the groove." They had made a complete adjustment, to use the psychiatrist's term.

To what had they adjusted? To the mores of Hollywood; to the acceptance of jive and jitterbugging as the pivots of existence; to the absolute necessity of "belonging" and of keeping "queers," or "drips" out of the gang; to the frequent carrying (or so I was informed by the school medical department) of contraceptives. When young people were being vitiated right under our eyes, it was clearly the duty of teachers, if they really belonged to a profession, to take steps to save the human material with which they dealt day after day. The teachers of the public school did not meet this responsibility. Not only were they not prepared to do anything, but even if they had been prepared and willing, the system would have effectively prevented them.

There was no cohesive relationship between the parents of the children and the teachers who cared for the minds of the children during the day. Once a term, or sometimes only once a year, there was a "Parents' Night," when the teachers were on display, and such parents as were interested, came to the school and chatted about the progress of their offspring. In one evening the teacher was expected to have a constructive word for as many as tens of hundreds of parents as presented themselves. There was rarely if ever a follow up of this relationship unless the student fell into serious disgrace.

My heart was no less heavy when I surveyed the teachers. They were deeply concerned with the standing of their pupils in Regents examinations, tests prepared in Albany to assure standardization of teaching in the public school system. They were also deeply concerned with the rating given them by the head of their department and by the principal of the school. Every so often they took a course in some graduate school because, in order to qualify for the salary increment, evidence had to be presented of a continued interest in intellectual growth and development through attendance at courses. Many of the teachers found interest outside their work that gave their lives meaning. A few of those I knew were artists; others found satisfaction in a happy home life to which they rushed at the end of the school day. Several were tied up with Communism. Others found surcease in travel. As soon as school broke up for the summer, they rushed off as far as they could reach and still returned after Labor Day. Of my immediate circle, both men and women, there were those who in the space of a few summers had visited Guatemala, Colombia, Mexico, France, Finland, England, Sweden, Denmark, Czechoslovakia, and Russia. The most animated subject of conversation was always "What are you planning to do next summer?" Teachers who had visited certain countries were always giving pointers to those who had not. They came back laden with snapshots and endless amateur movies of tourist havens. If all the feet of movie film taken of all these trips were placed end to end, they would undoubtedly make one reel.

What was most striking in a general way about the attitude of the teachers was that they were not finding satisfaction through their work, but rather through the leisure-time activities which their salaries were able to afford them; their travels, their movie-taking, their amateur theatricals, and play-going, their sports, their artistic pursuits, their political activities, and, in the case of the women, their clothes. Once I had made this analysis, I found daily proof that it was, for the majority of teachers, a true one. I found that it was certainly true in my own case.

LABOR TROUBLE

After the exhilaration of serving for four terms as a young teacher with vigor and enthusiasm to spare, I began to wilt — to look at the syllabus as my natural enemy. Five times a day, a group of about forty students trooped into my room; five times a day they trooped out. There was the constant marking of papers, the constant keeping up with the syllabus so that my class would not fall behind in final examinations. At formal and informal meetings of teachers, where one might expect a re-dedication to a naturally tiring task, one found no dedication in the first instance. Culture and the meaning of one's life should be related to one's work. I had expected that my work would help me to save my soul. When I discovered that I, too, was finding meaning for my life outside my work and that it became more and more impossible to integrate my working life and my leisure-time life, I made up my mind that, come what may, I had to leave the assembly-line job that teaching had turned out to be. Hundreds of souls passed by me daily. I was forbidden by the system to treat them as souls. My job was to teach them where to put the commas, and leave God out of the whole thing.

As I taught for the fifth and sixth terms, events in Europe were rushing to their climax of carnage and destruction. The youngsters who would suffer in this carnage were before me — they were without principles, without adequate bases of conduct, even for normal situations, not to mention crises. Many of them came from stable homes, where right principles were taught. The general absence of a re-statement of such principles caused them to leave high school less secure in basic moral standards than when they had entered. During the seventh term of my teaching life, I was placed in charge of a series of assemblies dealing with the values of citizenship and democracy. The whole series was rather frenziedly put together in response to an order. Steeped as I was in the tremendous reality of American democracy, and in the need for good citizenship as the bulwark of true democracy, I found little joy in the task. In such assemblies, as I remember there was one such assembly every week, we could not talk of democracy as stemming from the fact that God had created human being as equals and as brothers, as co-heirs with Christ of His Kingdom; nor could we trace good citizenship back to obedience to the moral law.

The spiritual rewards which I had expected from the profession of education just were not there. At first, when I had quietly made up my mind, that for me as a Catholic and as a human being, work in an education factory with its syllabi, its bells, its routine, and its cold methodicalness was unbearable, I had thought of finding another job. I had even thought of entering another profession. But after nearly four years of teaching, I was cured of compromise. I would throw myself on God's mercy, and go off to do a piece of study and work on social reform based on Catholic principles.

ON STRIKE

One day, in the eighth term of my teaching career, I walked into the principal's office and told him that I was leaving. I explained that teaching in a public high school was not my vocation, and that I felt that while I was still young I had to study Catholic social principles and the possibility of putting them into action. He accepted my resignation with the understanding, I felt, of one who had once had perhaps the same struggle. "I guess it is time for you to go off and be Joan of Arc," he said, "but if it does not work out, we'll have your position for you." In a week, I walked out of the education factory. The reference to Joan of Arc, with her commands from God, and the certainly of her mission, was a hard blow to a young woman who was certain only of what was wrong, but in company with many others, was still groping rather blindly for what was right. Nevertheless, once the hand was on the plough there was no turning back. There was in store for me more than a year of isolation, loneliness and misunderstanding, and a time of need when my last penny was exhausted. It was only then that I was accepted for meaningful work in a Catholic cause at fifty dollars per month, a mite compared with what I would have received as a teacher.

MASS PRODUCTION

My story is not atypical, since the essential evils of the New York City public high schools are duplicated in every city of the

United States. Even towns, where some of the evils are absent, run to the same education pattern. Mr. and Mrs. Lynd, in *Middletown in Transition*,[1] have fastened on one fundamental evil — that of bigness. They are talking of the high school set up in a town of no more than fifty thousand souls. Even a town of this size " . . . faces the necessity of more and more routinized procedures." They add ominously " . . . and there is no sector of our culture where the efficiency of large-scale routines is capable of being more antithetical to the spirit of the social function to be performed than in education." In a further analysis of the factory system in education, they conclude: "And in the struggle between quantitative administrative efficiency and qualitative educational goals in an era of strain like the present, the big guns are all on the side of the heavily concentrated controls behind the former."

It is very easy to pose the problem of the "curse of bigness" in the school system of a democracy. In a democracy all the children must receive an education, and how can they receive it unless schools are big enough and there are enough of them? On this score, I am afraid there is no solution unless a new spirit informs our educational system. I agree with the Lynds; the big guns are behind quantitative administration efficiency — the qualitative education goals are hardly even being kept in sight.

The problem of teachers, however, is a problem on the spiritual plane, and one that cannot be rectified by organizing into teachers' unions. It is very significant that organizations of teachers never strike out at fundamental wrongs. In their zeal to pass resolutions urging cost-of-living raises, the teachers never protest that all perfection is presumed to reside in the syllabus, and not in the teachers; never protest the progressive routinization of teaching procedures and of the entire school program.

---

[1] Originally published in 1937 as a sequel to their work *Middletown: A Study in Modern American Culture* (1929). — Ed.

INTEGRITY, June 1947

HIGHER WAGES?

The teachers themselves might probably be the last to realize it, but what is really eating at their vitals is not a lack of money, but lack of meaning in their work. As long as their world lacks spiritual depth and reality, they will need more and more money to indulge in travel, in leisure-time activities to make up for the routine emptiness of their days. Recently there was a strike of teachers in the town of Buffalo. All the teachers who received salaries went out on strike and interrupted the education of those entrusted to their care. The only teachers in Buffalo who remained on the job were those who received no salary but who found joy and peace in the cherishing and care of growing human souls. Thus it was that only the parochial grammar schools remained open to exercise their function.

It is now 1947. The carnage that we foresaw in the thirties has come and gone. Numbers of the boys who were my students were killed in battle; one has lost his mind after serving heroically in combat; one has committed suicide.

The crisis in the teaching world is more acute but has taken other forms. Now, instead of having long lists of prospective teachers and no positions, there is a serious teaching shortage. When there were other types of work to be done, work that allowed more freedom, and that possibly stressed less routinized procedures, the teachers trooped out of the classrooms. Life tenure did not have the same attraction in a time of business activity. No more terrible comment could be made on the spirit of our school system than this — that at the first opportunity to leave and find other life work, teachers left their posts, and young college graduates shunned the field of teaching. There is no doubt that the creative spark has largely been removed from the profession — either by the factory system of the overly large school, or by the unnatural supervision and restraints of teaching in a small country school. (The separate problems of one-room school houses cannot be covered here.)

There is a naïve belief that the crisis in the teaching world, and the shortage of teachers, can be cured by higher salaries. The papers are filled with the day-to-day agitation by teachers' groups for higher salaries, cost-of-living raises. The only thing that has not been used as a rallying cry has been longer-than-life tenure. The teachers actually in the system are unhappy, and they are convinced that more money can be used to escape temporarily from a dull job. Such a solution is based on the purest *non sequitur*. The problem is a spiritual one, and the teachers are not going to make their lot a happier one by agitating for, and receiving, more money. At best, the money can only be a palliative to a profession that needs a basic moral reorientation, in a school system that needs basic re-dedication.

FUTURE BUSINESS

I have not here indicated a wholesale solution — precisely because there is not a wholesale, widely applicable panacea. For Catholic teachers, however, there are solutions. Those Catholics who are forced at present to teach in schools that reduce spiritual work of training and preparing souls for living to a routinized, mechanical parroting of facts, can, in many cases, refuse to compromise further. They can refuse to be time-servers, because as Catholics they are responsible to their Father Who is in Heaven for every moment of time that they spend on earth. This means that they will leave the schools where they are not bringing young souls to God. There are many cases, of course, of men and women with families to support, where immediate egress is not possible; only the Lord can judge in these cases, where school systems are organized on a smaller, more human basis, where parents of all faiths are in contact with the school, and where a rounded progress for each student can at least be attempted.

SOLUTION OR DISSOLUTION

The main question at hand, however, is whether at this point of crisis on the American world scene, compromise is any longer possible or justifiable.

Catholic teachers do not want to seize the public educational system, but at the same time some Catholics now feel that they cannot in a time of terrible change form part of a system that is not preparing the young to meet the crisis. Many teachers justify their continuance in the public high school system by the fact that after school hours they are able to break through the routine and really help on an individual basis those students who are searching for light. In this way Protestant teachers help Protestant children, Jewish teachers help Jewish children, Catholic teachers help Catholic children, agnostic teachers gather to themselves their own, and those whom they have brought to agnosticism, and Communist teachers consort with Communist young people. They feel that an honest job as a manual worker, as a trolley car conductor, is earning one's bread by the sweat of one's brow, but that giving silent assent to a system of education that damns and dams up the natural idealism of youth is at best a questionable way of saving one's soul.

This is not aimed to be a negative little diatribe suggesting that teachers walk out of public high school and let the whole thing go to rot. There are still thousands upon thousands of children in these schools, and those who take it upon themselves to leave must immediately set about the work of reconstruction by Catholic means. These means, of course, are predicated upon a practice of poverty by the reformers, and would not include any country-club-like private schools for the rich, which besides their own faults are irrelevant to children now having to go to public schools. Catholic schools themselves have to a certain extent been visited by secular standards, and they often accept all or most of the wrong premises which have set our educational system off the road of truth. Even the crowning of the Virgin (which is done weekly during May on the well-cut lawns of our exclusive girls' schools) cannot in itself Catholicize these same institutions.

This record is the account of one who came to a point where further compromise with teaching in an education factory was impossible. She feels that there are many such — she also feels that time is running out.

There must be those Catholics who will find positive Christian means to help solve a crisis which is at base spiritual.

SANDRA KELLEY
New York

The Thirst for Theology

WE LIVE IN AN INTELLECTUAL HODGEpodge, in a society that can't see the woods for the trees, but that has corps of "experts" out in the forest studying the bark, watching the moss grow, and counting the leaves. Suppose you were to go to one of these experts, or even to the president of one of the colleges at which he was trained, and ask a simple question such as: "Tell me, on what principle do you decide which trees to cut down and which to allow to grow?" or "What are woods for, and who made them?" or "What is the significance of the fact (as you have determined after a life study) that oak trees thirty years old average 46,501 leaves a season as compared with 65,834 in elm trees? Suppose you were to ask these questions, and suppose you got in return nothing but puzzled looks. Would you not suppose you were in a nation of slightly crazed men?

What we need is not more detail, but some perspective; not yet more facts (as often as not erroneous ones), but some principles; we need some last ends, some first directives, some clear light, some *meaning*. We are thirsting, in a word, for theology. Theology is the science which will give us the last ends, the first principles, the meanings, the clarity and the directions which alone will make sense of the world and ourselves.

But theology is the one science which is generally withheld from us. This is due to the taint of liberalism, which has even affected Catholics. The liberal view is that it is not cricket to be told the answers and to go on from there, and that it is positively unmanly to have any certainty. It is all right to *look* for the final answers, only you must do so blindfolded, and *never, never* find them. So the liberal world goes groping about, and we Catholics often neglect to use the fullness of our revealed truth out of mistaken deference to those who cannot accept revelation because they cannot figure it out themselves. Instead of theology, we have been feeding on the insufficient food of philosophy, apologetics and devotionalism.

THE INADEQUACY OF PHILOSOPHY

Both theology and philosophy deal with the last things; the former as we know them in the blinding light of revelation, the latter as we can partially and inadequately discern them through the exercise of our own reason. They are the same last things in either case and therefore there is no incompatibility between the two sciences. Moreover, each is a legitimate and necessary science. It is only when philosophy, which is the lesser of the two, is overemphasized at the expense of (or exclusion of) theology that a disorder is created.

The philosopher is a man lost in the dense, dark forest jungles who, if he is sufficiently clever and his mind is not warped by intellectual pride, may conceivably deduce the existence of the sun from the life of the trees around him, although, of course, he would know very little about the sun. The theologian, on the other hand (be he erudite or a simple Christian versed in the catechism) is a man seated on the mountain overlooking the forest, who has only to open his eyes to know far more than the most clever philosopher can ever deduce.

Philosophy is useful as auxiliary to theology; it is in no way a substitute for theology. When we are thirsting for the fullness of truth it is painful to be set back into an intellectual framework approximating that of the Greek, pre-Christian philosophers. Philosophy belongs to the natural order, while all our problems are in desperate need of supernatural light. Now that Christ has redeemed us it is impossible to rationalize all our problems as though there had been no Redemption. The more we try to do so, the more we come out with the wrong answers to our problems. Only so much can be deduced from the natural law, and among the things that cannot be deduced is the all-important fact of grace. Too much straining with the intellect in disregard of Faith, and you have a picture of the good life which includes the right to collective bargaining, to a living wage, good health, etc., etc., but which has no place for the folly of the Cross. We have no right to build a picture of life or of society confined to the natural law, to the philosophical level; to do so is, in effect, to postulate a this-worldly end for man. Such an approach completely misses the paradoxical nature of Christianity. If we had been able to figure out philosophically that we would have to die to ourselves in order to live, we would not have needed the light of Faith by which seeming contradictions such as this grow ever more luminous.

Naturalism is one of the great heresies of the day. The secular world is intent on bringing about the millennium within the natural sphere; we are always besought to lend help to schemes for replacing the *bad* natural with the *good* natural, but it is naturalism itself (not nature) which has to be replaced by a consideration of man's supernatural end, and the understanding and use of the supernatural gifts whereby it is to be obtained.

One frequently finds among Catholic college graduates this over-balance of philosophy. They will have spent a whole semester on the proofs for the existence of God (which was, in a sense, unnecessary for them, since they already believe in God by Faith), yet have no working knowledge at all of, say, God's Providence.

With the non-Catholic we tend to make the same error; to instruct him on his own natural level instead of introducing him to the fact of supernatural life. It is a rare non-Catholic who doesn't know that the Catholic Church forbids contraceptives (a not very inviting piece of knowledge from his point of view); but a surprising number, even of college graduates, have never even heard of the Blessed Sacrament.

THE OBSOLESCENCE OF APOLOGETICS

Apologetics, which is the science of explaining and defending the Faith, is in itself honorable, and has been very useful in its day. But it is now obsolescent. Nobody ever asks the questions

The Thirst for Theology

to which apologetics is prepared to reply.

Apologetics characterizes a defensive Church, and the Church is no longer defensive. The real enemies of the Church today are not muck-raking the Church's past, but are fabricating lies out of whole cloth. One is faced with the alternatives of ignoring them or denying them flatly. Meanwhile the majority of Americans are not so much enemies of as strangers to the Church.

Both Hitler and Stalin have developed to its highest point the art of the lie. So have their fellow-travelers in America. If you try to argue with them you will find yourself completely at a loss to establish a rational basis for discussion. Would you like to argue your interpretation of the facts of the case against their interpretation of the facts of the case? It is impossible, because you will not even be able to agree as to what are the facts of the case. There will be two sets of facts, the true set and theirs. This is what is happening with Russia in the U.N. and in the Big Four attempts at making a peace. You cannot argue with Russia about whether or not she ought to remove her troops from such and such a territory if she flatly denies having troops there.

The same sort of thing happens here, with people who are not necessarily Communist. Msgr. Sheen gave a talk on the godlessness of psychoanalysis. But now, it appears from indignant letters in the public press, that the psychoanalysts have been much maligned. Either they do not take after Freud, or else they and Freud both revere the human personality, are profoundly respectful of religion, etc., etc. You can't argue with them on that basis. And they will not argue with you on the basis of, say, setting forth their beliefs in regard to God, the human soul, or the meaning of happiness.

Our learned opponents are also indifferent to the law of contradiction. If you pointed out to them that they have contradicted themselves several times in the same conversation, they would only say, "What difference does that make?" With such men you do not argue.

Among the less learned you find, even where they have good will, that they are so ignorant and their minds are so warped by sentimentality, that here again the art of apologetics is wasted energy. Usually they just do not even ask the questions which the apologist is prepared to answer, and if they do, they do not mean it seriously. If someone says "You Catholics have bad popes," the best thing to do is to say, "Name three." Then, after they have failed to name even one, and mutter something about having heard about it somewhere, you can favor them with a comparison between our present holy Holy Father and all the statesmen of the western hemisphere rolled into one.

Mr. Sheed has often pointed out the futility of apologetics. You wear yourself out, as he says, proving that God exists, and then your audience walks away muttering, "so what." They do not even know what God means. In their darkness and despair of our godless society they have not even dreamed that there could be Someone Who loves them and cares one iota whether they die or live, whether they sin or behave themselves.

DEVOTIONALISM

It is a dangerous thing to substitute devotionalism for a sound understanding of theology. Devotionalism is here used to mean feverish attendance at novenas, plus an accumulation of pious external devotions, which is fed not with the solid food of doctrine but with exhortations on the emotional level. The more energy with which devotionalism is pursued, the more dangerous it becomes. At best it degenerates into a gross sentimentality, at worst into madness.

When devotionalism concentrates, as it so easily can, on the charismatic aspects of religion, it can easily degenerate into superstition. It is not unusual to find people seemingly pious, who can converse endlessly about this or that mysterious or miraculous happening, yet who are not conspicuously virtuous and who evidently are devoid of a real interior life.

THEOLOGY FOR THE LAITY

Since, then, there is such a general need for theology, what is the best way in which it can be supplied to the laity?

The important thing about theology for the laity is that they should not get a watered-down course in seminary theology, much less a full course in seminary theology. The laity are not supposed to be diminutive theologians. To suppose so would be an error analogous to that which would have pious laity become little monks and nuns in the world, adopting conventual practice in so far as possible. We are called to be saints, but the path to sanctity must be according to our states in life. We are all called to know God, but here again there are different approaches to the same Truth. To suppose otherwise is to feel that the clergy or religious are somehow more a part of the Church than are the laity. But we are all equally members of the same Body; some eyes, some ears, some hands.

The difference is one of function, and it is according to the difference of function between the clergy and the laity that theology should be differently learned by each.

The similarity between the clergy and the laity as regards theology is this, that it is the same truth in either case, and should in both cases, since it is truth about God, be auxiliary to one's sanctification. The difference between the two cases is that the clergy must learn theology also in order to teach it as such, whereas the laity learn it chiefly for practical application in their personal and daily lives. From this difference spring the chief characteristics of theology for the laity:

1. The laity will have what might be called the "psychological" approach to theology rather than approaching it from the internal order of the science itself. For the laity the *Summa Theologica* will be a reference book rather than a textbook. They will not start at the beginning of it, but wherever they can find principles which apply to the problem which they are considering. The Benziger publishing house is going to publish an English edition

of the *Summa* with an index which will give detailed references to theological problems such as come up in different professions. It ought to be very useful.

Since the laity's interest in theology will be preeminently practical, they will not be under the necessity of remembering it so much as of absorbing it. The layman does not, for instance, have to remember all the daughters of sloth or pride, but only such as interfere with his own sanctification. As a matter of fact, one can informally observe that the laity are much more vulnerable to pride and to sterile pedantry in their theological knowledge than are clerical theologians.

2. It follows as a corollary to the above that the laity will always have to lean on the clergy for theological guidance. Those who claim the right to pick and choose the theology they will study, will never lose their dependence on those who have the fullness of theology, nor is it fitting that they should, since the laity are dependent upon and subordinate to the clergy in the hierarchical structure of the Church. This does not mean that a lay person cannot study by himself (indeed he is obliged to study according to his state in life), but only that he must seek guidance from his confessor or an advisor from time to time, the more so if he is engaged in any public use of theology.

3. It should be clearly understood that if the layman's theology is to be partial in regard to extension, it must nevertheless be deep. In fact, it is impossible to have too much understanding of the theological principles which apply to one's state in life. All too little is known about the Sacrament of Matrimony by many a husband and wife, whereas they ought continuously to grow, if not in study of it, surely in understanding of it. Catholic doctors have to know sharply the Church's teaching as it pertains to their profession, and in general this knowledge is readily available on the technical level, more generally ignored now on the broader level of professional obligations to charity, modesty, etc. The psychiatrist and psychologist, on the other hand, will need some

intensive study of St. Thomas' treatise on man, not to mention books on ascetical and mystical theology. Theology pertaining to economics and the social order is still *terra incognita* for the most part, despite the papal encyclicals. It is our habit to seize upon the natural principles set forth by the popes in disregard of their theological admonitions, so ending up at one with the liberals and other curious bedfellows.

SYSTEMS OF THEOLOGY FOR THE LAITY

To say that the laity can pick and choose is not to suppose that their study of theology must be hit or miss, but only that it does not follow the scientific order of the theological science. It normally should follow an organic order of its own, and this it can do in several ways.

1. Liturgy

The liturgy, which marks the rhythm of the life of the religious must also be a background influence in the life of the laity, teaching them the Church's great mysteries through the seasons of the Church year, and great spiritual principles through the psalms, for such of the laity who have time to read part or all of the Divine Office or one of the Little Offices. This is not to mention the Mass, which is the great teacher, but in another sense than we are here considering. But unless one has an exceptional lay vocation it is impossible to lead any sort of *full* liturgical life in an urban society geared to commercialism. What can be done with the liturgy in a closed, intensely Christian, rural community, is well exemplified by the Grail. On its farm in Loveland, Ohio, the Grail builds the whole pattern of its life around the liturgy, following not only the rhythm of the Church Year, but also using the blessings and sacramentals, as well as holding up saint after saint for emulation and admiration.

One thing especially obvious at the Grail is the richness of the liturgy which provides far more than enough material with which to plan a community program. I once visited a Catholic camp where a well-meaning but inept attempt was made to provide not very well instructed children with a sense of Christian observance by mechanical rather than organic reference to the liturgy. So Christmas was "celebrated" in the first week of August, Easter in the second week, and so on. The camp directors would have taught the children much more had they just relaxed and taken the Church Season as they found it, amplifying the day's liturgy by fitting drama and practices. Three days at the Grail would have been a revelation to them.

2. Scripture

Learning theology through scripture is learning it the way Christ first taught it, by parable, by admonition, by principle, and overwhelmingly by His own life. And so it is learned by the legions of those whose excellent custom it is to read a little every day from the Bible. The problem here is whether scripture can be used as a group instruction method. Its obvious use is, of course, in parish sermons. But apart from that, is it a suitable basis for a study club or college class?

There have been but few attempts, and most of them have not been notably successful. The difficulty is not so much in the scriptures as in finding a suitable priest director of the group or course. Owing to the rationalist attacks on the Bible, seminary courses in scripture have had to concentrate on the refutation of rationalist heresies, on sundry historical and technical studies valuable in themselves but not conducive to simplicity in approaching the word of God. What the layman needs to know is how to interpret the words of Christ in his own life.

Our danger today is not that we shall too literally interpret the scriptures (following the fundamentalist Protestants) but that we shall not take the Bible seriously enough, believing that when God says, for instance, that it is hard for rich people to be saved, that He means it is hard for rich people to be saved, and not that He means that it is hard for nasty rich people to be saved except in capitalistic America.

There are many new and useful helps to the study of scripture. One way and another they throw into unfamiliar perspective the words which have, through over-familiarity without meditation and practice, come to be taken for granted. Msgr. Knox's translations are very useful in this regard. So also is Fr. Stedman's little manual of daily readings, which is a re-arrangement of the order of the text.

3. Catholic Action

The genius of Catholic Action lies in the fact that it is organic. It is not so much something which has been invented, as something which has been discovered. The thing that is organic about Catholic Action is that it follows the natural process of reasoning: see, judge and act. Therefore it is, to over-simplify, a way of learning practical theology, with the immediate purpose of putting it to use. The "act" part of the inquiry technique is made possible because Catholic Action begins with the most obvious and pressing problems which confront its members, and therefore keeps the study in the realm of their own personal lives. It also automatically adjusts the dose to the capacity of the people concerned.

Catholic Action suggests the study group by way of contrast. The reason that study groups are over and over again failures is not because they do not teach theology (and often more of it and more clearly than Catholic Action) but because their approach is not organic, and therefore the study either fails to interest people, or makes the students academic and their study unfruitful. A Catholic Action cell must be homogeneous, which guarantees common problems and allows for common action. Study groups are all too often not homogeneous, or if they are they do not take advantage of their homogeneity.

Another contrast is between the passivity of the study group and the activist participation of those in Catholic Action. The activity of study groups is usually on the part of the clergy, and the passivity on the part of the laity. The result is that the outstanding fault of the Catholic laity is the lack of initiative.

Another familiar sin of study groups is their tendency to concentrate on other people's shortcomings. What good does it do housewives to study euthanasia? They might better be studying Christian home life. Meanwhile the doctors, who might well be studying Communism, eyes averted from the sins of industrial-capitalism. When will we learn that the world problem has to be solved locally?

4. Theology in Higher Education

How should theology be taught in college? It is already the consensus of opinion that it *should* be taught and a number of experiments are being made. I would like to suggest that the key is *not* advanced catechetical studies, or a diluted seminary course, but *integration*. There is such a tension already between secular courses of study and religion, even in Catholic colleges, that students have shown conspicuous resentment when God is mentioned in the so-called ordinary courses. Because of the separation of the departments of religion and other studies, students have lost the feeling that God is relevant to His creation. The synthesis must be restored. This cannot be done for the saying so, because there are not many teachers who can teach integrated courses, but it looks like the only answer, and therefore something will have to be done about it. An integrated college course is the only realistic way of teaching today.

How do you integrate religion with a secular course? It will not be done on a superficial level, but on the most profound level. Take history, for instance. Who since Bossuet has really attempted to show history as the unraveling of God's Providence? Yet is it not so? Is not the Incarnation the overwhelmingly most important of all *historical* events? It may even be well not to teach Church history separately any more in colleges, in the interest of showing that the Catholic Church is not a side issue in history, but the focal point of history. In order to do the integrating job in history we will need scholar-saints, who will take account of all the facts, yet always see the undiminished brilliance of Christ in His Church. If the Church really is Christ it will always look like Christ unless there are defects in the beholder, and this in the midst of recurrent crucifixions and betrayals. Catholic college graduates are more given to explaining how none of our sins really reflect on the Church than they are to the much more profound view that even our sins contribute mysteriously to God's greater glory and to that of His Church.

Economics is a subject which is crying for religious light. Garrigou-Lagrange, speaking of spiritual blindness, remarks that it makes people look for the explanation of our ills in economic cycles or over-production instead of seeing them truly as God's punishment upon us because large numbers of men have turned away from God as their last end and placed their last end in money or material prosperity. It is in this light that the economic system should be seen as the invention of men who have turned away from God. It would be folly, therefore, to teach that economics is just the way things work, to which morality is irrelevant. Rather let us show that the law of supply and demand is no law whatever, and is in fact reversed in practice (we create demands so as to get rich by supplying them). Let the college students look clearly at the fact of almost universal economic ruin. Let them see the sharp contradiction which exists between economic endeavor and Christian ideals of detachment and mortification. Let them go to the roots of true economics to see that it is God Who gives real wealth and that our practices should be harmonious with His laws.

Even *English composition* would be considerably changed in an integrated college course. Writing is now a glamour profession at which you can get enormously rich if you have the facility of style which you are willing to put at the service of contentlessness.

Catholic colleges have no honorable course but to turn their back on current practice and teach writing as an apostolate, putting the major emphasis on what is being said rather than on superficialities of style.

If Catholic colleges are going to teach *Sociology* they will have to transform the usual contents of such a subject. If the descriptive part is really to be valid, it will be necessary, besides describing the sordid living conditions of the poor, to describe the sordid living conditions of the rich. Then it might become apparent that what is really terrible is universal materialism and loss of religion.

Psychology is another subject which will require drastic transformation. This should be seen as the study of the soul, taken from a certain point of view, showing the spiritual organism, and how it is meant to work and what happens when, as frequently now, its nature is violated.

And so also with the other courses. It does not so much matter what framework of teaching is employed (whether the tutorial system, or through great books, or through certain courses as at present), so long as the integration is there. The integration will first of all have to be in the teachers and then, if such a system is used, in the textbooks. One sign of returning health in education will be the re-emphasis on perfecting the *teacher*. The cursory suggestions given above for accomplishing the integration should not be taken to indicate that the process is obvious and easy, but that it is largely *terra incognita*, awaiting exploration in the direction indicated.

One cannot imagine that a Catholic college with a truly integrated curriculum would be accredited by a secular system of accreditation. That would be just as well, because that would spare the college the necessity of sending its teachers to schools where they would be taught useless and erroneous things. Maybe if someone would dare to take the lead, Catholics would soon be setting the pace in education matters. To date all the daring educational experiments have been made by non-Catholics and are doomed to failure despite the sincerity of the experiments, because they lack the first principles.

Of the religion course which should be taught in addition to an integrated curriculum, there just is no space to treat here.

5. Retreats and Spiritual Direction

The theology which is most important to everyone has been left until last. It is the theology which pertains directly to one's own sanctification. Apart from reading spiritual books on one's own, this theology is chiefly gained from spiritual direction and retreats. As things are at present both of these sources are somewhat wanting. It is hard to find a spiritual director who will seriously undertake to help one to become a saint. Even retreats are ordinarily on the cozy side. One gets a warm glow of satisfaction from having set aside a day or two for God, but the stimulation is largely emotional. The usual retreat is geared low, like the parish mission, for those in a state of mortal sin, or nearly so. The few theological retreats that are given, whether Catholic Action or other, are far more fruitful. These abound in real solid principles of what the spiritual life consists in, and how necessary it is for salvation and a fruitful life. Not a few people's lives have been completely transformed by such retreats.

THE SWORD OF THE SPIRIT

One of the most hopeful signs in the Church is the growing army of laymen who are armed with the sword of the spirit, which is the word of God. One finds them in offices, in factories, on street corners and at cocktail parties, explaining and defending the Faith. It is largely owing to theological instruction of one or another sort that this army is supplanting the mute, unapostolic Catholic laity of former days.

CAROL ROBINSON

The Real McCoy

He maintains that Truth is subjective
Yet he is extremely objective
About the validity of the dollar.
Only to greenbacks with the print
Of the United States Mint
Is he receptive.
For one so insistent –
Isn't he inconsistent?

           CATHERINE CHRISTOPHER

Advice to Her Daughter On Starting to School

Now listen to mother, my darling
Frequently make a scene.
As soon as you're disregarded,
Roll back your eyes and scream.

For we haven't the money to spend, dear.
And you're not a Madame Curie,
And the only way to know yourself
Is to act like a little fury.

For problem children get help, dear.
They're examined; they're probed; and they're tested.
You may be a genius in disguise!
At least you'll be fed and rested.

For life is geared to the "difficult."
Your behavior must never be formal.
For teachers find that they have no time,
For the child regarded as "normal."

           CATHERINE WALSH

Secular Education— Some Years After

I SEE BY THE PAPERS THAT MY ALMA MATER is raising some many millions of dollars. A new library. A new dormitory. Some running expenses. It costs a lot to run Wellesley. I myself, or rather my father, paid $1,000 a year for four years so that I could be educated there, and that was only about half what it cost the college to put me through my paces. If you add to that the cost of unlearning what they taught me — but you can't add that, because it was largely a spiritual cost.

It is not that I don't have a certain gratitude to my college. It is gratitude for what was intended to be kindness, but turned out to be unkindness; for seeming light that turned out to be darkness; for guidance by the halt and the blind.

But before I beat Wellesley's breast (because it has not yet itself received the grace to view its own sins with humility and horror), let me beat my own. If Wellesley is no credit to me, neither am I any credit to it. Nor was I its joys as an undergraduate. There were nobler, brighter, more diligent students at every hand. The seeds the college sowed were bad, but the ground they fell on was as bad or worse. Neither my home training nor my previous schooling nor my own virtue provided auspicious foundation on which to implant a higher education, so if the higher education wasn't so high after all, it is yet not fully responsible for the end product.

I did not study very hard at college, so I was guilty of sinning by sloth. If I had studied harder I would have learned more untruths. It has been useful for me to reflect on this dilemma, as I have seen it repeated a thousand times since, in my own life and in the lives of my friends. If your job is selling cheap, badly-made and unnecessary dresses, the better salesman you are the more you sin by deceit and by adding some more materialism to a materialistic world. But if you are a poor salesman and lacking in diligence, you take money under false pretenses. Or suppose it is your job to file correspondence about comic strips. The more seriously you take your job the more the fool you are; the less seriously you take it, so much the less do you deserve the salary which you think you must have in order to eat.

Now I see that it is the devil who has maneuvered so many of us into such untenable positions, and that the only way out is God's way, which is to strike out in the direction of His righteousness, letting one's daily bread follow as it will. The answer to the Wellesley dilemma (had I known it) would have been to leave and to seek truth elsewhere. It was what I came to in the end, but only after a wasted youth, out of which only God could bring good.

ON THE CREDIT SIDE

Wellesley has plenty of minor virtues. It is breathtakingly beautiful, both in its natural surroundings and in its semi-monastic architecture. It is not bourgeois. Wealth is neither paraded nor worshipped; luxurious comfort is not held up as an ideal. The college has, or had, a tradition of scholarship. We obtained our information at first hand (from Spinoza himself and not someone's comments on, or condensations of, Spinoza). There were no courses in such non-academic subjects as feeding babies or department-store buying. There was still a lingering admiration for Philosophy and Greek majors, despite the fact that they were a handful compared with the hordes of those majoring in Psychology (which was then largely a matter of memory work). No one ever dreamt of teaching shorthand, typing, or indeed any subject bearing on gainful employment, the contention being that Wellesley undertook to train the mind and that anyone who could manage somehow to scrape together money enough for four years of it could find enough more money for three months at a secretarial school.

Wellesley students came largely from upper middle class, professional families. They were healthy and intelligent, usually possessed of high humanitarian ideals. The college had a definite religious foundation, in consequence of which it attracted the daughters of Protestant missionaries, as well as a sprinkling of their Chinese and Japanese converts. In my day the college motto, "Non ministrari sed ministrare," was still jokingly translated, "Not to be ministers but to be ministers' wives," yet the religious strain had worn a bit thin and the joke was no longer very funny. Every year one girl was chosen as "most typical of Wellesley," which really meant that she represented the ideal rather than the typical. It was a very high ideal, naturally speaking: wholesome, self-possessed, extrovert and gracious; without affectation and with marked nobility of character. There were always a few Negro girls in school and no noticeable race prejudice. One of the student's parents used as a matter of course to entertain Negro friends at their Bronxville home, a fact which caused but little comment at college.

THE DEBIT ACCOUNT

Despite these advantages, and many others, I was more nearly finished by than graduated from Wellesley. Four years left me with:

1. A vague but persistent feeling of superiority.
2. An intellectual curiosity run riot.
3. A militant immorality.
4. A set of wholly erroneous convictions.
5. No plans for the future.
6. A mind closed to the supernatural.
7. A profound ignorance of the purpose of life, the existence and nature of God, and all the rest of the really essential truths.
8. A growing despair (unacknowledged).

I cannot absolve my alma mater from responsibility for this state of affairs, even after due allowance is made for other contributing factors and my own exceeding lack of intellectual and moral virtues. I shall show in part how it came about.

RELIGION AT WELLESLEY

Wellesley is not so much a secular college as a sectarian college which has ceased to be Christian. It is of pious Protestant origin, as are most New England colleges, and its charter insists on the compulsory study of the Bible. In my day the clash between what the founder had in mind and the ultra-liberal religion of the faculty had reached an uncomfortable stage. Grace was still said at meals, but chapel attendance was no longer compulsory; the personal lives of the teachers continued to follow the Christian pattern in which they had been reared, which they themselves directly or indirectly undermined the whole of Christian ethics in the classroom. The required study of the Bible was in process of being telescoped into insignificance, after having first been completely perverted.

Wellesley fell hook, line and sinker for the higher biblical critics. It was not until long afterwards that I discovered most of the higher critics had then already eaten their words, unbeknownst to Wellesley.

If you want to damn religion by indirection the thing to do is to study it from a literary point of view, or anthropologically, or historically. We studied the Bible historically. All I remember from one year on the Old Testament is that the Pentateuch was said to have been written by a number of different people designated by letters of the alphabet and that this was supposed to have invalidated it somehow. No mention that I recall was made of original sin, of the singular mission of the Jewish race, of the nobility of the patriarchs, of the foreshadowing character of Old Testament events, or of the messianic prophesies. One could have spent one's time more valuably in a Baptist Sunday school.

The New Testament course was Wellesley's masterpiece, on a par with the "Man and Nature" course at the University of Wisconsin in the production of atheists. We studied only the synoptic gospels, Matthew, Mark and Luke, as John was supposed to have been written by someone else at a far later date.

All we heard of St. Paul in the required course was that he was the publicity agent responsible for the phenomenal spread of the teachings, not in themselves singular, of an obscure Jewish prophet named Jesus Christ.

The synoptic gospels were first reduced to St. Mark, as being (so they said) the earliest, most matter of fact, and therefore the most accurate. Mark does not describe Christ's birth: therefore there is nothing extraordinary about it. The miracles are then explained away; all diseases being reduced to epilepsy or neuroses, while such tales as the multiplication of the loaves and fishes became illustrations of the disciples' tendency to exaggerate. Christ's teachings were then twisted to support a theory of narrow Judaic preoccupation. By this time we had reached the triumphal entry of Palm Sunday (really so insignificant as to have caused no stir in Jerusalem and only seemingly important in retrospect). The Passion of Our Lord was considered the tragic end of blunderings and miscalculations, and the whole story ends abruptly as Christ dies in desolation on the Cross. And what of the Resurrection? It's a made-up story, later interpolated into the manuscripts.

A very pious Quakeress taught us these things. She opened every class with a prayer and frequently pointed to the nobility of Christian teaching, now that it was shorn of superstitious coating. Pretending to praise that which you have just destroyed is a common technique these days. You find it used in the popular expositions of the wonders of sex: three hundred pages of carnality, every fiftieth of which bows and says, "Love is so wonderful, especially married love." Its use is also flagrant in the standard obstetrical textbooks for nurses (Catholic and non-Catholic), which treat of woman as a biological exhibit, while carefully inserting periodic praise of motherhood.

For the most part Wellesley students succumbed to the enlightenment without protest. Who were we to argue with "the reading in the original Hebrew is…," and "all present-day scholars agree that ... "? Besides, our previous religious training usually amounted to a dubious baptism, some Sunday school stories, a dash of sentimentality and a dose of adolescent idealism. I took part in what was probably the most famous protest. Our teacher had been explaining away the Last Supper. It was, of course, an uneventful celebration of the Jewish Passover, to which sentiment later attached significance. Someone had been so foolish in the morning class as to have defied this interpretation because it clashed with what she had always been taught and firmly believed. There was a recent convert to Catholicism in our class who arose in her defense, defying the whole historical method. I joined her, but only for the love of a good fight, since I was already an atheist. The brightest girl in school, a Jewess of amazing intelligence, chimed in and the uproar lasted until the teacher walked out white with rage, long after the closing bell had rung.

Nothing I learned at college stuck with me so long and clearly as did the fourteen reasons why Christ wasn't divine, according to the Gospel of St. Mark. In the end it took a large miracle of grace to get me to reconsider Christianity at all. I sometimes wonder if that convert's prayers were instrumental in getting me another chance. She talked to me a lot and even took me to Boston to Mass, but I was a million miles away and impenetrable. Meanwhile the Quakeress was revealing the heartening news that a Dutch scholar was on the brink of actually being able to *prove* that Christ had really lived. "You know," she said, "we really have no proof now, in case we are challenged."

PHILOSOPHY AT WELLESLEY

Now that the supernatural order had been explained away, I in my folly went on to the destruction of the natural order. I majored in Philosophy.

We studied every major philosopher from the pre-Socratics to John Dewey, except all Christian philosophers. It was as though

Secular Education—Some Years After

human thought had been suspended during the 1900-year interval separating Aristotle and Descartes. Indeed, that was the precise opinion of the head of the Philosophy department, who put it thus: "When you are ready to give up thinking, become a Catholic."

Philosophy was taught cafeteria style. All the philosophers were presented to our view and no reason was given why one should be preferred to another. I didn't realize this at first and spent a miserable afternoon in consequence. The dean was conducting a seminar in modern philosophy. The very few students attracted to this study were sitting around the dean's dining room table while one student read a paper on John Dewey. The rest of them were taking copious notes so that on an examination they would be able to say: "John Dewey says so and so." I made the mistake of listening critically and discovered that Dewey's idea of the purpose of life was the pursuit of certain "ends" until they opened up new "ends," which would in time reveal still more "ends," etc. At the end of the reading I burst out with, "But that doesn't make sense!" There followed an argument, which was concluded by the dean's icy: "I would hardly say that the greatest living philosopher is talking nonsense."

I was miserable all through tea and only in later years discovered how right I had been.

As I said earlier, we were scholarly at Wellesley and read our text in the original. A list of our philosophy books would read like an extract from the Roman Index. Nothing pleases me more than to be forbidden ever again to share the intellectual writhings of post-Christian thinkers. I spent the better part of two weeks once in a beer parlor in Natick trying, with another girl, to make head or tail of Hegel. "Being is non-being, and the union of the two is becoming. . . ."

Still, the big things I learned in Philosophy came not so much from books as from teachers. Foremost was that there is no truth. This one was well hidden under verbiage about the love of truth and the nobility of searching for it; but we were never to find it. You have only to scratch any secular college graduate to find him infected with this same conviction; indeed it is held by the whole of secular society. The fact that she claims to know the truth is really the stock objection to the Catholic Church in America today, made by people who are so far from having disproved her claim that they actually do not know what the claims are, but only that they are to certainties and not to opinions, prejudices or possibilities.

The next important thing I learned in Philosophy was that there is no free will. I'm ashamed to have picked up this error because it was presented quite baldly and I could easily have used my brain in support of my common sense. Psychology and science students were persuaded more subtly, but the same determinism infected almost everybody. Its most popular form of expression was either the sentimental "You must not call these people bad, but sick," or the useful, "I couldn't help it because I was so badly brought up." One would be very mistaken to suppose that our theoretical determinism eliminated harsh judgments in the practical order.

I also picked up a certain working philosophy of life, a sort of courageous despair, amoral and rather on the sentimental side. I bore a much stronger resemblance to the Professor of Philosophy than to any of the philosophical systems we studied, most of which were in the purely speculative plane anyhow.

Lest anyone suppose that my Philosophy professor was a uniquely vicious man, let me hasten to assure them that he was by no means either vicious or singular. Indeed, it was because of his personal charm and exceeding kindness that his erroneous ideas were taken so to heart and did so much harm. He was a devout admirer of Alfred North Whitehead, whom I understand to have the same sort of soul-devastating effect on his Harvard students. The late Morris R. Cohen, famous Philosophy Professor at C.C.N.Y., who wrote "The Faith of a Liberal," is the exact counterpart of my teacher. Now there is another book out by a disciple of Professors Cohen and Whitehead. It is "Nature and Man," by Paul Weiss, who is Professor of Philosophy at Yale, and it follows the tortuous mental twists of Whitehead. I quote:

> The past conditions the future as a limited but not yet determinate realm within which a range of occurrences can take place. A concrete course in time is necessary in order to determine and thereby realize the future. The result can be known in advance as a possibility, not as an actuality.

My personal conclusion on this type of thing has long been that these erudite gentlemen are trying, in their intellectual pride, to invent the doctrine of God's Providence, but on the natural level.

It was not a pleasure to read of the death of Morris Cohen. I searched the obituary in vain for any sign that he had at last humbled himself before God.

CONTRASTS

You would misunderstand the curious nature of our instruction if you did not take into account the example set us by our superiors, which was on the whole exemplary. So far as I knew the faculty, I admired them. One of my teachers practiced voluntary poverty. Another bore with great patience the arthritic pains with which she was racked. It would not at all surprise me to learn that many other faculty members led lives of heroic personal sacrifice.

Furthermore, there may have been Catholic influence making itself felt here and there. Vida Scudder, who was to me only an illustrious retired member of the faculty, was, as I have since discovered, the great American authority on St. Catherine of Siena. A curious saint to preoccupy a non-Catholic. My art professor had influential ecclesiastical connections through which she was admitted to a view of the papal robes. How far beyond liturgical beauty her admiration for the Church extended I do not know. She may even have been trying to inculcate us with a pre-Raphaelite bias in art for all I managed to grasp of that subject. The college choir was partial to Gregorian Chant, which it sang without integral relation to the Sunday church service, of course. There were also a few Catholic teachers, mostly in the foreign language departments, with a consequent limited influence.

While the faculty continued their exemplary lives of noble pagan stoicism, or even of Catholic gropings, the student body took to heart their teachings and was noticeably degenerating. The students' favorite subject of private discussion was that of moral principles, which was argued endlessly. Under the circumstances the only argument for high moral principles was expediency, although the argument was given a hundred different ways. Expediency is the least strong deterrent of immorality and my informal observation was that it lost ground at an alarming rate.

At about this time the college took on a psychiatrist as advisor on student problems. Up until then the official attitude toward moral problems was non-existent, but could have been presumed to favor conventional Protestant moral standards. With psychiatry entered Freud and the all-explanatory sex. Rumors were that the psychiatrist was working to remove the inhibitions of the college girls.

THE VOCABULARY OF AN EX-CHRISTIAN

The commonly accepted connotation of certain key words will furnish an excellent indication of the spiritual state which underlay the polite Protestant covering of our lives at Wellesley:

SIN was a word which was never used, except facetiously or historically. When we did in fact sin, we had "done something wrong" or "made a mistake." The idea of sin as an offense against God would not have occurred to most of us, as we found ourselves unable to conceive a "personal" God. It goes without saying that anything we found ourselves unable to conceive of therefore didn't exist.

MODESTY, in the usual Christian sense, was another word missing from our vocabulary. It is quite true, as I have since read in ecclesiastical writings, that those outside the Catholic faith are incapable of understanding the delicacy of conscience involved in the Christian virtue of modesty. We might, in an extreme case, have labelled a costume indecent, but we would only have mocked a dress to call it modest. Our campus clothes were pretty modest, as a matter of fact, but we were not modest. We had long since lost our sense of shame, and nudity, whether informally in the dormitory or officially at the elaborate physical examinations presided over by the hygiene department, was more or less taken for granted.

SUPERNATURAL meant phony psychic phenomena, like crystal gazing. We were strict naturalists. If there was a higher intelligence than ours in the universe, it was of the same sorts as ours. But generally we credited what higher powers there might be with having lower intelligences than ours: blind force, or energy, or chance. So much for God. As for angels, it never crossed our minds that they might really exist, fallen or otherwise.

All the words which are more or less related to the supernatural went by the board with it. Sacrament, grace, mystical: they were words which we seldom heard and to which we attached no meaning. "God is Love" was written conspicuously over the choir of the chapel and was given as the designation of a special autumn Sunday. Still, the idea of the theological virtue of charity was certainly lacking to almost all students.

HUMILITY was no virtue to us, whether in practice (for the most part) or in theory. It suggested to us a sort of base groveling, a lack of the ever-desirable self-confidence. Instead of humility we used the word modesty to indicate a person who doesn't brag about his attainments. We would have thought St Thérèse of Lisieux was lacking in modesty for saying "I was made for great things." We had never heard that humility does not involve the denial of good qualities but the acknowledgment of them as from God.

SANCTITY was an unfamiliar word, and certainly not an ideal of character. Our ideal characters were strictly on the natural plane of greatness. We admired Abraham Lincoln, Florence Nightingale and Walt Whitman, and we would have gone right along with those who say St. Teresa of Avila was a prize psychoneurotic. That is, we would have if we had ever heard of her.

Our ideals of conduct were on the natural level too. We thought it would be a wonderful thing to find a cure for cancer and to give money to reputable charities. We were scrupulously honest according to our conception of honesty. There was practically no cheating at college and theft was limited to an occasional kleptomaniac. Most of us came from families which wouldn't have dreamt of taking anything not theirs and would have been disgraced to accept relief if jobs could still be had scrubbing floors. Yet most of our fathers were responsibly involved in banking, corporations, railroads, insurance companies and Wall Street, places where (it is said) robbery on a large scale sometimes takes place. That curious clinging to what might be called "petty honesty" is still a conspicuous "virtue" of the graduates of our best colleges, especially those engaged in such business as publicity, radio and publishing. The Harvard graduate who assures us that X-AX is gentle and harmless, feels he preserves his integrity by freely admitting in the bosom of his closest friends that the stuff is probably poison.

Some of our natural ideals of conduct were far less attractive. We were coming around to the idea that no fair-minded wife would force her husband to continue living with her after he had lost his love (romantic lust) for her. We rather thought it would be unfeeling to bring children into a world not fully prepared (financially) to take care of them. There was even a growing admiration for the man she loves to marry her for any other reason than pure romantic love (lust) at a time suited to his convenience.

RESULTS

So after four years we were turned out into a world which had, on the whole, even worse ideas that we had. It was a world desperately in need of salvation, but we were in no position to save it.

What happened to most of my friends was that they spent the next several years adjusting themselves downward to a world they couldn't lift up.

What's the point of studying English literature in order to spend your life reading unbelievably bad manuscripts for a publishing house with quite other than literary ambitions?

Why master higher mathematics in order to measure the capricious ups and downs of the stock market?

Had we disciplined our minds in order to do what was called "advertising research" but was really counting by ones?

Why had we bothered so with our brains if we were going to end up exhibiting our physical charms as Powers models?

The only thing ruthless commercialism had in common with our academic past was the irrelevancy of God to both types of life.

It is no wonder that none of my collegemates I know now lead a joyous, purposeful life. Some have married, some not. Some have made money, some not. One killed herself. Most have reached a working compromise (not very stable) with circumstances as they found them.

Only a few remain actively tormented by the contrast between the mediocrity and materialism to which the world invites them, and the hollow in their hearts which aches for God.

M.B.W.[1]

1   This was almost certainly written by Carol Robinson since she graduated from Wellesley College and referred to things that she often mentioned in her other works.

INTEGRITY, June 1947

At M.I.T. trigonometry
  Is advanced by men of vision.
Original Sin and the pickle we're in,
  Has been solved by nuclear fission.

BOOK REVIEWS

On Making a Good Confession

PARDON AND PEACE
By Alfred Wilson, C.P.
Sheed & Ward

Here is a practical guide to the oft-times regarded as insuperable problem of giving an intelligent account of our sins. The impact of pagan principles on today's Christians is infinitely more subtle than in the days of the pagan Roman Empire. The devil is the matinee idol of our times. Monsieur Verdoux playing fast and loose with morality and getting away with it! An unaccountable fluctuation in the price of a certain stock reveals a $10,000 a year "man of distinction" has been playing fast and loose with the welfare of widows and orphans. A camera enthusiast atop the Empire State Building carefully adjusts his lenses to capture the suicide leap of a tortured soul with one leg up on the parapet a few feet away. The line at the Paramount starts forming at 7:00 A.M. in Times Square. The tabloid gives us this day our daily surfeit of violence. "One-fourth of the budget of New York State is spent in the care of mental cases," says the newspaper. "Peace and there is no peace."

Too often, the approach to Confession is to compile a large budget of sins without an appropriate list of resolutions to match. Small wonder that we become weighed down with the burden of sin and thereby prejudice our chances of achieving an intelligent purpose of amendment, and the peace of mind which flows from absolution. Behind this Jansenist fussing lurks a latent desire to be self-sufficient and a lack of confidence in the goodness of God.

One of the chief obstacles to our reception of the Sacrament of Penance in its fullness, according to Fr. Wilson, is the lack of spiritual reading in our lives. We spurn the wisdom of Sacred Scripture and the counsel of St. Ignatius, St. John of the Cross, and St. Teresa of Avila for the pontifications of ex-cab drivers turned human relations experts, or fortune-tellers, astrologers or erudite psychiatrists with little regard for common sense or morality.

This is a wonderful book for priests and lay people both. It is written in a familiar style, and is besides very entertaining. Fr. Wilson has furnished the faithful with a year's supply of funny stories.

Pardon and Peace is nothing if not comprehensive. It covers everything from the advantages of confession and what constitutes a sin, to confessional manners; along with lots of detail and sound advice about examining your conscience and getting rid of scruples. It is one of the most welcome Catholic books published in recent years. Please everyone buy a copy.

JOHN MURPHY

Spiritually We Are Semites

THE REDEMPTION OF ISRAEL
By John Friedman
Sheed & Ward

It's an interesting fact that the one problem most widespread and most commonplace today, is a problem that can only be explained on the highest level of penetrative thought. The enigma of the Jew is a religious mystery. He is everywhere, yet nowhere is he at home. He is accused of the one thing of which he is least capable, a global political plot. He is criticized as capitalist and as communist, as mystic and materialist, as a culture-vulture and a boor. The nearer he achieves assimilation (as in Germany), the more marked is he for specific persecution. The more autonomous he remains (as in England), the less is he singled out as victim. His salvation lies in the place where he has been least likely to seek it, in that other branch of Israel, the Roman Catholic Church.

This book is a meaty nutshell-full of the Jewish historical mystery. It is a brief 122-page essay which scans the passage of the Jew from Abraham to Henri Bergson, all in the light of Divine Revelation. It logically subdivides this history into three epochs:

a. The Egyptian Epoch
b. The Babylonian Epoch
c. The Universal Epoch

These epochs in turn are divided into three phases common to each:

a. First Phase – Sin
b. Second Phase – Punishment
c. Third Phase – Salvation

Today, Mr. Friedman insists, finds the Jew more than halfway through the third and last phase of the final epoch. The material aspect of the regained Promised Land is the current return of the Jew to Palestine. Political Zionism, however, because it places the Nation before God (the sin of the Jew), is a factor which militates against salvation. The spiritual aspect of the regained Promised Land is found in those souls converted from Judaism to Catholicism, of which Dr. Friedman is one. Retaining their identities as Jews, these men, as new apostles of Christ, are the nucleus of a redeemed Israel. Re-grafted upon the Vine of Christ, they constitute the monumental answer to the enigma of the Jew.

All of which should give the Catholic who embraces an untenable anti-Semitism something to *think* about. When there is no Jew and no Gentile but all one in Christ, the anti-Semite will be a lonely man indeed.

ED WILLOCK

INTEGRITY, June 1947
Garment Rended

LEON BLOY—PILGRIM OF THE ABSOLUTE
Introduction by Jacques Maritain.
Selections by Raissa Maritain
Pantheon

    Raissa Maritain and her husband, Jacques (who does the introduction) are in an excellent position to present these extracts from some of Bloy's writings. It was to him they turned in suicidal desperation in their search for a *raison d'etre*, a hungering of the soul for the Truth which is God—the Absolute. Leon Bloy's words will come as a startling shock to American Catholics. His deliberate self-humiliations and his denunciations of the smugness and complacency of his fellows permit of no compromise. He spent the greater part of his life in utter misery and destitution; yet he persisted in his relentless viewpoint. For example, in his indictment of the Modern Christians:

> You have no idols in your homes, that is to say, you don't burn incense before wooden or stone images while adoring them. You don't blaspheme. The Name of the Lord is so far from your thoughts that it would not even enter your heads to 'take in vain.' On Sundays you do God the overwhelming favor of appearing in His Church. It's more the thing to do than anything else would be, it sets a good example for the servants, and after all it makes no difference one way or another. You honor your fathers and mothers in the sense that you don't, from sunrise to sunset, bespatter their faces with gobs of filth. You do not kill either with the sword or with poison. That would be displeasing to mankind and might serve to scare your customers away. And finally, you don't go in for too scandalous debauchery,

you don't tell lies as big as mountains, you don't rob along the highways, where you can so easily be waylaid yourselves, nor do you rob banks, which are always so admirably guarded. So much for God's Commandments.

More than 300 passages are included in the book, and a very fine index gives their French sources.

JOY ANDERSON

The Problem of Love

THE MIND AND HEART OF LOVE
by M.C. D'Arcy, S.J.
Henry Holt

There are few men and women who have not had the experience of conflict between the impulse of selflessness and the drive of selfishness; few, also, are they who have had the time or the ability to face in a speculative manner the problem of these conflicting loves or to attempt to solve it. The problem may be stated simply in this fashion: is there a way to reconcile the apparently contradictory impulses of selflessness and selfishness? Or must one or the other conquer and cast out the other?

Fr. D'Arcy has given much thought to the problem and this work gives us the fruit of his investigations. There are two purposes in the work that should be distinguished. There is, first, what might be called the documentation of the problem, the accumulation of the evidence of its existence. This purpose has been attained most brilliantly by the author. The reader is made keenly aware of the existence of the two loves, their pervading presence throughout the universe on every level of being, and the difficulties their conflicting tendencies give rise to.

The second purpose of the book is the presentation of a solution to the problem of love. That Fr. D'Arcy has attained his second purpose is questionable. In seeking the solution, the author was aided by intellectual contact with several others who were engaged in a similar pursuit. Much of the book is devoted to an exposition of their opinions; the author, then, shows how his own thoughts were developed through a criticism of these opinions. This is an ancient and fruitful method of enquiry. Some of the authors discussed are: de Rougemont (*Passion and Society*), Nygren (*Eros and Agape*), Rousselot (*Probleme de l'Amour au Moyen Age*), and Hunter Guthrie (*Introduction au Probleme de l'Histoire de la Philosophie*).

Fr. D'Arcy leans heavily on the contribution of Hunter Guthrie, although he brings in elements of Rousselot's theory that are, in fact, incompatible with Guthrie's thesis. The one element of Rousselot's explanation that would ultimately solve the problem, the Thomistic theory of the relation of the whole and the part, is passed over lightly on the authority of Gilson, who chose to ignore St. Thomas' clear indication of his own adherence to this solution and suggested that the doctrine of men and angels as images of God was the key to the solution, as though there were a choice between the two.

It might seem that the whole problem is of little practical value and of interest only to philosophers. This is far from true; the problem has urgent practical applications, especially in the spiritual life and in political life. Recent controversies over the relation of the individual to the common good, the human person to society, are fundamentally resolvable into this question of love. There is, in fact, urgent need for a clear solution to the problem of love which would manifest the possibility of reconciling the apparently contradictory impulses of love. Fr. D'Arcy has contributed much toward a clarification of the problem and its solution.

JAMES M. EGAN, O.P.

Book Reviews

The Story of Fatima

OUR LADY OF LIGHT
Translated from the French of Chanoine C. Barthas
and Pere G. Da Fronseca, S.J.
Bruce

For the third time in less than a hundred years, our Blessed Mother revealed herself on earth to repeat substantially the same message to the world. *"Men must correct their faults and ask pardon for their sins. In order that they no longer offend Our Lord, who is already too much offended... continue every day to say the beads."* Her intermediaries in each case at La Salette, Lourdes, and in our own century, at Fatima, Portugal, were all humble peasant children. With increasing urgency she has insisted that the world repent for its sins, particularly for sins of the flesh.

This book with its authoritative description should help increase the already spreading devotion to Our Lady of Fatima. Portugal has already shown the modern world, had it only eyes to see the truth, the blessings which come to a nation that returns to love and devotion to Christ and Mary. Within twenty-five years it had been transformed from a chaotic, revolution-torn, persecution-ridden country, to a peaceful, stable nation imbued with the spirit of Catholicism in its social, economic, and political life.

It remains to each of us individually to accept in our own lives the message of Fatima, and do penance for ourselves and for our fellows.

DOROTHY WILLOCK

The Green Revolution

RECLAMATION OF INDEPENDENCE
By Willis Dwight Nutting.
Berliner & Lanigan

The man who was beating himself on the head with a hammer, stopped to remark to his friend, "If you have nothing but negative criticism to offer, please keep quiet." A few moments later he was carried away screaming. This lunatic is brother to the less violent individual who counters every criticism of the present social order with the same remark. In both their tortured minds is embedded the notion that some inexorable force, law, or authority demands that they keep on doing what they're doing. They both fail to realize that if they but stopped, things would show a rather startling improvement. The reasons for stopping our self-inflicted economic mayhem, the manner of stopping, and the positive moves that should occupy our resultant sabbath, are the subject of this book.

Mr. Nutting advocates a Green Revolution as a means toward regaining the human liberty we have lost under the present System, and as the sole means of forestalling the otherwise inevitable state of tyranny toward which we move. I have seldom seen the case for a decentralist, agrarian and craft economy, so logically and unemotionally developed. He first points out to us very convincingly that specialization in methods of work has created an abnormal interdependence. We are all consumers dependent not upon a man or upon a class, but upon a System. So involved has this interdependence become, that no one can state with certainty just who or what controls it. The rich as well as the poor are slaves to these wheels within wheels. They are equally dependent for their supper upon that mad magic that puts the food on our tables, and the clothes on our backs. Consequently:

> ... the proper function of the System is our greatest concern. It must work or we perish. Our instinct of self-preservation demands that we make it work. Nothing else is important. Our existence on this earth depends on it. Nothing else — personal preferences, the hopes, ambitions and plans of individuals, *and even human rights* – must take second place, for what are preferences, or hopes or rights if we are not alive to enjoy them?

This state of affairs, Mr. Nutting insists, does not make for human freedom. The organization of one class against the other fails to advance human freedom one iota, and he gives as evidence the strongly organized unionism of Germany and Italy offering but slight resistance to dictatorship when it arose. My own evidence is the present seeking after legislation by our American labor unions, which if granted, would as Mr. Belloc prophesied make one class *under law* subservient to the other. To perpetuate the System, the American worker at present would gladly accept well-paid servility to freedom, by their own testimony.

At great length, the author suggests ways and means to bring about a quiet revolution which would be characterized by more and more people becoming less dependent upon the System and more dependent upon their own skill of hand, or, at least, dependent upon a small local cooperating community. This is the Green Revolution similar in most details with that advocated by Chesterton, Belloc, McNabb, Maurin, Borsodi, and company. It would be essentially a land and craft movement.

Agreeing wholeheartedly with Mr. Nutting's diagnosis and treatment of the social problem, I must say his optimism is greater than mine. Not because he hopes to see results, for so do I, but because he implies that the impetus for such a movement can be forthcoming from men's innate desire for human freedom. I do not believe that this is strong enough today to hope for any such heroic manifestation. Human freedom is an expression without meaning until qualified by an answer to the question, "Freedom to do what?" Without the proper motives and admirable desires of Mr. Nutting, many men might consider his ultimate community a deprivation of that licence they now enjoy as slaves. His optimism is the same as that of which our founding fathers were guilty, and resulted in their idealism hardly outliving themselves.

Apart from Christianity as it is interpreted and lived out by the Church of Christ, men will find themselves ill-equipped to achieve or maintain any social order compatible with dignified freedom for the person, for this civic liberty can only come as by-product to a Christian religious life. The self-denial, altruism, and hopefulness necessary to make the Green Revolution possible could only be the natural consequence of supernatural virtue. Man must first come to realize that he is ultimately neither dependent upon a System, nor his own productivity, but upon the Providence of God. Freedom thus sought would be the kind of freedom of a Beneficent Father, where neither ambition for one's own ends, nor envy for another man's possessions can get a foothold. We need not wait upon the day when all men are of this persuasion but certainly the first heroic steps can only be taken by men Calvary-bound.

Mr. Nutting's Green Revolution integrated with 1947 Christianity is the social dish for our famished age. The Revolution, however, will not be an end, but an effect.

Reclamation of Independence is a valuable contribution to those libraries which we hope will soon be discarded as less attractively fertile than compost heaps. Until that day the book itself will give you some delight as a thing well done. It is the first from Messrs. Berliner & Lanigan and the beautiful format leads us to believe that these gentlemen share Mr. Nutting's enthusiasm for craft skillfully executed. Copies may be ordered direct from the publishers.

EDWARD WILLOCK

Recent Titles
AROUCA PRESS

Integrity, Volume 1:
The First Year (October–December 1946)
Ed. Carol Jackson, Ed Willock

Christ Wants More:
Ignatian Principles and Ideals on Prayer and Action
Fr. Frank Holland, S. J.

Breaking the Chains of Mediocrity:
Carol Robinson's Collected Works (The Marianist *Articles)*
Carol Jackson Robinson

The Eightfold Kingdom Within:
Essays on the Beatitudes and the Gifts of the Holy Ghost
Carol Jackson Robinson

Liberalism:
A Critique of Its Basic
Principles and Various Forms
Louis Cardinal Billot, S.J.
(Newly translated by Thomas Storck)

The Pearl of Great Price:
Pius VI & the Sack of Rome
Christian Browne

www.ingramcontent.com/pod-product-compliance
Lightning Source LLC
Chambersburg PA
CBHW071801080526
44589CB00012B/641